T0333294

1000 Checkmate Combinations

Victor Henkin

Translated by Jimmy Adams and Sarah Hurst

BATSFORD CHESS

First published in the United Kingdom in 2011 by
Batsford
43 Great Ormond Street
London
WC1N 3HZ

An imprint of Pavilion Books Company Ltd

Originally published in Russian by Russian Chess House Limited

ISBN: 9781849947251

A CIP catalogue record for this book is available from the British Library.

26 25 24 23 22
10 9 8 7 6 5 4 3 2 1

Reproduction by Rival Colour Ltd, UK
Printed and bound by CPI Group (UK) Ltd, Croydon CR0 4YY

This book can be ordered direct from the publisher at
www.pavilionbooks.com, or try your local bookshop.

Contents

		Page
Don't reinvent the bicycle *by Mikhail Tal*		5
Before you open the book ...		7
1.	The Rook	10
2.	The Bishop	35
3	The Queen	46
4.	The Knight	68
5.	The Pawn	88
6.	Two Rooks	98
7.	Rook and Bishop	127
8.	Rook and Knight	160
9.	Two Bishops	190
10.	Two Knights	202
11.	Bishop and Knight	214
12.	Queen and Bishop	237
13.	Queen and Knight	274
14.	Three Pieces	296
15.	Solutions	320

Don't reinvent the bicycle

…The master has sacrificed a piece. You don't know what this sacrifice is going to lead to yet, and, holding your breath, you follow the ensuing events. But then the situation becomes clear: the master declares checkmate against his opponent. How did he find that combination? How did he discern it among the dozens of other moves and possibilities?

When I'm studying a specific position, above all I note its peculiarities, the reciprocal positioning of the pieces, their connections. And suddenly (in the majority of cases this occurs intuitively) somewhere nearby the indistinct features of some new teasing and appealing position become faintly perceptible. It isn't on the board yet, of course, but everything points to the fact that it may arise. The hunt for the blue bird begins. Often the calculating of variations turns out to be a Sysyphean task. The position in your mind's eye hardly ever comes about, even if your opponent joins you in a 'cooperation'. Some piece is on the wrong square, some pawn is getting in the way…

But it can happen that the tedious calculation of variations brings real results. Move for move you get exactly the same position that you saw from afar. And if the circle of variations has been exhausted, then … Then you can start the combination.

A successful combination provokes admiration not only in the spectators; it also becomes a 'starring moment' for the chess player himself. But although each of us thinks that we've created something original, in fact, even if it's subconsciously, we've only reproduced something that we've already seen or encountered somewhere and sometime.

Most chess combinations have already squeezed into the Procrustean bed of standard plans. From the methodological standpoint this is essential, but from the point of view of an artist it's sad.

I myself hate to admit that I'm an imitator of chess science. And it's no coincidence that Emanuel Lasker said that before participating in tournaments he wished he could forget everything he knew, just to play freely and uninhibitedly without burdening himself with knowledge, so that during a game he wouldn't have to remember what theory recommended and on which page.

That's only a dream, alas. The joy of great discoveries has been left in the distant past. Information has swamped the entire world, including the chess world. The century has dawned, I would say, of pathologically increasing knowledge. Chess has now achieved such a level that inventing something fundamentally new is unbelievably difficult. Everything's been done, almost everything …

But still it came as an enormous surprise to me that a three-digit number of typical mating finales exist, which are already included on the 'black list' of chess theory, and the chess player's task has been reduced to forcing a non-typical position to become a typical one.

There's no doubt that very complicated combinations are encountered in chess that can be found only by a player who is endowed with sharp tactical vision and who possesses an excellent ability to calculate. But no matter how complicated and original the combination itself is, as a rule it leads to a position that yields to a specific evaluation. And the most important thing is to see this in time and correctly evaluate the final position.

Of course, chess creativity hasn't been restricted once and for all by established boundaries. Every player improvises to the extent of his talent and imagination. But in places where you just have to know things you shouldn't reinvent the bicycle.

This book isn't just an anthology of mating combinations. The last check isn't necessarily the final chord of a game. It's the note that nearly always sounds the leitmotif for many combinations associated with winning material or achieving other advantages. Mating finales are encountered rather infrequently in high-level tournament practice, but they are always present out of frame, just as the multiplication table stands invisibly behind the most complex mathematical formulae. In this book you'll find numerous examples where merely the threat of mate turned out to be the decisive factor in the battle.

There hasn't been a book like this before in our chess literature. The author has done an enormous amount of work selecting and systematising the material. An experienced master, who in the recent past himself participated in competitions and had a reputation as a staunch tactician, he has retained a particular taste for the last check.

This book is easy to read. It has been written clearly, in vivid language, with the soft shading of the author's inherent humour.

This book will be particularly useful for chess players who are starting their creative life. It serves as a solid guide to the world of chess combinations, explains the significance of many of the 'road signs' and shortens the road to mastery.

In *Masters of the Chessboard* Richard Reti writes:

"There is a widespread but mistaken notion that the art of combination in chess cannot be learnt and that it is all down to an inborn power of calculation and imagination. But any experienced player knows that most combinations, indeed, practically all of them, are devised by recalling known elements, as, for example, the famous bishop sacrifice on White's h7, which will not give the advanced player anything much to think about.

It would be a grateful task to write a complete theory of combinations, which would have to demonstrate the ever recurring types, and show what principal factors must be kept in mind in judging the correctness of combinations and in carrying them out."

Precisely that work is in front of you.

Mikhail Tal
Former World Chess Champion

Before you open the book ...

The chess code with its characteristic brevity defines mate as a check to which there is no defence. With a declaration of mate against the enemy king the goal of the chess game is considered to have been achieved and the game ends.

According to the modern rules, 'declaring mate' doesn't at all mean pronouncing the word out loud. It's enough to make the move, after which the mating position arises on the board. However, this wasn't always the case. Up until the end of the 19th century an irrefutable check was announced with the words 'check and mate'. This served as a kind of proof that checkmate hadn't been given accidentally (a 'blind mate', as they used to say in Russia. This term can be found in the late 19th-century *Brockhaus and Efron Encyclopedic Dictionary*), but as a result of precise calculation.

'Here White (Black) announced mate in such-and-such a number of moves' – may be encountered in many notes to games not only by Steinitz and Chigorin, but also by later commentators.

Mating positions have long been considered the crown of chess creativity. In the distant past the rules of the game were distinguished from the modern ones by the slower movement of certain pieces (in particular, the queen and bishop), so mating finales were encountered extraordinarily rarely and were highly valued by our predecessors. Especially beautiful and unexpected endings received their own names.

In later times, when reform of the game of chess, as Dutch historian Antonius van der Linde put it, abolished the eastern slowness and started 'hurried chess', mating positions ceased to be museum pieces. But even today checkmate can't be seen on the board that often: chess players try to put an end to their torments and resign, as a rule, before the final gong.

Still, the goal of the game of chess remains unchanged – to give mate to the enemy king. All of the chess player's thoughts are subordinated, in essence, to this goal. As a rule a single piece strikes the final blow against the enemy king. But the pieces rarely act alone. Before one of them manages to announce 'check and mate', its assistants must do a fair amount of work, and sometimes even give themselves up as a sacrifice.

In the same way as a composer makes the sounds of a captivating melody out of chaos, the chess player creates a beautiful game, trying to find the best move out of the innumerable quantity of variations. The chess player, like the composer, is governed by the laws of harmony. Harmony in chess is the cooperation of the pieces. We can boldly state that the class of a person's play is to a large extent determined by their ability to distribute their fighting forces in such a way that they support and complement each other. The nature of the connections between pieces depends on their individual characteristics, the tasks they are carrying out, and, of course, the concrete peculiarities of the position.

The clearest cooperation between pieces is manifested in the attack on the enemy king. Here every piece reveals its capabilities. The essence of a game of chess is expressed in its ideal form precisely in mating scenarios.

This book is devoted to methods of finding mating combinations and ways to implement them. We'll examine typical finales and get to know the technical methods of achieving them.

As all the pieces are individual in terms of their range of action and rules of movement, each of them has its own favourite 'profession'. In this sense the chess pieces can be compared to an ice hockey team, in which each player has worked out shots at goal from different points on the rink. The same can also be said about the determining of roles in a joint attack on the king. Some pieces prefer to play 'for a pass', and others aim to 'shoot the puck' on their own.

In the book we'll examine over 200 mating positions. With the aim of systematising the material they are divided up into 14 chapters according to their formal features, i.e. based on the number and type of pieces directly participating in the creation of the mating constructions. Examples are given at the end of each chapter for you to solve by yourself.

As you move from chapter to

chapter, you'll soon realise that exactly the same methods are used to solve the most varied tactical problems: deflection, enticement, a double attack, blocking and so on. You'll also notice the rather important circumstance that not only individual tactical ideas, but also entire combinations, repeat themselves in chess practice, often at intervals of decades or even hundreds of years. This regularity increases the value of accumulated experience. Numerous cases are included in the book where knowledge of games by the great masters of the past and present has helped to quickly and accurately solve the most complex tactical problems.

I recommend that you read this book without a chessboard. This method will not only help you to develop your tactical vision, but will also make the use of technical means of achieving your aim become automatic.

You shouldn't take 'tactical medicine' in large doses. Even the most beautiful combinations can set your teeth on edge if you swallow them with the greed of a hungry pelican. On this topic there are many wise sayings, for example a Chinese one: 'Don't bite off more than you can swallow', or a French one, 'Too much of anything is a bad thing... ' In general, as the satirical pseudonymous Russian author Kozma Prutkov said, "One cannot embrace the unembraceable!".

You should get to know the combinations carefully, thoughtfully, without distractions or hurry, returning again and again to the examined positions. Best of all, limit your daily ration to two or three 'dishes'.

A few words about the examples for solving by yourself.

Easy examples deliberately alternate with more complicated ones. The 'lottery' principle of the lucky ticket makes the solving of exercises more like the process of searching for a combination in a tournament game. You see, it is not possible to predict earlier what precise tactical opportunity will show up during play. The combination could be simple and lying on the surface, so to say, but it could also turn out to be a ring tossed to the bottom of the chess ocean. Chess is full of the unexpected.

As well as examples from practice the tasks include problems and studies. It's also useful to solve these without a board – this will help you to develop the technique of calculating variations. Of course, if necessary there's nothing to stop you from setting up the pieces on a chessboard.

This book is aimed at the broad spectrum of chess amateurs and can be used both for independent study and by chess teachers as a textbook. I hope that it will bring you many pleasant minutes and will inspire you to achieve new chess feats.

1. The Rook

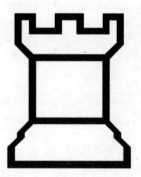

In chess literature the rook is usually portrayed as a sort of clumsy oaf, lazy and sleepy. This is evidently because it dozes in its corner for a while. But, like Russian folk hero Ilya Muromets, who stayed at home for his first 33 years sitting on an oven, the rook transforms itself the moment it sees an open line in front of it.

You mustn't think that the rook exists only for a rook endgame. As Savielly Tartakower said, "between the opening and the endgame God created the middlegame." When after castling short the pawns on the kingside are still in their initial positions, the king cautiously listens for salvos from the enemy batteries and, if shells start falling in direct proximity, orders one of its infantrymen to take a step forward, so that in the event of a check on the last rank it can safely change its command point.

However, it often happens that in the heat of the chess battle there isn't enough time to open up a 'little window', and then the check can be fatal. The strongest specialist in this field is the rook. It's the one that thanks to its 'linear profession' delivers the decisive blow along a rank.

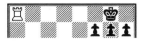

Similar situations arise with an insufficiently solid defence of the last rank.

It doesn't take much imagination to visualise the queen in place of the rook, which doesn't spoil the scenery at all.

The weakness of the first rank in the game Geller – Ostojic (1969) is obvious. However, the black rook can occupy the f1 square only with the support of its friend, which, alas, is pinned by the enemy queen. On 1... ♖e4 White will reply 2 ♕d5. The moves 1 ... ♖f6 or 1 ... ♔g7 suggest themselves. But these moves leave the queen a path to retreat to e1.

1 ... ♕e4! leads to the goal, attacking the queen and freeing the rook from the pin. Now White either loses the queen or is mated on f1.

The first rank is in danger here, too. The d1 square, towards which the black rook is gazing unequivocally, is only defended by the queen. And in general White's rear isn't protected by any kind of solid cover.

Black wins by deflecting the queen with two tactical blows:

1 ... ♗a4! 2 ♕xa4 ♕b5! 3 ♕xb5 ♖d1+ or **3 ♕b3 (c2) ♕f1X**.

In the game German – Walter (1926) the critical e1 square is guarded by two white pieces. The forces of attack and defence are balanced for now. However, the move **1 ... ♕c2!** deflects one of the pieces from its duties. On **2 ♗f4** follows **2 ... ♕xc1+**.

In this case we come into contact with the direct destruction of a piece that is defending the rear. Here is another example:

Smyslov – Lilienthal (1941): **1 ♕xd6!** Black resigned.

In the examples I've given the weakness of the last rank was generally visible enough and the idea of exploiting it lay on the surface. Let's now get acquainted with a combination from the game Adams – Torre (1921).

At first glance Black's position doesn't give cause for concern. But there are two serious flaws in his position: the absence of a 'little window' for the king and insufficient defence of the e8 rook which is opposing White's doubled rooks. Thus the motif of the combination appears, the implementation of which is associated with a series of brilliant moves aimed at deflecting the black queen or c8 rook from the defence of the critical e8 square.

1 ♕g4! ♕b5. It's clear that Black couldn't take the queen because of 2 ♖xe8+. Nor did 1 ... ♕d8? 2 ♕xc8 ♖xe2 3 ♕xd8+ etc. work. The black queen is tied to the defence of the e8 rook. That is why 2 a4 suggests itself, to drive the queen off the a4-e8 diagonal. But that move loses: 2 ... ♕xe2! 3 ♕xc8 (3 ♖xe2 ♖c1+) 3 ... ♕xe1+ 4 ♘xe1 ♖xc8. The aim can be achieved only by exceptionally beautiful queen sacrifices.

2 ♕c4!! ♕d7 3 ♕c7!! ♕b5 4 a4 ♕xa4 (4 ... ♕xe2 5 ♖xe2) **5 ♖e4! ♕b5** (5 ... h6 6 ♕xc8 ♕xe4 7 ♕xe8+) **6 ♕xb7!**

Now all the squares on the a4-e8 diagonal are exposed to fire from the white pieces, and the e8 rook is left defenceless. Black resigned. Six moves in a row the white queen offered herself as a sacrifice for the sake of victory!

Knowledge of this classical combination allowed master Rovner to easily and quickly find a win 25 years later in a game with Kamyshov (Black).

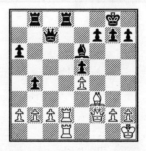

It isn't difficult to notice a superficial resemblance of this position to the previous one. Its solution is very similar, although less impressive: **1 ♕a7! ♕a5 2 ♕xa6! ♕c7 3 ♕a7!** Black resigned.

In the absence of a 'little window' it is particularly dangerous, as we've just seen for ourselves, to oppose the major pieces on the files. A very simple example is the ending of the game Ickes – Flood (1960).

If the white rooks try to take one of the opponent's pieces, the other one immediately strikes a blow in response on the first rank. Exploiting this, Black intensifies the pressure on the open line: **1 ... 罝gc8!**, and White resigned, as there is no way to defend the c1 rook, and if it moves away then 2 ... 豐xa1 3 罝xa1 罝c1+ is decisive.

This position requires more careful study. A direct attempt to double the rooks with the move 1 ... 罝fa8 not only doesn't lead to the goal, but even loses due to 2 豐xa8+, and Black is mated.

The attack on the a1 rook must be undertaken by a more cunning method – **1 ... 豐b2!** Now the white rooks are helpless, and the queen will not manage to come to the rescue, as after 2 豐d1 there is a mate after 2 ... 豐xf2+.

Janowski (White) used a similar method against Burn (1907).

With his last move (罝f8-e8) Black offered an exchange of rooks, justifiably believing that White couldn't play 1 罝xe8+ 罝xe8 2 豐xd7? 豐xd7 3 罝xd7 罝e1+ or 1 罝xd7? 罝xd7

2 豐xd7 豐xd7 3 罝xd7 罝e1+. However, he hadn't counted on a third variation, which actually did occur in the game: **1 豐xd7!** Black resigned. After 1 ... 豐xd7 2 罝dxd7 the rooks are inviolable, and he is a bishop down.

And here is another 'great opposition'.

Patasias – Purdy (1954): **1 ... 罝dc8 2 罝xc7 罝xc7! 3 豐a3** (3 豐d1 is better) **3 ... 豐a4! 4 豐b2 豐xa2 5 豐a1 罝c2! 6 罝f1 罝xf2!** White resigned.

If the last frontier is guarded by the queen, then the idea of deflecting it is often combined with the threat of a double attack. The black queen's whimsical manoeuvres in the game Lowcki – Tartakower (1935) led to a forced win.

1 ... 豐c5+ 2 當h1 豐c4! The threat of a double attack by the rook on f1 ties down White's play – this is the leitmotif of the whole operation.

3 當g1 豐d4+! 4 當h1 豐e4! The first attempt at deflection (5 罝xe5 豐xe5).

Of course, he couldn't play 4 ... ♕e3? 5 ♕xe3 ♖f1+ 6 ♕g1 – a blunder that even experienced players often make.

5 ♕c1. The rook must be defended, on 5 ♕d1 would follow 5 ♕f4. But if 5 ♕g1, then 5 ... ♕e2 forcing the win of the queen (6 ... ♖f1).

5 ... ♕d3! (again threatening check on f1) **6 ♔g1 ♕d4+ 7 ♔h1 ♕d2!** The black queen has arrived at the appointed place. This is not only deflection, but also a double attack as, in addition, the g5 rook comes under fire. White resigned.

A weakening of the last rank can be provoked by an exchange, as happened in the game Bernstein – Capablanca (1914).

1 ... ♘xc3 2 ♖xc3 ♖xc3 3 ♖xc3. Now it is impossible to continue the attack by means of 3 ... ♕b1+ 4 ♕f1 ♖d1?, because the black king doesn't have a 'little window' either, and after 5 ♖c8+ it perishes first. This is evidently what Ossip Bernstein was counting on, believing that Black merely intended to win back the pawn – 4 ♕xa2. But Capablanca had something completely different in mind.

3 ... ♕b2! White resigned (4 ♕e1 ♕xc3; 4 ♕d3 ♕a1+; 4 ♖c2 or ♖d3 – 4 ... ♕b1+).

Material can also be sacrificed with the same goal.

Novichkov – Luzganov (1963): **1 ... ♘xe4! 2 ♖xe4** (it was better to accept the loss of the pawn). **2 ... ♕b7!** Deflection is again combined with a double attack. White resigned (3 ♕e1 ♕xe4).

And here is an example where a knight inflicted the final double attack.

Capablanca – Fonaroff (1918): **1 ♘h6+ ♔h8 2 ♕xe5! ♕xe5 3 ♘xf7+**. Black resigned, as after 3 ... ♔g8 4 ♘xe5 he is a piece down, and in the event of 3 ... ♖xf7 he is mated.

Let's also mention the feat accomplished by the bishop in the game Sznapik-Gaprindashvili (1976).

White cheerfully played **1 ♖a3** ('with an inevitable mate'), but it turned out that the women's world champion had been waiting for exactly that. There followed **1 ... ♛xc1+!** **2 ♕xc1 ♗xb2!**, and it was soon all over.

Pawns can also take part in deflecting the enemy forces from the defence of the last rank.

Lilienthal – Aronin (1948): **1 ♕c3!** **♕b6 2 ♕b2! ♕d6** (2 ... ♕a5 3 ♕b5!) **3 f4!** On 3 ♕xb7 or 3 ♕xe5 Black would move the king along to f8 and retain chances of defending. Now, though, the white pawns take on the task of deflecting the queen.

3 ... exf4 4 e5 ♕e7 5 ♕xb7! ♕e8 **6 ♕b8 ♖d6 7 ♕xd6**. Black resigned.

The threat of deflection usually arises in cases when the enemy pieces are overloaded by having to defend two or more critical squares. When they are attacked, these pieces lose the ability to 'multi-task' and are forced to leave one of their posts.

Deflection as one of the fundamental tactical methods of attacking the eighth (or first) rank is encountered in the most surprising forms.

In the game Mikenas – Bronstein (1965/66), in an apparently absolutely peaceful position Bronstein literally stunned his opponent with the blow **1 ... ♖xa3!!** There you have a real bolt from the blue! You can play 100 games for the sake of one move like that.

Meanwhile, this paradoxical capture – a means of deflection in its purest form – actually deflects one of three pieces from the defence of the first rank: the queen, the rook or the pawn. And although the following variations are simple (2 ♖xa3 ♕e1+ 3 ♕f1 ♕xf1X; 2 bxa3 ♕xa1+ 3 ♖b1 ♖e1+ 4 ♖xe1 ♕xe1+ 5 ♕f1 ♕xf1X), finding such an appropriate turn is only within the powers of a player with sharp combinational vision.

Another unexpected attack has something in common with 'Bronstein's move', one that was found by Black in a game played in Yugoslavia (1949).

White, evidently, was already getting ready to celebrate victory, when a 'natural disaster' suddenly occurred – **1 ... ♖c5!!**, and nothing can prevent catastrophe.

In the game Jaya – Staudte (1958) White decided to win back the piece with all conveniences – **1 ♖xf6** – thinking that in the event of check on the first rank, the rook would instantly go back where it came from. But after **1 ... ♕xe6!** he 'missed the train'.

Olafsson (Black) was able to attack with an exceptionally beautiful move against Tal (1975).

1 ... ♕f4! 2 ♖e7! (also inventive, but, alas, not enough) **2 ... ♖f8! 3 ♕a5**. No better is 3 ♕e2 ♗xf3 4 ♕xf3 (4 gxf3 ♕g5+) 4 ... ♕d6 or 3 ♕c1 ♗xf3 4 gxf3 ♕xf3 5 ♖d2 ♕g4+ 6 ♔h1 ♕g5.

And now the Icelandic grandmaster missed the chance to play 'like Tal'

against Tal – **3 ... ♕g5!!**, putting the queen under attack from two enemy pieces and attacking a third (the e7 rook).

He continued **3 ... ♖d1+** and after **4 ♘e1** won with the same move **4 ... ♕g5!**, but now with only one exclamation mark.

Let's spend some time on another typical method that is associated with deflection.

Engelhard – Schultz (1958). Check on f1 is parried by the reply ♕e3-g1. But after **1 ... ♖c1+** the queen is deflected off the diagonal.

Fontein – Euwe (1939): **1 ... ♖c1!** Here a similar move deflects the f1 rook, opening up the first rank for an attack – **2 ♖xc1 ♕d1+**. White resigned.

The arsenal of tactical resources that can exploit a weakness on the last rank is extremely varied. Here are two examples on the theme of blocking.

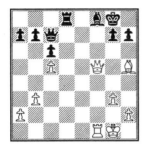

Reti – Bogoljubow (1926): **1 ♗f7+ ♔h8 2 ♗e8!** The connection between the black pieces has been severed, and the f8 bishop has been left without support. Black resigned.

Tserendagva – Purevzhav (1949): **1 ... ♗d4+ 2 ♔h1 ♕xd3! 3 ♗xd3 ♘f2+ 4 ♔g1 ♘xd3+ 5 ♔h1 ♘f2+ 6 ♔g1 ♘d1+.** White resigned.

Sometimes the aim is achieved by means of a strong secondary threat.

Gragger – Dorn (1958): **1 ♘e7+!** (first freeing up the d-file with tempo, and the enemy rook is deflected from the eighth rank) **1 ... ♖xe7 2 ♕xf6!** (and now another defender of the rear

is annihilated, while simultaneously threatening mate on g7). Black resigned (2 ... ♕xf6 3 ♖d8+ or 2 ... ♘g6 3 ♕xe7 ♘xe7 4 ♖d8+).

Sometimes the threat of mate on the last rank is created by a zwischenzug. In the game Cornfield – Huckle (1965) this led to the win of a piece.

1 ♘f6! ♕xg4. Otherwise the g7 square can't be defended. 1 ... ♕d2+ 2 ♔h1 is no help, and the e7 rook is unassailable, as the c8 rook is in the firing line.

2 ♘xe8! After this 'interim' capture the threat of mate on f8 arises, to which there is no better defence than 2 ... h6. But then White simply takes the queen. Black worked out what this 'exchange' operation was turning into for him, and capitulated.

In the famous first game of the match for the World Championship of 1927, Alekhine (Black) won a pawn from Capablanca with the help of two attacks based on a pin.

1 ... ♘xc2! 2 ♖xc2 ♕xf4. The situation wasn't changed by 2 ♕xc2

♕xc2 3 ♖xc2 ♗xf4 either.

Here is a collective find by polar explorers on Uedinenie Island, playing Black against employees from the editorial office of the newspaper *Pravda* (1978).

When the inhabitants of the Arctic 'coldly' announced their next move – **1 ... ♕xb2!!**, even the journalists couldn't 'write off' the double pin.

In the position from the game NN – Richter (1957), you won't immediately grasp whose rear is in more danger. Once you know it is Black's move, you'll want to play 1 ... ♕xe1+ 2 ♕xe1 ♖fxe8 with a clear advantage, but a rather protracted endgame.

Kurt Richter finished the battle in two moves: **1 ... ♖dxe8 2 ♕xe8 h6!** Threatening 3 ... ♖xe8, and a retreat by the queen leads to mate on f1. That is what opening a 'little window' on time is all about!

Now let's get acquainted with some methods of moving the major pieces

out to firing positions. Above all, you need open lines. Sometimes they can be created by a simple exchange.

Vashkau – Dibel (1957): **1 ... ♗xc4 2 ♖e5** (2 dxc4 ♘e2+) **2 ... ♖xd3 3 ♖xd3 ♘e2+ 4 ♖xe2 ♕c1+**. White resigned.

In the game Itsenko – Petrovskikh (1975) the black rooks were aimed at the c2 pawn, which was obstructing their path to the enemy camp. However, an immediate 1 ... ♖xc2 doesn't work because of 2 ♖xc2, and 2 ... ♕c1+ 3 ♖xc1 ♖xc1+ is impossible due to 4 ♖f1. So before boarding it is necessary to sever the connection between the defenders of the white king.

1 ... e4! The queen is deflected from the defence of the f1 square and the h5 knight. White is forced to take the pawn in connection with the threat of e4-e3. But now the main battery enters the action.

2 ♕xe4 ♖xc2! White resigned. After 3 ♖xc2 ♕c1+ he is mated, and in the event of 3 ♕xc2 ♖xc2 4 ♖xc2 ♕xh5 he is a piece down. True, by playing 3 h4 he could drag out his resistance.

In the presence of open lines it is very important to occupy them with maximum speed.

Lepek – Koonen (1962): **1 ♖c2! ♕xd4 2 ♖c4!** The queen has to be chased away from the d-file in order to destroy the defence of the file. If Black is going to be obstinate – 2 ... ♕d2, then he loses his queen: 3 ♖c8+ ♖d8 4 ♕xd2.

2 ... ♕b6 3 ♖c8+ ♖d8 4 ♕b5! Black resigned.

This position is from the game Novotelnov – Rovner (1946).

Black first 'drew fire on himself' – **1 ... ♗xf5! 2 ♗xf5 ♘xf5 3 ♖xf5**, then quickly seized the open lines – **3 ... ♖ed8 4 ♕c4** (so that on 4 ... ♖d1+ there'd be the defence 5 ♖f1) **4 ... ♖ac8 5 ♕e2 ♖xc2 6 ♕xc2** and in conclusion he struck a blow on the theme of deflection that is already familiar to us – **6 ... ♕c8!** White resigned, as the choice between mate and losing a rook is unpleasant enough.

Neikirch – Botvinnik (1960): **1 ... ♕d8! 2 ♕xe6+** (Black also wins easily after 2 ♕d2 ♕xd2 3 ♗xd2 ♖d8 4 ♗e3 ♖d1+ 5 ♗g1 ♖d2) **2 ... ♖f7 3 ♕e1 ♖e7!** White resigned.

"The final position," Mikhail Botvinnik wrote, "is interesting because although all the white and black pieces are situated on the edge of the board, Black's pieces are so far-ranging that there is no defence. From the point of view of composition the artistic influence would be stronger if Black's bishop were on a8."

But that's getting into chess 'connoisseurship' ...

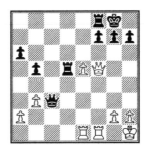

In the game Gutmayer – Swiderski (1928) after **1 ♖c1!** Black immediately landed in a dangerous situation. The seizure of the c-file threatened the last rank, as its rook defender was chained to the f7 square.

The mistaken reply **1 ... ♕xe5** (correct is 1 ... ♕d3) allowed White to resolve the matter with a straightforward combination – **2 ♕xf7+ ♖xf7 3 ♖c8+ ♖f8 4 ♖cxf8X**.

Black also loses on a queen retreat to a5: 2 ♖c8 ♖dd8 3 e6! ♖xc8 4 exf7+ ♔h8 5 ♕xc8 ♖xc8 6 f8=♕+ ♖xf8 7 ♖xf8X.

In this variation we become acquainted with yet another typical tactical operation that exploits the weakness of the last rank – pawn promotion. And although the pawn perishes on the battlefield at the moment that it receives the 'marshal's baton', like d'Artagnan, it has fulfilled its duty to the end.

One of the technical methods of advancing a passed pawn to the promotion square is illustrated in the game Nedeljkovic – Szilagyi (1957).

1 ... ♘xd4! (this exchange allows him to open the c-file) **2 cxd4 f2+! 3 ♔h1 ♖c1!** White resigned.

Simple? Very simple, even. But future grandmaster Gurgenidze (White) missed a similar opportunity in 1959 against future world champion Spassky.

White played 1 fxg7?, and after 1 ... ♖xf2 2 ♖xf2 ♔xg7 the game soon ended in a draw. Meanwhile our already familiar method won immediately, **1 f7+! ♔h8 2 ♕d8!**, with the only difference that this time the queen substituted for the rook.

By means of an elegant deflecting queen sacrifice Alekhine ended his encounter with an unknown amateur (1939).

After the natural **1 ♖c8 ♖xc8** (1 ... ♕xd7 2 ♕f8+) the battle ended with the far from obvious move **2 ♕e7!**.

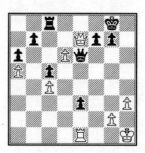

It was already easier for Geller (White) in his game with Ivkov (1973), when he played the 'Alekhine-style' **1 d7!**, forcing his opponent to capitulate immediately.

Mating situations in which the rook delivers a linear blow can also arise on the files. In these cases it is as if the board does a 90-degree turn.

As you can see, blocking the enemy king as much as possible is the main theme of all mating scenarios. This is achieved by a variety of tactical methods.

In the game Salter – Brigg (1947) the white knight was pinned, but there is an opportunity to free it: **1 ♕g8+!** (at the same time the rook is drawn to the king and blocks it) **1 ... ♖xg8 2 ♘g6+!** (and now the h-file is opened) **2 ... hxg6 3 ♖h1X**.

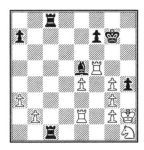

Here, Fischer's operation (Black) against Bisguier (1966) is reminiscent of a 'square circle'.

1 ... ♖xh1+! 2 ♔xh1 ♖c1+ 3 ♔h2 hxg3+ 4 ♔h3 ♖h1X.

Albin – Bernstein (1904): **1 ... ♖e6! 2 ♕d7 ♖d6 3 ♕a4** (3 ♕h3 is more stubborn, but White's position remains unenviable) **3 ... ♕e2 4 ♖f1** (White still suspects nothing, but he can't escape his fate after 4 h3 ♗xf2+ 5 ♔h2 ♗g3+ 6 ♔xg3 ♖g6+ either) **4 ... ♕xf3! 5 gxf3 ♖g6X**.

A very beautiful finale, it is similar to the 'epaulette mate' which we we will discuss later.

Very often pawns take part in an attack on a castled position. By penetrating to the sixth (or third) rank, they drive a wedge into the king's barrier of pawns and securely close the 'little window'. In these cases the rook can deliver the final blows according to the plan we have already seen.

Deflection as one of the tactical methods of exploiting a weakness in the most distant rank is the main element of the operation here, too.

Opocensky-Alekhine (1925): **1 ... ♖e8! 2 ♕d1 ♕xf3+!** White resigned.

The pawn on h3, as we've just seen, creates additional combinational possibilities, as it serves as a supporting point for the attacking pieces.

So, in the game Terpugov – Kan (1951) White could have exploited this circumstance with the move **1 ♕f6!** The threat of mate on g7 forces Black to take the queen – **1 ... ♕xf6**. But then a second threat comes into play - **2 ♖xe8X**. (In the game White missed this opportunity, but still won after 1 ♘h5 ♔f8 2 ♘f6 ♖xe3 3 ♘xh7+ ♔e8 4 ♘f6+ ♔e7 5 ♘d5+ ♔d7 6 ♕xd8+ ♔xd8 7 ♘xe3, as the h6 pawn freely promotes to a queen.)

The knight sacrifice **1 ♘f6+ gxf6 2 exf6** in the game Levenfish-Riumin (1936) immediately led to a win, as the threat of 3 ♕g3+ could only be repelled by moving the queen to c2, e4 or g4. However, disaster came from another direction – **3 ♕xf8+! ♔xf8 4 ♖d8X**. (In the game 1 ♘g3? was played)

Here we've become acquainted with yet another tactical element – enticement of a piece (in this case the king) to an unfavourable square. Alekhine used the same method against Reshevsky (1937).

1 ♖xb8+! ♔xb8 2 ♕xe5+! Black resigned, as after 2 ... fxe5 3 ♖f8+ he is mated.

Here a double deflection of pieces from critical squares was accomplished by Duras in one of his games in a simul (1910).

1 ♖c1+ ♔b8 2 ♕b4+ ♔a8. Now that the opponent's king has been driven back into the corner, he needs to seize the eighth rank. This is achieved by the subsequent deflection of the rook from the e-file and the queen from guarding the rear squares.

3 ♗f3+! ♖xf3 4 ♕e4+! Black resigned.

Among the tactical methods that exploit a weakness in the last rank, we'll show you the 'double pin'.

In the game Mikenas – Aronin (1957) the white queen is pinned on a diagonal by its black counterpart, and after **1 ... ♖d8!** it was also pinned on the file. White resigned.

The constricted position of the enemy king often serves as the motif of a combination. Methods of attracting the opponent's pieces in order to force a self-block are illustrated in this position by Phillip Stamma (1734).

1 ♖g2+ ♔f8 2 ♘d7+! ♖xd7 3 ♖e8+! ♔xe8 4 ♖g8X.

In this position from the game Keres – Petrosian (1959) the white king's space is severely constrained, which allows Black to prepare a decisive attack, first with a sacrifice and then with a series of forcing manoeuvres.

1 ... ♖g3! 2 hxg3 hxg3 3 ♖fd2. A pawn wedge has been established on g3, and White's opportunities are now severely restricted. Tigran Petrosian starts transferring his major pieces to the h-file, while each of his moves contains a concrete threat.

3 ... ♕h4 4 ♗e2 ♖h7 5 ♔f1 ♕xf4+! White resigned (6 ♕xf4 ♖h1X).

When pieces are serving their king unflaggingly by crowding around it and restricting its mobility, a rook, in conjunction with a pawn, is capable of creating various mating constructions.

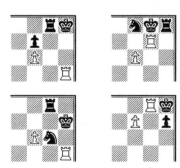

In 1750 the Italian chess player Ercole del Rio found an impressive mating scenario.

White mates in 4 moves

1 ♕a6! ♖b8 2 ♗c6 ♕c8 (now White must act energetically, as mate on h3 is threatened) **3 ♕xa7+! ♔xa7 4 ♖a1X**.

The final blow was possible thanks to the constrained position of the enemy king. A similar idea still repeats itself in different forms to this day. Here are some examples given in chronological order.

In the game Capablanca – Roubicek (1908) it would be unfavourable for White to continue 1 ♖a5?, as Black could then give perpetual check (from the squares f4, f2 and f1). Capablanca finds a forced solution, winnowed from del Rio's position: **1 ♖xa7+! ♕xa7**,

and only now **2 ♖a5!** with the inevitable finale 2 ... ♕xa6 3 ♖xa6X or, on any other second move by Black, 3 ♕xa7X.

Former women's world champion Vera Menchik used a typical method of achieving a similar final construction in her game against British champion Sir George Thomas (1932).

1 f6+. White chases her opponent's king away and gets the opportunity to occupy the h6 square with her queen, as 1 ... ♔xf6 is impossible because of 2 ♕g5+ ♔g7 3 h6+ ♔g8 4 ♕f6 with an unstoppable mate.

1 ... ♔h8 2 ♕h6 ♖g8 3 hxg6 fxg6 4 ♕xh7+! Black resigned (4 ♔xh7 5 ♖h1+).

Grandmaster David Bronstein, confirming that everything in chess has already been studied – you just have to know it and remember it – copied the women's world champion's entire combination in a game with Keres (1950).

1 f6+ ♔h8 2 ♕g5 b3 (2 ... ♘e5 3 ♖f4) **3 axb3 ♕b4 4 bxc4** (4 ♖f4 was already possible here, but Black nevertheless wasn't in any condition to prevent the fateful finale) **4 ... ♕xa4 5 ♖f4 ♕c2 6 ♕h6**. Black resigned (6 ... ♖g8 7 ♕xh7+).

A similar mating scenario served as the guiding star in a tactical operation by Tal (White) against Andersson (1976).

White has already 'tuned up his lyre', as they say, but an immediate diversion – 1 ♕h6 ♖g8 2 ♖h4 (2 ♕xh7+? ♔xh7 3 ♖h4+ is not possible due to 3 ... ♕h5) doesn't lead to success because of 2 ... ♘f8. Implementation of the combination, as we can see, is hindered in one case by the queen and in the other by the knight. However, there is a means of removing these obstacles.

1 ♗b6! ♖c8. The bishop is unassailable. On 1 ... ♘xb6 already possible is 2 ♕h6 ♖g8 3 ♖h4.

2 ♕h6 ♖g8. If 2 ... ♘xf6 (reckoning on 3 ♖xf6 ♕d1+ 4 ♖f1 ♕xg4), then 3 ♖h4 ♘h5 (otherwise 4 ♖xf6) 4 g4 ♖g8 5 ♖xf7 ♕d1+ 6 ♖f1 ♕d5 7 ♖xh5 gxh5 8 ♕f6+ ♖g7 9 ♗d4, and White wins.

3 ♖d4! A move aimed at chasing the queen from the fifth rank so that it can't cover the h-file on the h5 square. In the

event, say, of 3 ... ♕c6 the main idea of the operation comes into play – 4 ♕xh7+ ♔xh7 5 ♖h4X, and after 3 ... ♕e5 the d7 knight is simply lost. So Ulf Andersson gives up his queen for rook and bishop, which, however, doesn't save the game.

3 ... ♘xb6 4 ♖xd5 ♘xd5 5 ♖f3! By renewing the threat of 6 ♕xh7+, White forces the exchange of rooks, after which Black's queenside becomes indefensible.

5 ... ♖c3 6 ♖xc3 ♘xc3 7 ♕e3 b4 8 ♕a7 ♖f8 9 ♕c5 ♖b8 10 ♕d6. Black resigned.

The closer a pawn gets to the promotion square, the more dangerous it becomes. Akiba Rubinstein once even said that a pawn that has reached the sixth rank is no less strong than a piece.

The joint actions of a rook and a passed pawn allowed Kotov (Black) to successfully realise an attack against Stoltz (1952).

1 ... f2 2 ♗g2 (2 ♘g3 ♕f3+ 3 ♗g2 f1=♕+) **2 ... ♕f3!** White resigned (3 ♕xb7+ ♔h8 4 ♗xf3 ♖g1X).

In the next position (1896) White achieved the maximum blocking of the king and, by destroying a piece that was defending a critical square, delivered an 'epaulette mate'.

1 ♕a8+ ♘b8 2 ♖xd8+! ♖xd8
(2 ... ♔xd8 3 ♕xb8+ ♔e7 4 ♕d6X
doesn't save him either) **3 ♕xb7+!
♔xb7 4 ♖a7+ ♔c8 5 ♖c7X**.

Similar mating finales even occur in
the endgame.

N.Grigoriev, 1937

White can't immediately promote his
pawn to a queen, as on 1 b5 Black
replies 1 ... ♖h5 with a draw. On the
other hand, if the black king manages
to get to f6 before the pawn reaches b6,
it avoids defeat, as the e6 square is
inaccessible to the white rook.

1 ♔c2! Only here. In the event of
1 ♔a2 ♖d3! 2 b5 ♖d5 3 ♖b1 ♔e5
4 ♔a3 (or 4 b6 ♖a5+ 5 ♔b3 ♖b5+)
4 ... ♔d6 5 b6 ♔c6 6 b7 ♖a5+ Black
gets a draw.

1 ... ♔f5 2 b5 ♔f6 3 b6 ♖h8. The
continuation 3 ... ♔f7 4 ♖b1 ♖h8
5 ♔c3 ♔e6 6 ♔b4! ♔d7 7 ♖c1 led to a
theoretically lost endgame for Black.

4 ♔c3 ♖b8 5 ♖b1 ♔e7 6 ♔c4 ♔d7

7 ♔b5 ♔c8 8 ♖c1+! It still wasn't too
late to make a mistake: 8 ♔c6? ♖b7
9 ♖h1 ♖c7+ 10 bxc7 – stalemate or
10 ♔b5 ♖c2, and then 11 ... ♔b7 (b8)
with a draw. Now, though, exploiting
the unfortunate position of the black
pieces, White constructs an unexpected
mate.

8 ... ♔b7 9 ♖c7+ ♔a8 10 ♖a7X.

A rook supported by pawns can also
create mating situations in the centre of
the board.

In the game Goldenov – Zakharian
(1960) the white king is shut in a tight
corridor on the f-file by its own and
opposing pawns. The second rank is
inaccessible to it because of the threat
of b2-b1=♕+. It is on these peculiarities
of the position that the precise
manoeuvre by the black rook is built.

1 ... g4+ 2 ♔f4 ♖a5! (threatening
3 ... g5X) **3 e5 ♖a4+! 4 e4 ♖a3!** White
resigned, mate on f3 can only be
prevented at the cost of a rook.

In reply to the mistaken move **1 Rd1?** (Gligoric – Commons, 1972) Black returned the favour with the mistake 1 ... **Kb7?** Meanwhile, the Yugoslav grandmaster's carelessness could have cost him dearly, if Black had found an elegant combination based on the advanced position of the white king: **1 ... Ne5+! 2 Bxe5 Rxd1 3 Bxc7 e5!**, and the mouse-trap has snapped shut (4 ... Rxd4X).

The black king found itself in a similar situation in the game Fischer-Durao (1966), but the American grandmaster didn't miss his chance.

1 b4!, and Black resigned, as there is

no satisfactory defence to the threat of 2 Ke3 and 3 Rxc5X (1 ... cxb3 2 Kd3 Rxa4 3 c4+ or 1 ... Ke4 2 Rxc4+ Kd5 3 Kd3).

The mating ideas in the game Wenzel – Gronau (1975) are combined with the threat of promoting the a7 pawn.

1 g5+ Kf5 2 Kf3! (threatening 3 Rf7X) **2 ... e5 3 Re7!** (another mate is imminent – 4 Rxe5, and 3 ... e4+ 4 Kg3 doesn't save him) **3 ... exd4 4 cxd4 Ra3+ 5 Re3** (this way the exchange of rooks is forced, and the a7 pawn becomes a queen) **5 ... Rxe3+ 6 Kxe3**. Black resigned.

Exercises

1. Maric – Gligoric, 1964

Black to move

Take the a2 pawn? Or...

2. Minic – Honfi, 1966

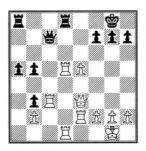

White to move

Into the thick of it.

3. Fomina – Zaitseva, 1978

White to move

Short circuit.

4. Parma – Forintos, 1977

White to move

'Rolling, overloading ... '

5. Makogonov – Flohr, 1942

White to move

As if from a crooked rifle, but right on target.

6. Paly – Merkulov, 1969

White to move

Is 1 ♖e1 good?

7. NN – NN

White to move

1 ♖xf6 and White wins?

8. Friedman – Regedzinsky, 1938

Black to move

1 ... ♖xc6 (such an annoying pawn). But what is White thinking?

9. Buchner – Andersen, 1961

Black to move

And he continued 1 ... ♖a8. What would you play for White?

10. Tal – Holm, 1970

White to move

"Advance! And woe to Godunov!"

11. Selyavkin – Belousov, 1973

White to move

Ducks in a row.

12. Keres – Levenfish, 1947

White to move

Keres never missed these kinds of attacks.

13. Keres – Levenfish, 1949

White to move

Two years later against the same opponent ...

14. Keres – Troger, 1960

White to move

And again Keres!

15. Sterk – Barasz, 1912

White to move

One, two, three!

16. Chigorin –
Levitsky and Nenarokov, 1899

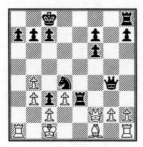

Black to move

1 ... ♖he8 is possible, of course, but there is something more beautiful and more decisive ...

17. Alekhine – Kohnlein, 1908

White to move

Give and take.

18. Malich – Kort, 1971

White to move

An attack on the left.

19. Rigo – Szell, 1978

White to move

How to break down the defences?

20. Guldin – Bagdatiev, 1963

White to move

Draw fire onto yourself!

21. Reshevsky – Fischer, 1971

Black to move

1 ... ♕f4 2 ♔g1? (time trouble, 2 ♕b5 is correct), and now ...

22. Bettner – Patterson, 1958

White to move

On 1 ♕xe7 Black has prepared 1 ... ♕d4+ winning the a1 rook. But does White need it?

23. Tukmakov – Kochiev, 1978

Black to move

1 ... ♕xc4 2 ♖xc4 ♖xa2 preserved equality. Black played **1 ... ♖xa2?** immediately.

24. Teschner – Portisch, 1969

White to move

1 ♖xd5 – '!', not '?'. Why?

25. Tuk – Asenova, 1969

White to move

And she decided to win a pawn: **1 ♗xc7 ♖xc7 2 ♖xb4**. What reply hadn't she counted on?

26. Fershter – Byvshev, 1960

Black to move

Against the mate on h7 there is the defence **1 ... ♘e4 2 ♖xe4 ♖xf6** and on **3 exf6 – 3 ... ♗xe4**. But what else?

27. E. Vladimirov – Kharitonov, 1977

White to move

Don't miss the moment!

28. Henkin – Mudrov, 1956

White to move

By hook or by crook.

29. Gligoric – Nievergelt, 1959

Black to move

1 ... ♗xf4? But we're not afraid of bishops.

30. Vints – Videla, 1955

White to move

Three checks under the curtain.

31. Isakov – Pitskhelauri, 1978

Black to move

1 ... ♕xg3! But what to do about the reply **2 ♕xd5+** ?

32. Tseshkovsky – Alburt, 1975

White to move

Where the king is going is a big secret.

33. Koshnitsky – Wolfers, 1971

White to move

A solo dance. But there is a simpler tango.

34. German – Ranfeld, 1976

Black to move

Queens don't retreat!

35. Westerinen – Hubner, 1974

Black to move

Close the door!

36. Taverne – Grodner, 1952

White to move

Well, who wouldn't pin the rook – **1 ♗b1?** But Black wins ...

37. Cortlever – van der Weide, 1968

White to move

Remove the sentry!

38. Stephenson – Blaine, 1962

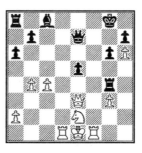

White to move

Like snooker.

39. Vodopyanov – Kantsyn, 1974

Black to move

You have to die to be resurrected.

41. Sznapik – Bernard, 1971

White to move

A trick with a costume change.

40. Ivkov – Eliskases, 1958

White to move

Queen on the prowl.

42. Stahlberg – Alekhine, 1930

Black to move

How to break through the tunnel.

43. NN – Lazarevic, 1972

Black to move

Alas, **1 ... ♛xf1?** Play 'fortissimo'.

2. The Bishop

'Like an elephant in a china shop,' we say in Russia when we want to emphasise someone's clumsiness and awkwardness. (The Russian word for the chess bishop is 'elephant'.) But an 'investigative experiment' was once conducted. Some crank brought a real elephant (what we don't know is whether it was an African elephant or an Indian elephant!) into a real china shop and left it alone with the glass and porcelain. And what do you know? The elephant behaved so delicately that it didn't break a single cup, although out of curiosity it felt all the fragile wares that were set out on the shelves with its trunk!

All kinds of tales are told about the chess 'elephant', too. They say it is straightforward, not too smart, and in general suffers from colour-blindness – it sees squares of only one colour. Where is the bishop by comparison with the rook, let alone with the queen!

But it is precisely on that strict subordination that the discipline of the chess army is based. While by military rank the bishop is lower than the queen and rook, in many battle episodes this circumstance is an advantage rather than a deficiency. It is easier to throw a less valuable piece onto the sacrificial altar of the attack. As for the particular qualities of the bishop, its dagger blows are sometimes so unexpected and effective that even the queen herself may envy them.

Fridrik Olafsson was once asked to demonstrate the shortest game of his life. "Here it is," the grandmaster said, laughing.

Bocdvarsson – Olafsson (1947): **1 f4 e5 2 fxe5 d6 3 exd6 ♗xd6 4 ♘f3 ♘c6 5 h3?? ♗g3X**.

The game Teed – Delmar was no less of a joke, although it was played in a past century (1896), which perhaps mitigates Black's guilt somewhat: **1 d4 f5 2 ♗g5 h6 3 ♗h4 g5? 4 ♗g3 f4 5 e3 h5 6 ♗d3 ♖h6?**

7 ♕xh5+! ♖xh5 8 ♗g6X.

In both examples the dagger blow by the bishop became possible thanks to the total blocking of the enemy king, the weakness of the diagonal leading to it and ... the utter helplessness of one of the players. However, the finale may be preceded by an impressive prelude.

NN – Pillsbury (1899): **1 ... ♕f1+!** (forcing White to block the g1 square) **2 ♗g1 ♕f3+! 3 ♗xf3 ♗xf3X**.

The beautiful final position attracted the attention of chess composers. Vladimir Korolkov (1935) managed to express the idea of blocking the enemy king with a similar mating setup in the most economical and artistic style. Possibly this study will seem difficult to some readers, but its solution brings enormous aesthetic delight.

*White to move
and win*

The position is literally snatched from a practical game. It appears that Black has only just sacrificed a rook and his pawns have moved inexorably towards becoming queens. The impression has even been created that he must win, as the white pawn on d6 is easily stopped by the king. But still ...

1 d7 ♔e7. The end? As it is impossible to stop the black pawns ...

2 ♖b8! The first surprise. The rook waits in ambush, so that in reply to 2 ... f1=♕ possible is 3 d8=♕+ ♔xd8 4 ♗a6+ ♔c7 5 ♗xf1 ♔xb8 6 ♔xh4 with a win. But Black also has something up his sleeve ...

2 ... &xg3! Black is threatening not only 3 ... f1=♕, but also 3 ... &xb8. The problem isn't solved by 3 ♔xg3 f1=♕ 4 d8=♕+ ♔xd8 5 &a6+ ♔c7 6 ♖b7+ ♔c8 7 ♖b6+ ♔c7 8 ♖b7+ ♔c8 9 ♖xa7+ ♔b8 10 ♖b7+ ♔a8 with a draw, as White can't take the queen without losing the rook.

3 ♖a8! Continuing to play 'cat and mouse'. Now the rook finds itself beyond reach of the black pieces. But the battle doesn't end with that.

3 ... f1=♕ 4 d8=♕+ ♔xd8 5 &a6+, '... and White wins', many people would say. But ...

5 ... &b8! There you go! Right on an undefended square and also in a pin! And the main thing is that the bishop is given up with check. However, after 6 ♖xb8+ ♔c7 there is a draw, as we already pointed out in the notes to Black's second move.

6 &xf1 ♔c7. It is becoming clear that the king is heading for the b7 square to brick up the rook in the corner. This must be hindered.

7 &a6! e2! Another counter-argument: deflecting the bishop.

8 &xe2 ♔b7. Black has put his plan into action, but White has the last word.

9 &f3!! ♔xa8. It isn't difficult to grasp that after 9 ... a6 10 &xc6+ ♔xc6 11 ♖xb8 White easily stops the a-pawn.

10 &xc6X.

There are no words to express my admiration for this magnificent finale! There isn't a single extraneous piece on the board, and in the whole game not a single unnecessary move was made.

With the help of pawns the bishop manages to end the battle in the most unexpected situations.

The finale that occurred in the game Denker – Gonzalez (1945) is seldom encountered in serious tournament practice, but it goes without saying that you should bear this possibility in mind.

It seems very unlikely that the b2 bishop, which is blocked by the f6 pawn, will deliver the decisive blow against the enemy king in three moves. Nevertheless, this is achieved with the help of two tactical methods.

1 ♘xf7+! (freeing the diagonal; the queen gets to h6 without losing a tempo). **1 ... ♘xf7 2 ♕h6!** (deflecting the f7 knight, which is blocking the f6 pawn). Black resigned. On 2 ... ♘xh6 there follows 3 f7+ with mate on the next move. We should note that 1 ... ♖xf7 2 &xf7 ♘xf7 3 ♕h6 ♕g8 4 ♖e1! didn't help, and there is no defence to the threat of 5 ♖e8.

White's combination ended with an original queen sacrifice in the game Salwe – NN (1906).

Black has created dangerous threats (in particular, e3-e2+ or ♕h4), but on the other hand his king isn't feeling very confident.

1 ♖xd4. This sacrifice (a forced one, it's true) not only eliminates the main enemy, but also weakens the dark squares in his opponent's camp.

1 ... ♕xd4. No better either is 1 ... ♖xd4 2 ♕c7 (with the threats of 3 ♕h7+ and 3 ♗e5). If Black didn't take the rook, playing instead 1 ... ♗xf3, then he would also get mated: 2 ♕d8+! ♔g7 (2 ... ♕xd8 3 ♗e5+) 3 ♗e5 ♕xe5 4 ♖d7+ ♔h6 5 ♖h7X.

2 ♕d8+ ♗g8. A familiar situation has arisen: the opponent's king is blocked by the bishop and its mobility has been restricted as much as possible. In order to deliver the final blow it is necessary to deflect the black queen from the long diagonal.

3 ♕h4+! Black resigned, as in the event of 3 ... ♕xh4 4 ♗e5+ he is mated, and after 3 ... ♔g7 4 ♕xd4+ ♖xd4 5 ♗e5+ he is back where he started.

George Salwe's combination looks even more attractive if you take into account the fact that the brilliant Polish master found it in a simul, and what's more a blindfold simul!

In certain circumstances the king can come under an irrefutable attack by the bishop not only in the corner of the board, but also in the centre.

In the game Vanka – Skala (1960) White lured the enemy king out of its refuge to meet its own demise with a stunning sacrifice: **1 b4!** (opening the long diagonal for the bishop with tempo) **1 ... ♕d8 2 ♕xf6+!! ♔xf6** (2 ... ♔g8 3 ♗b2) **3 ♗b2X!**

In order to find a hidden combinational opportunity, you must, of course, display attentiveness, tactical insight and the well-known share of fantasy, but certain indicators can still serve as a starting-point for the ensuing search. Above all these are the constricted position of the enemy king and the presence of free diagonals for the bishops.

The following straightforward, but by no means obvious combination is a credit to one of the strongest female chess players in Russia.

Domsgen – Kozlovskaya (1975): **1 ... ♕xe4+!** White resigned, as on

2 ♔xe4 an unbelievable mate follows –
2 ... ♗c6X!

The law of hospitality doesn't apply in a chess game. Here are a few cases when the enemy king was exterminated by a furious bishop after an 'invitation to visit'.

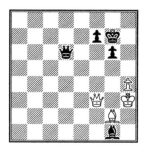

Zilberstein – Veresov (1969):
1 ... ♕h2+ 2 ♔g4 f5+ 3 ♔g5 ♕xg2+! 4 ♕xg2 ♗e3X.

In the game Klyukin – Gergel (1971) the reprisal took place on the far edge.

1 g6! (this isn't simply an exchange, but a prelude to a six-move combination).

1 ... fxg6 2 ♖xe6! ♕xh4 3 ♖xc6+ ♔b4 4 a3+ ♔a4 5 ♖c4+! bxc4 6 ♗c6X.

A problem by A. Zhoze (1966) is solved by a circuitous bishop manoeuvre. *(see next diagram)* **1 c3 ♔a5 2 ♗h6 ♔b5 3 ♗d2 ♔a5 4 c4X**.

Now let's look at a number of positions in which the bishop ends the battle in close cooperation with the king. As the king usually only gets

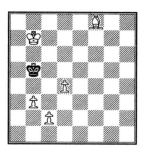

White mates in 4 moves

complete freedom of movement in the endgame, we can't avoid a chess composition.

The setups shown here seem artificial. Nevertheless, they are genuinely achievable.

A.Troitsky, 1895

White to move and win

1 ♗h6+ ♔g8 2 g7 ♔f7.

A win is also achieved in the case of **2 ... e6+ 3 ♔d6 ♔f7 4 ♔e5 ♔g8 5 ♔f6 e5 6 ♗e3 h5** (6 ... e4 7 ♗h6) **7 ♗g5 e4 8 ♔g6** or **2 ... e5 3 ♔e6 e4 4 ♔f6**.

3 g8=♕+!! A paradoxical move, leading to a delightful finale.

3 ... ♔xg8 4 ♔e6! ♔h8 5 ♔f7 e5 6 ♗g7X.

A very beautiful study. But still, the final position wasn't new. Its traces lead back to the twentieth year of the nineteenth century.

We have before us a position from a game between two great French chess players – Deschapelles (White) and La Bourdonnais. It is difficult to say how this 'abstract canvas' arose, because the early moves haven't been preserved. But still, chess historians consider this position authentic, and not composed. According to Yakov Neishtadt (*The Uncrowned Champion*, Moscow, 1975), a game existed in France in those days called 'Partie des Pions' ('Pawn Game'). One of the players could take any piece from the board and replace it with a few pawns, on condition that they didn't cross a line of demarcation. It is possible that this game was also played according to these rules.

White's position seems completely hopeless, but Deschapelles finds a brilliant idea: **1 ♘xh6+ gxh6** (1 ... ♔h8 2 ♘f7+ ♔g8 3 ♕xg7+! ♔xg7 4 ♗f6+ ♔g8 5 ♘h6X) **2 ♕h8+!! ♔xh8 3 ♔f7! ♖f8+ 4 ♔xf8**, and mate by the bishop on f6 is irrefutable.

Almost 'according to Troitsky'! But ... 70 years earlier.

Similar finales are also encountered in problem composition.

A.Cheron, 1936

White mates in 3 moves

1 ♘f5 (with the threat of ♖h1+) **1 ... ♗xh8 2 ♘g7!** (zugzwang) **2 ... ♗xg7 3 ♗xg7X**.

E.Gutman, 1935

White mates in 6 moves

The mating mechanism is already in motion and you only have to find the white bishop's shortest route to the long diagonal. As the black rook is preventing this, the manoeuvre is drawn out to six moves.

1 ♗d6! Not 1 ♗b4? immediately because of 1 ... ♖c7!, and White not only doesn't give mate, but is also losing in general: 2 ♔xd1 ♔b2. No good either is 1 ♗a3 due to 1 ... ♖b7. The manoeuvring should be done in a way that doesn't allow the rook onto the c- and b-files.

1 ... ♖f5 2 ♗b4 ♖f3 3 ♗c5 ♖f4 (3 ... ♖c3 4 ♗d4) **4 ♗a3 ♖b4 5 ♗xb4**, and it is mate on the next move.

A.Troitsky, 1916

White to move and win

White's task is to force the black king to occupy one of the squares on the b1-f5 diagonal. Then a diagonal check from below wins the queen on h7.

1 ♕d4+ ♚g5 2 ♕f6+ ♚g4 3 ♕f3+ ♚g5 4 ♕g3+ ♗g4. The main motif – 4 ... ♚f5 5 ♕d3+.

5 ♕h4+!! A sound of thunder. If 5 ... ♚f5, then 6 ♕f6+ ♚e4 7 ♕d4+ ♚f5 8 ♕d3+ or 5 ... ♚f4 6 ♕f2+ ♗f3+ 7 ♕xf3+ ♚g5 8 ♕g3+ ♚f5 and again 9 ♕d3+.

5 ... ♚xh4 6 ♗f6X!

O.Wurzburg, 1896

White mates in 3 moves

1 ♗h3! (now on any move by the king or e-pawn White replies 2 ♕g4 with unavoidable mate on c8 or d7). **1 ... a5 2 ♕a6+!** (the same sacrifice as in Troitsky's study) **2 ... ♚xa6**

(2 ... ♚a8, ♚b8 or ♚c7 – 3 ♕c8X) **3 ♗c8X.**

This is a position by del Rio (1750). The task is mate in three. **1 ♘e6+! ♕xe6** (1 ... fxe6 2 ♕f8X or 1 ... ♚g8 2 ♕b8+) **2 ♕h6+! ♚xh6 3 ♗f8X.**

If pawns also take part in the attack, then the range of mating finales expands.

There are well-known cases when the bishop turns out to be more adroit than the queen, and not in some limited area of the board, but in positions where the pieces have complete freedom of movement.

S.Kaminer, 1925
(ending of a study)

White to move and win

1 &d8+! (forcing Black to block the last free square for his king). **1 ... g5 2 &a5!** Now Black can only move his queen (2 ... g4? 3 &xd8X), and she cannot go to all the squares. She has to guard the second rank, so as not to allow g2-g3X, and also the e1 square from where the bishop can deliver a fatal blow.

2 ... ♕e2 3 &c7! (creating the threat of 4 &g3X and keeping the d8 square in his sights in case of an advance of the g5 pawn) **3 ... ♕f2 4 &d6!** Precisely here, in order to retain the possibility of transferring to the h4-d8 diagonal. Black finds himself in zugzwang: he is not able to keep the g2 pawn pinned and to defend the g3 square.

4 ... ♕f4+ (hoping for 5 &xf4 gxf4 with a draw) **5 g3+ ♕xg3+ 6 &xg3X**.

The idea expressed in the study by S.Kaminer is by no means abstract, and tournament practice is the best confirmation of this.

This position from the game Wachtel – Musial (1953) even seems to be more favourable for Black. However he loses in one move!

1 ♖e5! Threatening 2 ♖xc5+ bxc5 3 &c7X, and after the forced **1 ... ♖xe5 2 &xe5** there is no defence against 3 &c3X or (in the case of 2 ... b5) 3 &c7X. Therefore Black resigned.

If, in the game Jung – Szabados (1952), Black had managed to play 1 ... ♘f5, then he could have looked forward to the future with hope. But White found a combination that is already familiar to us.

1 &xg7! ♖xh4 2 ♕xh4+! ♔xh4 3 &f6+ g5 4 &c3! From this square the bishop controls both critical squares – e1 and f6. Black resigned – any move by him leads to defeat. The queen cannot leave the second rank because of g2-g3X, on 4 ... ♕f2 follows 5 &e5!, while on 4 ... g4 5 &f6X. It is remarkable that the study was repeated in the game almost 'verbatim'.

But this study did not come out of the blue. It is possible that its idea was inspired by a combination from the game Schlechter – Meitner (1899).

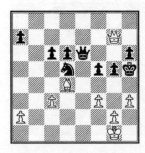

1 g4+ fxg4 2 hxg4+ ♔h4 3 ♕xh6+! ♕xh6 4 ♔h2, and, despite the extra queen, mate with the bishop on f2 can be delayed only by one move.

In their memory chess players keep 'photographs' of the most striking positions from practice and theory. The final mating position was certainly in the mind's eye of Tal (Black), when he set Geller a disguised trap in the premier league of the USSR championship in 1975.

White to move. It seems that he can calmly take the knight on e7, since after **1 ... ♕g1+ 2 ♔g3 ♕f2+ 3 ♔g4 ♕xg2+ 4 ♗g3 h5+ 5 ♔h4** (5 ♔f4 ♗e5+ or 5 ♔g5 ♕xg3+) Black has no more checks and White's threats are irresistible. But precisely at this moment Tal had hit upon **5 ... ♕e4+! 6 ♕xe4 ♗f6X!**.

However Geller spotted the trick, played 1 ♘b5 and soon won.

*　*　*　*

44. Kube – R.Braun, 1977

Black to move

After 1 ... ♘fg8 he could still play on. However there followed 1 ... h6 and ...

45. Mann – Pann, 1962

Black to move

The white king is trembling, but holding on. But is he holding on? Count to three ...

46. Mosionzhik – Gorniak 1969

White to move

Who is straining to get into the action?

47. Eliskases – Berensen, 1960

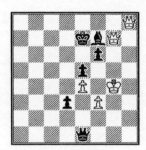

Black to move

1 ... ♕g1+ Draw. But why not 2 ♔f5?

48. Jackson – Marshall, 1899

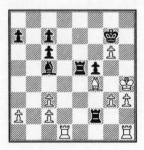

Black to move

1 ... ♔xg6 (intending 2 ... ♗e7+) 2 ♗g5. What then?

49 Gazic – Schmidt, 1978

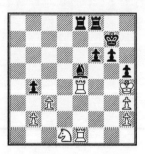

Black to move

Don't wait a minute.

50. Ending of Study by T.Gorgiev, 1938

White to move and win

A race to queen. Yes, but with care ...

51. After A.Guliaev

White mates in 3 moves

A 'turnaround' study – see No.98.

52. Study by A.Troitsky, 1897

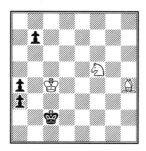

White to move and win

An old, old story.

53. L.Kubbel, 1922

White to move and win

6 moves in all. But what moves!

* * * *

"A combination is a forcing variation with a sacrifice."

M.Botvinnik

"On the chessboard there is no place for lies and hypocrisy. The beauty of a chess combination lies in the fact that it is correct."

Em. Lasker

"A combination is a distinctive explosion on the chessboard, during which the usual 'everyday' calculation and concepts lose their significance. In modern chess, beauty is more often found in analysis, while brilliant blows, as a rule, remain behind the scenes."

I. Bondarevsky

"The combination is a beautiful flower, nurtured by fantasy, love, care and logic."

D. Bronstein

"We should prize not victory but interesting combinations."

L.Tolstoy

"Combinations in chess are basic, elementary, and it is impossible to become a good chess player without having fully mastered them. But, together with this, it is always necessary to delve into the character of the position and not combine just for combination's sake."

R.Reti

"Calculation in chess requires constant training."

M.Tal

"In modern chess, beauty frequently lies in the analysis, while brilliant blows usually remain behind the scenes ..."

L.Evans

3. The Queen

In the distant past the rules of chess differed considerably from those of today. One of the most inconspicuous pieces was the queen. It moved only to an adjacent square along the diagonal. The enemy queens, just like opposite coloured bishops, never met each other, while kings easily avoided fleeting threats by choosing squares inaccessible to the queen. And so centuries passed, until some unknown reformer suddenly asked: "what in fact does the queen do?" And it became clear that the queen was good-for-nothing. So to combat its idleness it was converted into the most active piece, making it work like a rook and bishop together. "A queen for all purposes" – was the new name given to this chess piece in our country, and legitimised in *the Dictionary of the Russian Acadamy*, published in 1774. (In those days, the queen could also even move like a knight, but this rule did not catch on since it was opposed internationally.)

The name of the queen justified itself immediately. It became the terror of the chess board. Assuming the role of bishop, then rook, the queen rapidly appeared in any sector of the battle, instilling fear in the enemy, generating panic in its ranks.

Who would have guessed that after **1 ... cxd4??** in the game James – Miles (1974) the white queen mates the black king by force on the h8 square! Let's see how it happened:

2 ♗h7+ ♔h8 3 ♘xf7+! ♖xf7 4 ♘g6+! ♔xh7 5 ♘f8+ ♔g8 6 ♕h7+ ♔xf8 7 ♕h8X.

The queen lands on h7 like a bishop, while the decisive blow on h8 is delivered like a rook. This combination of manoeuvre and attack occurs in a great variety of mating attacks involving the queen.

In the game Craddock – Mieses (1939) White played **1 ♘xf6+?**, reckoning only on 1 ... gxf6. Mieses, however, surprised his opponent with the reply **1 ... ♕xf6**. After **2 ♗xc6+ bxc6 3 ♕xb8+ ♔d7 4 ♕xh8** Black continued **4 ... ♕f3!**, and the white king found itself in a mating net (5 0-0 ♗h3). There followed **5 ♔d1 ♕xe2+ 6 ♔c2 ♕xc4+ 7 ♔b1 ♕d3X.**

In the final position the queen could also be substituted by the light-squared bishop. But in the following 'game' the queen is inimitable.

1 e4 e5 2 ♕h5? ♔e7?? 3 ♕xe5X.

This tragi-comic situation will bring a smile to everyone, apart from his majesty the black king. The position demonstrates the maximum power of the queen, who is able to deny the enemy king four squares without the help of other pieces.

Here we are dealing with a variation of the so-called 'epaulette mate', the classic position of which is shown in the following schemes.

With a small stretch of the imagination, the black pieces on both sides of the king can be taken as epaulettes on the shoulders of the captive commander in chief. The 'epaulette mate' was highly prized by our chess predecessors.

Here is a position from a book by the Italian G.Lolli (1763). *(see next diagram)*

1 ♕f6+ ♔h6 (1 ... ♔g8 2 ♕e6+ ♔g7 3 ♕e5+ shortens the end by two moves) **2 ♕h4+ ♔g7 3 ♕d4+ ♔h6 4 ♕f4+ ♔g7 5 ♕e5+** (the queen was heading for this square when starting her manoeuvre.) **5 ... ♔h6 6 ♖h5+! gxh5 7 ♕f6X.**

Let's expand the combination with tactical elements.

Rakic – Govedarica (1975): **1 ♖h5+** (deflecting the g6 pawn and blocking in the king) **1 ... gxh5 2 ♕f6X**.

Steinitz – NN (1861): **1 ♖d8+!** (the queen is diverted from her control of the e6 square) **1 ... ♕xd8 2 ♕e6+** (the king is driven to a blockaded square) **2 ... ♔h7 3 ♖xh6+ gxh6 4 ♕f7X**.

And here is a more intense tactical operation, complicated by counter threats.

Golan – Stiff (1950). Black's last move was 1 ... ♕f8-b4? (correct was 1 ... ♕f8xe8). In view of the threat of mate on b2 he was counting on winning the queen. And this is what came of it.

1 ♘g5+! hxg5 2 ♗g6+! ♖xg6 3 ♖h1+ ♖h6 4 ♖xh6+ gxh6 (4 ... ♔xh6 5 ♖h1X) **5 ♕f7X**.

In the following mating finishes the second 'epaulette', as it were, is only implied as it is the edge of the chess board.

The basic technique of deflecting pieces covering critical squares, was encountered in the game Gerter – Scheipl (1957).

1 ♖c8+! Black resigned, since after 1 ... ♖xc8 2 ♖xc8+ ♘xc8 the queen gives mate on d8. A similar blow was delivered by Alekhine in a game against Freeman (1925).

1 Ee8+ ♘f8 (now it is necessary to deflect the black queen from f6) **2 ♘h6+! Wxh6** (mission accomplished, it only remains to 'call' the king to f8) **3 Exf8+! ♔xf8 4 Wd8X.**

Efimov – Bronstein (1942). Here, quite unexpectedly, the e1 square became vulnerable, after White carelessly went for an exchange of bishops: **1 ♗xe6? ♘g3+! 2 ♔g1 ♗c5+ 3 d4 ♗xd4+ 4 Wxd4 ♘e2+! 5 ♘xe2 We1X.**

In all these examples, in the final account it was the weakness of the back rank that was exploited.

The queen can deliver a blow to the opposing side if she manages to get behind enemy lines.

Kveletsky – Roslinsky (1954): **1 We5+ ♔f8** (1 ... ♔h6 2 Wf4+) **2 Wf6!** Black resigned. He can defend against the threat of mate on f7 by taking the white rook, but then the queen mates on h8.

In the scheme of the 'epaulette mate', the f8 (f1) and h6 (h3) squares often prove critical.

In this position from the game Znosko-Borovsky – Duras (1909) it seems that the second rank is sufficiently well defended.

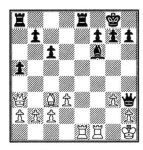

However, from h3, the queen keeps the rook f1 in her sights, and this factor ties down the possibilities of its 'twin' on e1: **1 ... Ee2!** White resigned.

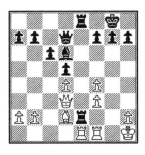

Pritchard – Cafferty (1957). Here the black rook is already on the second rank, and though it is attacked by the white pieces, the move **1 ... ♕h3!** leads to the same situation as in the preceding example.

We see how the queen simultaneously attacks two vitally important objects in the opponent's camp and gives assistance to her rook. The role of supporters may also be fulflled by other pieces.

Hort – Portisch (1973): **1 ♗g4+!** (freeing the diagonal for the bishop) **1 ... fxg4 2 ♕g5+** (driving the king into the corner and depriving the rook f8 of defence) **2 ... ♔h8 3 ♕h6**. Black resigned, since he cannot simultaneously defend the h7 square and the rook f8.

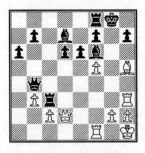

Tal – Platonov (1973): **1 ♗g3+!** (also here the king is driven into the corner, after which White exploits the pinned rook on c3) **1 ... ♔h8** (But better is 1...♗g7 2 f6 ♖f3!!) **2 ♕h6!**

Now Black's rook f8 and bishop f6 are both threatened. It seems that he saves himself with the move **2 ... ♖xg3**, but then follows **3 ♗g6!** with unstoppable mate on h7 or f8. This

'little trick' remained off screen, since Platonov preferred to resign.

Antoshin – Zvetkov (1965): **1 ♘f6!** Black resigned.

Let's look at another position, in which the critical square f1 was attacked with the help of 'telescopic sight'.

Jones – Dueball (1974): **1 ... ♖e1!** This move forces White to obstruct the first rank with his bishop and leave the rook f1 undefended since 2 ♖xe1 ♘f2+ leads to the loss of the queen.

2 ♗xe1 ♘b2! An example of a discovered double attack: the knight attacks the queen, while the black queen – the rook f1, albeit from an extremely long way away. White suffers material loss.

3 ♗c3 ♘xd1 4 ♖xd1 ♕e2. White resigned.

The final blow can also be delivered by promoting a pawn on the critical square. It is remarkable how fiercely the queen generates her own kind from the passed pawn.

In the game Chigorin – Blackburne (1898) there were three queens battling away, but the last word belongs to the fourth 'new arrival'.

1 ... ♕a5+ 2 ♖a2 (the a2 square is blocked, now there comes a decisive deflecting sacrifice) **2 ... ♕e1+! 3 ♘xe1 c1=♕X**.

Kuzmin – Kochiev (1976): **1 d5! ♖c3 2 dxe6! ♖xd3 3 exf7+ ♔h8 4 ♗b2!** Black resigned. A queen will appear on f8 with mate.

If the square g8 (g1) is occupied by a rook, and the king is on h8 (h1), the queen can deliver a conclusive blow from h6 (h3).

A variation from the game Taylor – Ghitescu (1956): **1 ... ♕g3 2 h3 ♖xh3+ 3 gxh3 ♕xh3X**. The h-pawn was eliminated by a rook sacrifice.

NN – Anderssen (1872): **1 ... ♗g2+! 2 ♖xg2 ♕f1+ 3 ♖g1 ♘g3+! 4 hxg3 ♕h3X**. Here the same pawn was deflected by the black knight.

(You will also come across NN repeatedly in the future. As a rule, this mysterious figure is an unknown opponent in a simultaneous display – but it cannot be excluded that he might simply be the product of some prankster's imagination).

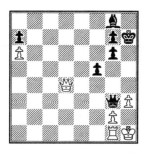

In the game NN – Elstner (1958) the advantage of the exchange is apparently not enough for White and he went after a pawn in a distant province – **1 ♕xa7??** But the surprising reply **1 ... ♗d5!** forced him to surrender since the threat of **2 ... ♕xh3X** can only be averted at the cost of his queen.

In the endgame, when the chessboard is more empty, the queen becomes even more mobile and is capable of controlling far distant sectors of the battle.

In the following study White manoeuvres in such a way that, by threatening mate on the 8th rank, he does not allow the freeing advance of the b7 pawn.

L.Borgstrom, 1950

White mates in 5 moves

1 ♔g5 ♗g8 2 ♕f3 ♗f7 3 ♕h3! From here the queen simultaneously attacks two critical points on c8 and h8. There is no defence. Mate in two moves is unstoppable.

Thanks to its high manoeuvrability, the queen can create a zugzwang position without help from the other pieces.

L. Grunenwald, 1971

White mates in 7 moves

Black would find himself in zugzwang if it were his turn to move: 1 ♕f6 ♔g4 2 ♕f8 ♔g5 3 ♕f7 ♔g4 4 ♕f6 ♔h5 5 ♕g7! (the deed is done, now everything goes like clockwork) 5 ... ♔h4 6 ♕g6 ♔h3 7 ♕h5X.

S.Limbach, 1950

White mates in 3 moves

1 ♕f5 ♗g4 2 ♕e4! ♔h5 3 ♕h7X.

The following splendid study is by the same composer. In the course of the struggle the white queen subsequently creates three identical zugzwang positions.

White mates in 8 moves

1 ♕e4! (a false trail would be 1 ♕d1+? ♖g1 2 ♕d5+ e4!) 1 ... b1=♕ 2 ♕xb1+ ♖g1 3 ♕b7+ e4 4 ♕xe4+ ♖g2 5 ♕b1+ ♖g1 6 ♕b7+ ♖g2 7 ♕e4! By travelling twice along the triangle e4-b1-b7-e4, the queen forces the king to leave his refuge.

7 ... ⚔g1 8 ♕e1X. This is not simply 'mate in 8 moves', but the only means of winning overall. Such compositions are called 'study problems'.

The final position and preceding play in the study by I.Grigoriev (1925) also looks as if it has been taken from practical play.

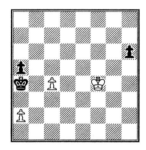

White to move and win

White's first task is to promote his pawn earlier than his opponent.

1 a3! h5 2 ⚔g3! h4+ 3 ⚔h3! As will become clear later, it is necessary to keep the black h-pawn 'alive'. Meanwhile Black is in zugzwang.

3 ... ⚔xa3 4 c5 a4 5 c6 ⚔b2 6 c7 a3 7 c8=♕ a2. Now the queen is moving closer to the enemy, exploiting the method called 'the staircase' in studies.

8 ♕b7+ ⚔c1 9 ♕c6+ ⚔b2 10 ♕b5+ ⚔c2 11 ♕c4+ ⚔b2 12 ♕b4+ ⚔c2 13 ♕a3 ⚔b1 14 ♕b3+ ⚔a1. Black would be in stalemate if the h4 pawn were not on the board and it would end in a draw. By freeing the way for the black pawn, White gets time for a decisive queen manoeuvre.

15 ⚔g4! h3 16 ♕c2 h2 17 ♕c1X.

The effectiveness of an attack increases dramatically if the queen has an outpost in the immediate vicinity of the enemy king. The pawn serves as a support when advancing to the 6th (3rd) rank.

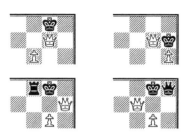

When the queen is the spearhead of the attack, as a rule it is not difficult to find a decisive blow. It usually comes down to eliminating the opponent's pieces that are defending critical squares.

1 ♕h6 ♘e6 2 ♘d6! Black resigned: after 2 ... cxd6 3 ♖xe6 the king perishes at the royal gate.

In the game Chikovani – Aufman (1952) White threatens to take the knight e6 with the rook and deliver mate on g7. No use is 1 ... ♖g8

2 ♖xh7+ ♔xh7 3 ♕h5X or 1 ... ♕d7 2 ♖e5, and the threat of 3 ♖xh7+ is irresistible.

Black tries to bar the way for the queen – **1 ... ♘g5** reckoning on 2 ♕xg5 ♖xe1+ 3 ♔f2 ♕g8. But the sacrifice **2 ♖xh7+** dispels his hopes. Black resigned. (2 ... ♔xh7 3 ♕h5+).

Saidenshur – Kolhagen (1936): **1 ♘c6!** In view of the threat 2 ♕xh7+ ♔xh7 3 ♖h4X Black must give up his queen, but the struggle is not over.

1 ... ♕c5 2 ♖h4 ♕h5 3 ♖xh5 gxh5.

Black is reckoning on counterplay along the g-file. But the h1-a8 diagonal is presently closed, which gives White a decisive tempo.

4 ♖b1! With the direct threat of 5 ♖xb7 and 6 ♘e7 (No help is 4 ... ♖g6 5 ♖xb7 ♖xh6 6 ♖b8+).

4 ... ♗xc6 5 ♖b8! This device of deflecting the rook from the critical square g7 is very typical. Black resigned.

The same danger awaits the king also when there is a pawn wedge on h6 (h3). In these cases the queen's route usually runs via the f6 (f3) square or the 7th (2nd) rank.

Let's take a look at three positions where the h-pawn is already established on the bridgehead and the queen is waiting patiently.

Kochiev – Ubilava (1975): **1 ♘f6+.** Black resigned (1 ... ♔h8 2 ♘xd5). Note how the knight forces the king to move away to h8 so that the queen can pay him a visit without any delay. 1 ♕f6? does not achieve its objective after 1 ... ♕f8.

Silberstein carried out a similar manoeuvre in a game against Dementiev (1968). The jumps of the white pieces resemble the childen's game of 'leapfrog'.

1 ♕f6 (the struggle would be confused after 1 ♘f6+ ♔h8 2 ♘d7 f6) **1 ... ♘e8 2 ♕e7! ♘c7 3 ♘f6+ ♔h8 4 ♘e8!** Black resigned.

Zhuravlev – Kapanidze (1977): **1 ... ♖xb1 2 ♖xb1 ♗f5!!** Interception.

The threat is 3 ... ♛f3+, and if 3 ♜f1, then 3 ... ♛e2. White resigned.

The scheme of advancing pawns to the 6th (3rd) rank in principle is very simple.

1 f6 g6 2 ♛h6 or **1 h6 g6 2 ♛f6**.

However in tournament practice such direct methods usually figure only as a threat. As a rule, advancing pawns and pieces to attacking positions is preceded by all sorts of tricks and attacking operations.

Yates – Naegli (1927). The immediate pawn attack 1 f6? is parried by the move 1 ... g6. But isn't it possible to replace the g7 pawn with a piece to give the game a different character?

1 ♗xg7! Black resigned, without waiting for the obvious finish – 1 ... ♔xg7 2 f6.

Arkhipkin – Prodanov (1977): **1 f6!** Black resigned. Mate is threatened on h7, while after 1 ... hxg5 2 ♛g6 both the commander and the soldier are established on a narrow bridgehead thanks to the diagonal fire-power of the bishop on d5.

Often the queen bursts into the enemy trenches first and waits for the infantry to come to her help.

In the following example this is achieved with the help of a sacrifice.

Spiller – Matchett (1956): **1 e5 ♜xc1?** 2 ♘f6+! exf6 3 exf6 Black resigned.

The same device, but in more complicated circumstances, was applied by Ravinsky (White) against Illivitsky (1952).

1 ♗f6! (White blocks the f7 pawn, not allowing it to advance, which it could have done after 1 e5) **1 ... ♗xf6 2 e5!** (in view of the threat of mate on h7 Black has no time to deal with the defiant pawn) **2 ... ♘xd3 3 exf6**

(Black's king is surrounded while White's easily escapes the checks) **3 ... ♘f2+ 4 ♔g1 ♘h3+ 5 ♔f1 ♗c4+ 6 ♘e2.** Black resigned (6 ... ♗xe2+ 7 ♔e1).

In establishing a pawn wedge at f6 (f3), particular care should be taken to assess its durability. Here is a typical example where an apparently dangerous pawn proved to be a 'paper tiger'.

Shvedchikov – Estrin (1977): **1 ♘f6+? exf6 2 gxf6.** The black king is looking down the barrel of a gun but it turns out to be a futile attempt ...

2 ... ♛xf2+! White resigned (3 ♔xf2 ♘g4+ or 3 ♔h1 ♛xf6).

Science fiction writers and brothers Arkady and Boris Strugatsky coined the term – 'zero-transportation', which means the instantaneous movement of a physical body from one point to another. How this happens (and whether it happens at all), nobody knows. But chess players have long since learned to project the pieces in the right direction with tempo, that is, without loss of time. Only here fantasy has got nothing to do with it.

The next tactical operation comes from olden times and it is a scheme which we quote from a book by the Portuguese Damiano (1512). White's task is to get his queen over to the h-file. This is achieved by consecutive sacrifices of two rooks:

White mates in 5 moves

White's task is to break through with his queen on the h-file. He achieves this with consecutive sacrifices of two rooks: **1 ♖h8+ ♔xh8 2 ♖h1+ ♔g8 3 ♖h8+ ♔xh8 4 ♛h1+ ♔g8 5 ♛h7X.**

This motif is often met in contemporary tournament practice. Here is a case where Damiano's combination was repeated in its pure form exactly 400 years later.

Mannheim – Regensberg (1912). White played **1 ♖h8+** and then as in the previous example.

In the game Sturua – Kozlov (1975) the white queen has already made an appointment with the black king on the g7 square, but cannot find her way there. The rook comes to her aid.

1 ♖g8+! Black resigned. After 1 ... ♖xg8 2 ♕xc1 he loses the queen, while after 1 ... ♔xg8 2 ♕g3+ mates.

The freeing of lines is one of the most typical tactical methods, making possible the breakthrough of the queen in the hot spots of the position.

It is not always put into effect by check, but usually with tempo, as is seen, for example, from the ending of the game Heemsoth-Heisenbuttel (1924).

White needs to free the g7 square for the queen, but there are two rooks in its way. One, for example, can be sacrificed on h7, but what to do with the other?

The situation is aggravated by Black's counter-threats on the c-file. But it is precisely this fact that draws White to a solution to the problem.

1 ♖c5! Not only defending the c2 square, but also attacking the enemy queen. In this way White moves the rook off the g-file with tempo.

1 ... ♕xc5 2 ♖xh7+ ♔xh7 3 ♕g7X.

In both this and the previous operation the main protagonists were the rooks, however the concluding transfer of the queen can be preceded by a whole cascade of sacrifices.

This is a position from the game NN – Mason (1948). Who from fiction would dare to predict that the black queen is ready to undergo 'zero-transportation' along the route c8 – h8 – h2, where seven pieces crowd the way! But look how cleverly they disperse ...

1 ... ♗b5! 2 axb5 ♘hg3+ 3 ♘xg3 ♘xg3+ 4 hxg3 hxg3+ 5 ♔g1 ♖h1+! 6 ♔xh1 ♖h8+ 7 ♔g1 ♗c5+! 8 ♘xc5 ♖h1+ 9 ♔xh1 ♕h8+ 10 ♔g1 ♕h2X!

All the black pieces have disappeared from the board, except the queen. But as they say, 'mate is boss'.

At heart, the queen is an aristocrat, 'dirty work' is not to her liking, she likes to engage in business only after her staff have cleared the way for a 'grand entrance'.

Mayet – Hirschfeld (1861): **1 ... ♗xd4+! 2 cxd4 ♖xg2+ 3 ♔h1 ♖xh2+!** (but not 3 ... ♕h4? 4 ♗xf4 ♕xf4? 5 ♖xf3) **4 ♔xh2 ♕h4+ 5 ♔g1 ♕g3+ 6 ♔h1 ♕g2X.**

With a pawn wedge on g6 (g3) the squares h7 (h2) and f7 (f2) become critical. And the queen's powers give her paths of access to them.

The h-file

Botvinnik – Keres (1966): **1 ♖b8!** Black resigned (1 ... ♕xb8 2 ♕xh4).

Trying to weaken the onslaught of the white pieces, Matanovic (Black) in a game against Spassky (1962) gave up the exchange: **1 ... ♖xd4.** But Spassky had already gathered speed: **2 ♖xf8+** (first eliminating the knight, which protects the h7 square) **2 ... ♕xf8 3 ♖h8+** (the h-file is freed for the queen, while the enemy king is deflected to h8) **3 ... ♔xh8 4 ♕h3+.** Black resigned.

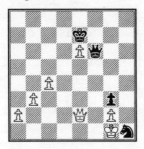

Dobberdin – Stark (1962): **1 ... ♕a1+! 2 ♕f1 ♕d4+ 3 ♔xh1 ♕h8+ 4 ♔g1 ♕h2X.** In this operation Black's knight was literally superfluous, but his queen forced White to block the f1 square.

The seventh rank

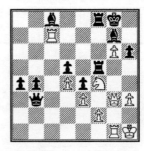

Blackburne – Lipschutz (1889): **1 ♖xg7+! ♔xg7** (1 ... ♔h8 2 ♖h7+ ♔g8 3 g7) **2 ♘h5+ ♖xh5 3 ♕c7+.** Black resigned (3 ... ♔f6 4 ♕d6+ ♔g7 5 ♕e7+).

Roizin – Sorokin (1952): **1 ... ♘b3+! 2 axb3 axb3+ 3 ♘a3 ♖xa3+! 4 bxa3 ♕c2.** The rank is indefensible because of the pin. White resigned.

Diagonal

Littlewood – Powell (1960): **1 ♗xh6
♖d1?** (1 ... ♖d4! 2 ♕b7 ♕a3) **2 ♕c4+
♔h8 3 ♗xg7+!** and Black resigned
(3... ♗xg7 4 ♕c8+ or 3 ... ♔xg7 4 ♕f7+).

Upon operations on the f7 (f2)
squares, frequently the corner square is
blocked.

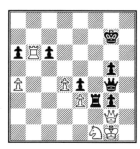

Bankov – Lysmyagin (1975): **1 ... ♖f2!
2 ♕h1** (2 ♕xg3 ♖xf1+) **2 ... ♖xf1+
3 ♔xf1 ♕d1+.** White resigned (4 ♔g2
♕f3+).

E.Vladimirov – Donchev (1975):
1 ♖xh7+ ♔g8 2 ♕c4+ ♖d5 3 ♕c8+!
This is stronger than 3 ♗xd5+? ♔f8
4 ♕c8+ ♕e8. It should not be forgotten
that Black has two queens on the board.
3 ... ♗f8 4 ♖h8+! ♕xh8 5 ♕e6+.
Black resigned, since he will be mated
on f7.

We now show some typical tactical
methods of engagement against a
bishop covering the king. When the
king is in the centre, the bishop usually
holds the defence on the e7 (e2) square
– and after short castling – on g7 (g2).

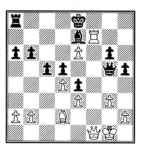

In the game Betbeder – Tiroler
(1930) the penetration of White's
queen into the opponent's position is
hampered by her own rook. If however
the rook moves to g7 or h7 ... 1 ♖g7?,
then Black, by playing 1 ... ♕f5,
maintains the balance. However his
objective is achieved by **1 ♖f8+! ♗xf8
2 ♕f7+ ♔d8 3 ♕d7X.** This is not only
a freeing of the f7 square (unblocking),
but also a deflection of the bishop e7.

Netheim – Hamilton (1961): **1 ♖h8+!**
(inferior is 1 ♕h5 ♖xf4, and the black
king can hide on f8) **1 ... ♗xh8 2 ♕h5.**
Black resigned.

Belyavsky – Michalchishin (1977).
If 1 ♕xg7 0-0-0! 2 ♕xe7 gxh2+

3 ♔xh2 e3 Black obtains dangerous counterplay. Belyavsky found a forcing way to victory. **1 ♕h5+! ♔f8** (1 ... ♔d8 2 ♕h8+) **2 ♕h8+ ♖g8 3 ♖xf6+!** (again a deflection of the bishop). Black resigned (3 ... ♗xf6 4 ♕xf6+ ♔e8 5 ♕f7+ ♔d8 6 ♕d7X).

A pawn reaching the 5th (4th) rank can also serve as an outpost for the queen. In these cases a mating finish arises when rear squares are blocked and its pattern is reminiscent of the 'epaulette mate'.

The motif of the combination in the game Kramtsov – Vaksberg (1938) was the cramped position of the black king.

1 ♖d7! ♕b1+ 2 ♗f1 a6 3 ♖xb7+! ♔xb7 4 ♕b6X.

Redelyi – Barati (1961): **1 ... ♖a1+! 2 ♗xa1 ♕a4 3 ♕g8+ ♔b7 4 ♕b3 ♕xa1+ 5 ♕b1 ♖xc2+! 6 ♔xc2 ♕c3X.**

The white queen took a sharp turn in the game Strekalovsky – Golyak (1974): **1 ♖h7+! ♔xh7 2 ♕h2+ ♔g7 3 ♕h6X.**

Pawns that take a direct part in the attack also restrict the mobility of the king, making possible the creation of mating situations.

The direction of the main blow can come on the back rank or an edge file.

Niederman – Szucs (1895): **1 ♗c8!!** Luring the rook to the c8 square, since the variation 1 ... ♕b1+ 2 ♔h2

♕xb6 3 ♗xb7 ♕xb7 4 ♕d6+ ♔c7 5 ♖a8+ leads to the loss of the queen.

1 ... ♖xc8 2 ♖a8+! ♔xa8 3 ♕xc8+ ♖b8. Now, when the back rank and a-file are free of pieces, the queen carries out its crowning manoeuvre.

4 ♕c6+ ♖b7 5 ♕a4+ ♔b8 6 ♕e8+ ♕d8 7 ♕xd8X.

In the game Sokolov – Mikhailov (1973) both kings find themselves in danger, however it's White's turn to move, and he carries out a combination in which an important role is assigned to the f6 pawn.

1 ♖a3! (defending against the mate on a1 and opening a path for the queen to h5) **1 ... bxa3 2 ♗d7!**

With the help of a tactical device familiar to us, White, with tempo, makes way for an approach to the black king. Insufficient was 2 ♗xc8 ♖xc8, and in view of the threat to the c2 square White will not manage to complete the attack (3 ♖xh7+ ♔xh7 4 ♕h5+ ♔g8 5 ♕g4+ ♔f8 6 ♕xc8+ ♕e8). Also no good is 2 ♕h5? ♗xh3 3 ♕xh3 a2+ 4 ♔a1 ♕xc2.

2 ... ♕xd7 3 ♖xh7+! ♔xh7 4 ♕h5X.

One of the most economical mating constructions is illustrated by a position given by D.Ponziani (1769).

1 ♗d8+ ♔a7 2 ♖xa6+! bxa6 3 ♕d7+ ♔b8 4 ♕c7+ ♔a8 5 ♕c8+ ♔a7 6 ♗b6+! ♔xb6 7 ♕b8X. There are black pawns on both sides of the king – the same fateful 'epaulettes'. Only the 'decoration' is made not on the front line but from the rear. For this a particular role is played by the b4 pawn.

Forintos managed to carry out an analogous idea nearly two hundred years later against Tomovic (1957).

Black's attack seems irresistible, but White found a forced win: **1 ♗d3+ g6 2 ♖h8+! ♔xh8 3 ♕f8+ ♔h7 4 ♕xf7+ ♔h8 5 ♕f8+ ♔h7 6 ♗xg6+! ♔xg6 7 ♕g8X.**

In particular, the great manoeuvrability of the queen should be borne in mind when there is play on different flanks.

A straightforward but typical manoeuvre decided the outcome of the encounter Fedorov – Vasiliev (1974). After **1 ... ♕g1** White found himself in a hopeless position since his queen will not succeed in coming to the aid of her king.

2 g5 h5! 3 g4 h4! White resigned: one of three mating finishes is inevitable: 4 ♔xh4 ♕h2X or 4 ♕a3 ♕h1X, or 4 ♕a1 ♕g3X.

A similar manoeuvre was made by Fischer (Black) against Mednis (1958).

1 ... h5! How to repulse the threat of 2 ... g4+? No help is 2 ♕b7+ ♔h6 or 2 g4+ hxg4 3 ♕xg4 ♕h1+ 4 ♔g3 ♕e1+, and then the white knight is captured. There remains the last possibility:

2 ♕xh5 ♕h1+ 3 ♔g4 ♕d1+!

Forcing White to block the f3 square, since on other replies he loses his queen.

4 ♘f3 ♕d7X.

And now here is a study in which the ending of the last game was reworked:

M.Botvinnik, S.Kaminer (1925)

1 ... ♕f2+ 2 ♔h3 (otherwise all the kingside pawns are lost) **2 ... ♕g1.** White resigned.

Despite his material advantage, White, in the game Lutov-Botvinnik (1925), lost because of the unfortunate position of his king.

1 g4+ ♔h4 2 ♗h6! Black has to take the bishop, since mate is threatened from h2. The queen is lured to a square where it will block in his king.

2 ... ♕xh6 3 ♕h2+ ♔g5 4 ♕d2+! ♘f4 (the blocking in is completed) **5 ♕d8X.**

62

54. Edelstein – Yazhe, 1957

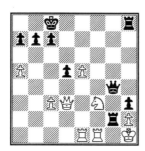

Black to move

And he played 1 ... ♖f8? But what would you do?

55. Lyaska – Ikart, 1974

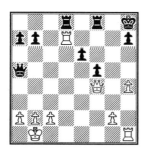

White to move

1 ♕d4+ is parried by means of 1 ... e5. Which move leads to mate?

56. Karner – Karpov, 1972

Black to move

1 ... d2? Come what may.

57. Tarjan – Karpov, 1976

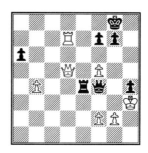

Black to move

In the rank of champions ...

58. Smejkal – Adorjan, 1972

White to move

Distract or attract!

59 Sindik – Cebalo, 1978

White to move

A blow that is necessary!

60. Aitken – Payne, 1962

Black to move

What follows on 1 ... ♛xe5 ?

63. Tisdall – Sax, 1978

Black to move

A suspicious 'vacuum' ...

61. Garcia – Romanishin, 1977

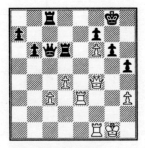

White to move

1 ♕h6? But then 1 ... ♖xf6. How can he secure this pawn?

64. Agzamov – Ruderfer, 1974

White to move

Open lines are not trifles.

62. Gratias – Muller, 1976

Black to move

A magical square.

65. Sobura – Surada, 1977

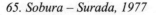

White to move

There is no third course.

66. Damjanovic – Lutikov, 1969

White to move

A favourite manoeuvre.

67. Morphy – NN

White to move

A familiar configuration? Get started!

68. Gambelli – Maroczy, 1889

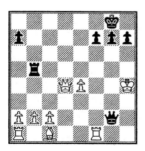

Black to move

An angry queen.

69 Borisenko – Simagin, 1955

Black to move

Even in the endgame ...

70. Ruchieva – Eidelson, 1976

Black to move

With Caissa's blessing.

71. Fleissig – Schlechter, 1899

Black to move

How to get the queen to d1?

72. Vladimirov – Agzamov, 1977

White to move

Packing the gun tight with ammunition ...

73. Willer – Hall, 1964

Black to move

White dreams of exchanges, Black – of an appointment with the king.

74. Matokhin – Kuzmin, 1970

Black to move

A king hunt.

75. Goltzov – Moiseev, 1970

White to move

Level headed heroes always take the roundabout route ...

76. Larsen – Englund, 1961

Black to move

The bishop d7 has the last word, but before then – two beautiful moves.

77. Study by I.Koers, 1916

White mates in 3 moves

Solitaire.

78. Study by A.Grunenwald, 1956

White mates in 3 moves

A queen in disgrace.

79 Study by A.d'Orville, 1837

White mates in 4 moves

Over the barbed wire.

80. Study by L.Borgstrom, 1956

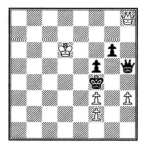

White to move and win

A lacy pattern.

*　*　*　*

"The possibility of an opportune conversion of material into force and force into material is a remarkable characteristic of chess, the most important in chess."

Spielmann

"You should embark on a combination only when your mind is perfectly clear, so you can calculate precisely all forcing moves, taking into account all possible replies in all variations to the very end."

I.Bondarevsky

"Many sacrifices do not generally require concrete calculation. It is enough to look at the arising position, in order to convince yourself that the sacrifice is right."

M.Tal

4. The Knight

The chess knight is a strange piece, unlike any other. "Where are you riding to, proud steed, and where will you lay down your hoof?" Manuals for beginners use many words to explain in an intelligent manner the intricate move of the chess knight. However let's quote the text of an old military song:

> Where the infantry does not trek,
> Where the armoured train does not torment,
> The heavy tank does not trundle,
> There flies the steel bird...

The knight, of course, is not as fast as the 'steel bird'. Moreover, in its speed of travel it is inferior to all the other chess troops, except the infantry. But in return none can compare with the knight, especially at that moment when, rearing up on its hind legs, it makes a 'half move' as if hovering over its target.

For this piece obstacles do not exist: one jump – and it is behind the menacing guards, the bristling fence of pawns. Here the enemy king hides behind impregnable walls and is surrounded by courtiers given over to the joys of chess, when suddenly ... "Mene, Tekel, Upharsin". Like the Babylonian king, Balthazar, he learns of his sentence in the midst of a noisy feast.

The 'smothered mate'. Its form is easy to understand yet striking, like a painting. It has been known since olden times and was already described in the very first chess book, published in 1497 by the Spaniard J.Lucena.

1 ♕e6+ ♚h8 2 ♘f7+ ♚g8 3 ♘h6+ ♚h8 4 ♕g8+ ♖xg8 5 ♘f7X! (The position has an additional solution: 3 ♘d8+.)

A main role in the mechanism of combinations is played by the 'double check', by virtue of which we now give it our attention.

More than five hundred years have since passed, but the 'smothered mate' not only continues to be seen in modern tournament practice, but also to amaze chess fans. And although from a once brilliant combination it has turned into a simple tactical device, a proud knight jump somehow highlights the triumph of mind over matter.

In this position F.Koehlein delivers mate in 6 or 9 moves. *(see next diagram)*

1 ♘b5+ ♚b8 2 ♕d6+! ♚a8 3 ♘c7+.

It becomes clear why it was necessary to give a check with the

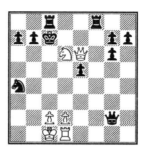

queen from d6 and not e5. The white knight is invulnerable since the rook f8 is under attack. This factor frequently accompanies combinations associated with the 'smothered mate'.

3 ... ♚b8 4 ♘a6+ ♚a8 5 ♕b8+ ♖xb8 6 ♘c7X.

Now let's see what happens if the black knight takes another route: 1 ♘b5+ ♚d8 2 ♕d6+ ♚e8 3 ♕xe5+ ♚f7 (3 ... ♚d7 4 ♕d6+ ♚e8 5 ♖e1+) 4 ♘d6+ ♚g8 5 ♕e6+ (again the queen is placed on a square from which it attacks a rook, this time another one) 5 ... ♚h8 6 ♘f7+ ♚g8 7 ♘h6+ ♚h8 8 ♕g8+ ♖xg8 9 ♘f7X.

The mechanism of 'double check' comes into actrion after an initial check by the queen along the diagonal.

In the game Evans – Larsen (1957) such a check was prevented by the rook f2. By sacrificing it, the Danish grandmaster frees the g1-a7 diagonal for attack: 1 ... ♖f1+! 2 ♖xf1 (2 ♚xf1 ♕f5+ 3 ♚g1 ♕c5+) 2 ... ♕c5+, and

White resigned, without waiting for the finish.

In this position from the game Morphy – Brien (1859) the diagonal leading to the black king is free of pieces but the execution of the combination is prevented by the queen's control of the e7 square. (1 ♕a3+ ♔e8). This means that it is necessary to drive it away.

1 e5 ♕g5 2 h4! ♕g4 (the job is done, the way is clear) **3 ♕a3+ ♔g8 4 ♘e7+ ♔f8 5 ♘g6+ ♔g8 6 ♕f8+ ♖xf8 7 ♘e7X**.

Dahl – Schperber (1968). White has already 'lit the fuse' but even here the final salvo on c7 is prevented by the black queen.

1 ♖d6! ♕xf3. Black also loses after 1 ... ♕c8 2 ♖a3. But stronger was 1 ... e5! 2 ♕xe5 ♖e8 (inferior is 2 ... ♖xg2+? 3 ♔f1 ♖e8 4 ♘c7+ or 3 ... ♕c8 4 ♖a3), and White still has to

find the difficult move 3 ♖g3! (3 ... ♖xg3 4 ♕xg3 or 3 ... ♕xg2+ 4 ♖xg2 ♖xg2+ 5 ♔f1 ♖xe5 6 ♖d8+).

2 ♖d8+! ♖xd8 3 ♘c7+ ♔b8 4 ♘a6+ ♔a8 5 ♕b8+ ♖xb8 6 ♘c7X.

The rapid advance of pieces to an attacking position is the key to success in carrying out such operations.

Bernstein – Metger (1907): **1 ♘eg5! fxg5 2 ♖xd7 ♕xd7 3 ♘xe5**. Black resigned. After 3 ... ♕e8 (3 ... ♕f5) 4 ♘f7+ ♔g8 5 ♘d6+ the queen is lost, while all other queen moves lead to a 'smothered mate'.

Handolin – Ojanen (1962): **1 ... ♘g4 2 ♗xe7 ♕b6!** (Black does not waste time taking the bishop – the threat of discovered check is irresistible) **3 ♔h1 ♘f2+ 4 ♔g1 ♘e2+ 5 ♘xe2 ♘h3+ 6 ♔h1 ♕g1+ 7 ♘xg1 ♘f2X**.

Sometimes it is possible to get round things even without a double check.

Dragunov – Odrykovsky (1961): **1 ♕h5!** (with the threats of 2 ♘e7+ or 2 ♘h6+) **1 ... ♔h8** (while here Black has no choice) **2 ♕xf7 ♕d8 3 ♘h6!** (threatening 4 ♕g8X, and on 3 ... gxh6 follows mate) **3 ... ♗d6 4 ♕g8+! ♖xg8 5 ♘f7X.**

Unzicker – Sarapu (1970). On his last move Black played ♖f8-d8, reckoning on capturing the knight d6. However White has at his disposal a hidden defence.

1 ♗f4! ♘xf4? (Black is hypnotised by the pin on the d-file) **2 ♕xf7+ ♔h8 3 ♕g8+!** (the rook is deflected from the saving file) **3 ... ♖xg8 4 ♘f7X.**

In the game Stolberg – Zak (1939) a similar operation was prepared by an interception: **1 ♖d7!** ♗xd7 (1 ... g6 is better) **2 ♕xf7+ ♔h8 3 ♗c4!** Surprisingly it becomes clear that Black has no satisfactory defence to the mating threat. After **3 ... ♘g6** it finishes in the familiar way: **4 ♕g8+ ♖xg8 5 ♘f7X.**

One of the indispensable conditions of the 'smothered mate' operation is a complete blockade of the enemy king. This is forced either with a sacrifice, as we have seen earlier, or a threat.

Alekhine – Lugowski (1931): **1 ♘e6+!** ♘xe6 (1 ... ♗xe6 2 ♕e7+ ♔g8 3 ♕e8X) **2 ♕e7+ ♔g8 3 ♕e8+** (forcing Black to block the last free square) **3 ... ♘f8 4 ♘e7X.**

The blockading operation can also be directed against a king in the centre.

In the game Ed.Lasker – Horowitz (1946) the namesake of the world champion had played the opening very badly. True, White has won a pawn but at a catastrophic lag in development. With a queen manoeuvre Black completely disorganises his opponent's piece coordination.

1 ... ♕a5! The threat of 2 ... ♘c2+ is unpleasant enough. On 2 ♕d2 would of course follow 2 ... ♘e4.

2 ♘d2 ♕e5+ 3 ♘e2 (otherwise this knight is lost) **3 ... ♘d3X**.

Once upon a time an old fellow by the name of Perkovsky used to come to the chess pavilion in the central park of culture and recreation in Moscow. He was one of those regulars who gave a special flavour to the park battleground. He was a pretty tough player, but what distinguished him was the fact that he liked to surround his king with 'over-protection' and construct quaint defences. These positions were called 'the Perkovsky box'. For his poor old king, it often became an eternal resting place. In chess jargon, this method is called 'self blocking'. Here are a few oddities on this theme.

Granter – Kemp (1894): **1 e4 c5 2 ♘f3 ♘c6 3 d4 cxd4 4 ♘xd4 e5 5 ♘f5** (not the best move because of 5 ... d5!, but ...) **5 ... ♘ge7?? 6 ♘d6X**.

Do you think this happens only in beginners' games? Not at all!

In the next game a Polish master was playing Black, and not anywhere, but in an international tournament and against P.Keres.

Keres – Arlamowski (1950): **1 e4 c6 2 ♘c3 d5 3 ♘f3 dxe4 4 ♘xe4 ♘d7 5 ♕e2 ♘gf6?? 6 ♘d6X**.

Grandmaster S.Reshevsky needs no introduction, but in a game against Margolith (1958) even he was embarrassed after: **1 d4 ♘f6 2 c4 e6 3 ♘c3 ♗b4 4 e3 c5 5 ♘ge2 ♘c6 6 a3 ♕a5 7 ♗d2 e5 8 axb4 ♘xb4 9 ♖xa5?? ♘d3X**.

The danger of 'smothered mate' appears every time when a knight takes part in the attack, and a king is hemmed in by his own pieces.

Rymyatsev – Lomonosov (1978): **1 d6!** More funny than sad. On 1 ... ♘a6 follows 2 dxc7 ♘xc7 3 ♘d6X. If 1 ... ♕c8, then once again 2 dxc7 with the same threat of mate on d6. Black must suffer serious material loss, therefore he resigned.

Schlage – NN (1934). The black king is already in a secure 'package' and it is enough to eliminate the piece

defending the critical f6 square –
1 ♕xd7. Black resigned.

In this position from the game Muller
– Weihacht (1937), the c2 square, from
where the knight b4 might deliver the
decisive blow, is defended by two
pieces – the queen b3 and the knight a3.
Black logically removes both these
obstacles.

1 ... ♘e4! 2 ♗h4 (2 ♘xe4 ♘d3X)
2 ... ♘c5! 3 ♕g3 (one piece is deflected
with a threat, the other eliminated at
once) 3 ... ♕xa3! White resigned.

Donner – Balcerowski (1962). How
to exploit the cramped position of the
black king? Like this: **1 h6!**, and Black
resigned, since 1 ... g6 2 ♘xe7+ ♕xe7
3 ♗g5 leads to the loss of a piece,
while 1 ... ♘e8 – to a 'smothered
mate': 2 hxg7 ♘xg7 3 ♘h6X.

The theme of 'smothered mate' has
been exploited time and again in
compositions. It was celebrated

particularly loudly in a study by
A.Seletsky (1933).

Looking at the deserted board, it
cannot even be imagined that in a few
moves the black king will be
imprisoned by his own pieces.

1 ♕g5! With the unambiguous threat
of 2 d8=♕. Not possible is 1 ... ♗xd7
because of 2 ♘f4, and the black king
falls into a mating net (3 ♗h5X).

1 ... ♔e6+ 2 ♔g1!. Only here is the
white king safely sheltered from the
checks.

2 ... ♔xd7. If 2 ... ♗xd7, then
3 ♗g4+ ♔f7 (3 ... ♔d6 4 ♕c5X)
4 ♘e5+ etc.

3 ♘c5+ ♔c8. Other moves lead to
the loss of the queen: 3 ... ♔d6
4 ♕g3+! ♔d5 (4 ... ♔e7 5 ♕e5+ ♔f7
6 ♗c4+ ♔g6 7 ♗d3+ ♔h6 8 ♕h2+
♔g7 9 ♘e6+) 5 ♗c4+! ♔xc4 6 ♕b3+
♔xc5 7 ♕a3+ ♔b6 8 ♕xf8. (Here, it is
true, there is some very sophisticated
analysis showing that Black could
construct a drawing fortress.)

**4 ♗a6+ ♔b8 5 ♕g3+ ♔a8 6 ♗b7+!
♗xb7 7 ♘d7!!** By now it is not chess
but magic! The threats are 8 ♘b6X and
8 ♘xf8, and the queen cannot leave the
back rank because of 8 ♕b8X.

7 ... ♕d8. Moving away the
queen and defending the b6 and b8
squares.

8 ♕b8+! ♕xb8 9 ♘b6X!.

The final position, where all available black pieces take part in the 'self-blocking' and the concluding blow is delivered by the sole surviving knight, makes a great impression.

In practical play such a finale is unlikely to occur. But here, perhaps, is something similar ...

Zhotov – Glebov (1975): **1 ♕c7!** A funny situation. White threatens 2 ♕b8+ ♖xb8 3 ♘c7X, and this finale can only be 'exchanged' on 1 ... ♗xa6 2 ♕xa7X or 1 ... ♖xa6 2 ♕xb7X. Therefore Black resigned.

Noting the personal merits of the knight, let us now consider how it performs in co-operation with its own king. These endgame positions have practical significance.

Here is an ending from one of the oldest studies.

1 ♔c2 ♔a1 2 ♘c1! In order to force a fatal advance of the pawn, Black exploits a zugzwang to 'stalemate' the black king.
2 ... a2 3 ♘b3X.

P.Stamma, 1737

On the move, White creates a zugzwang position that is similar to the preceding example: **1 ♘g3+ ♔h2 2 ♘f5 ♔h1 3 ♔f2 ♔h2 4 ♘e3 ♔h1 5 ♘f1 h2 6 ♘g3X.**
But if it were Black to move at the start then it would end in a draw.

A.Salvio, 1634

Here White wins irrespective of whose turn it is to move: **1 ♘f6 ♔h1 2 ♘g4 g5 3 ♔f1 h2 4 ♘f2X**.

Or **1 ... g5 2 ♘f6 g4 3 ♘xg4+ ♔h1 4 ♔f1 h2 4 ♘f2X**.

The same thing goes for the following position.

K.Jaenisch, 1837

1 ♘e5 ♔h2 (1 ... f3 2 ♘g4 f2 3 ♘xf2+, and then as in the main variation) **2 ♔f2 ♔h1 3 ♘g4 f3 4 ♔f1 f2 5 ♘xf2+ ♔h2 6 ♘e4 ♔h1 7 ♔f2 ♔h2 8 ♘d2 ♔h1 9 ♘f1 h2 10 ♘g3X**.

Or **1 ... h2 2 ♘g5 f3 3 ♘e4 f2** and now **4 ♘g3X** or **4 ♘xf2X**.

A similar mating finale is seen in compositions.

P.Keres, 1936

White to move and win

Though White is a queen up, Black's passed pawns are very dangerous. A mating combination leads to victory.

1 ♘c2+! ♔a2 (if 1 ... ♗xc2 2 ♕b8) **2 ♘b4+ ♔a1**. Also no help is 2 ... ♔a3 3 ♘d3 ♗xd3 4 ♕d6+ ♔a2 5 ♕d5!.

3 ♕a2+! bxa2 4 ♘c6, and there is no defence against the manoeuvre 5 ♘c6-d4 with mate on b3 or c2.

G.Grasemann, 1950

White mates in 4 moves

The scheme is clear: ♔e1-f2 and ♘h5-g3X. However after 1 ♔f2? the black knight is pinned and a stalemate position arises. The solution: **1 ♕d5+ ♔g1 2 ♕h1+! ♔xh1**, and only now **3 ♔f2**, since the knight f1 is freed from the pin.

In all the examples we have examined, a deadly role in the fate of the king was played by its own pawn. Sometimes this is replaced by a bishop.

Here is one of the best known miniatures.

A.Troitsky, 1924

White to move and win

The balance of the forces is equal, but White wins because of the poor position of the black bishop.

1 ♔h6 ♔h8 2 ♘h4 ♔g8. Black has no alternative, on 2 ... ♗g8 follows 3 ♘g6X. This motif is repeated and particularly loudly celebrated in the finale.

3 ♘f3 ♔h8 4 ♘e5 ♔g8 5 ♘c6 (there is a dual: 5 ♘d7 ♔h8 6 ♘f8 ♗g8 7 ♘g6X) **5 ... ♔h8 6 ♘e7!** (the knight comes up for the finish, the black king has no more moves) **6 ... ♗g8 7 ♘g6X.**

V.Bron, 1952 (ending of a study)

White to move and win

1 ♗a2! (by taking away the g8 square from the king, White starts to weave a mating net) **1 ... ♗b7.** Black tries to include the bishop in the defence. 1 ... h4 2 ♔f7 h3 3 ♔f8 h2 4 ♘f7+ ♔h7 5 ♗b1+ leads to a mating finish.

2 ♔f7 ♗a6 3 ♔f8 ♗d3 4 ♗g8 (threatening 5 ♘f7X) **4 ... ♗g6** (it seems that the bishop is in time...) **5 ♗h7!** Alas, the bishop g6 does not have a single free square. If there were no h5 pawn, Black would achieve a draw after 5 ... ♗h5.

5 ... ♗xh7 6 ♘f7X.

The following miniature is excellent.

V.Korolkov, 1951

White to move and win

The first move can be found without difficulty, since White's trump card for the attack is the f6 pawn.

1 f7. Now Black needs to hold up the pawn. For this purpose, no good is either 1 ... ♖f6 2 ♗b2, or 1 ... ♖g8 2 fxg8=♕+ ♔xg8 3 ♘e7+ and 4 ♘xc8.

1 ... ♖a6+ 2 ♗a3! A beautiful move, although there was no choice: 2 ♔b1? ♗xf5+ or 2 ♔b2 ♖f6.

2 ... ♖xa3+ 3 ♔b2. It seems that Black can already resign with a clear conscience, but there is interesting counterplay to be found for him.

3 ... ♖a2+! Clearly the rook cannot be taken because of 4 ... ♗e6+ with a draw. However it is not easy to save himself from the persistently pursuing rook: the white king cannot step on the diagonals a4-e8, a2-g8, b1-h7, f1-a6, h1-a8 and h3-c8, i.e. all those squares where the bishop might deliver a check, capturing the knight, pawn or freeing the 8th rank for the rook.

4 ♔c1! (after 4 ♔c3? ♖c2+ there was already no win) **4 ... ♖a1+ 5 ♔d2 ♖a2+ 6 ♔e3 ♖a3+ 7 ♔f4 ♖a4+ 8 ♔g5 ♖g4+!** If now 9 ♔xg4, then 9 ... ♗xf5+ 10 ♔xf5 ♔g7 11 ♔e6 ♔f8 with a draw.

9 ♔h6. By now there is no salvation in the rook sacrifice: 9 ... ♖g6+ 10 ♔xg6 ♗xf5+ 11 ♔h6.

9 ... ♖g8! 10 ♘e7! ♗e6 (the last line of defence...) **11 fxg8=♕+ ♗xg8 12 ♘g6X**.

Other pieces too might do a disservice to their king.

In a game such things are of course hard to see, but who knows ...

A.Troitsky, 1898

White to move and win

White has a great material advantage, but Black holds the initiative. He threatens 1 ... ♖b1+ or 1 ... g2. Nevertheless the cramped position of the king on h3 allows a decisive combination.

1 ♗c6! ♖b1+ 2 ♔e2 ♖xh1 3 ♗g2+! ♔xg2 4 ♘f4+ ♔g1 5 ♔e1! A tragi-comic position! Black is forced to brick himself up: **5 ... g2 6 ♘e2X**.

And here is yet another example of a surprising 'self bricking up'.

A.Gurvich, 1929

White to move and win

1 ♘b2! This quiet move contains the threat of 2 ♖h4!! with unavoidable mate – 3 ♖a4X or 3 ♗b4X.

1 ... ♖e4 The best defence. There is no salvation in 1 ... b5 2 ♖h4 ♘c6 3 ♖a4+ bxa4 4 ♘c4X.

2 ♗e3! ♘c6. Of course the bishop cannot be taken because of the 'fork' on c4.

3 ♗c5+ ♘b4 4 ♘d3 a5 5 ♗xb4+ axb4 6 ♖h8 Threatening mate on a8. On 6 ... b2 follows 7 ♖a8+ ♔b3 8 ♘c5+, while on 6 ... ♔a4 – at once 7 ♘c5+. There remains the only move.

6 ... ♖e6 7 ♖a8+ ♖a6 8 ♖xa6+! bxa6 9 ♘b2 Crowning the idea. The black king will die in prison. **9 ... a5 10 ♔a1 a4 11 ♘c4X.**

Which true connoisseur of chess beauty does not know the following study!

L.Kubbel, 1925

White to move and win

By exploiting the poor position of the black queen, White, with forcing manoeuvres, compels the opponent's king to flee to the other flank, where it will await the leader of the enemy forces. **1 ♘e3+! ♔g3 2 ♕g4+ ♔f2 3 ♕f4+ ♔e2 4 ♕f1+ ♔d2.** The knight is invulnerable – 4 ... ♔xe3 5 ♕e1+ winning the queen.

5 ♕d1+ ♔c3 6 ♕c2+ ♔b4 (otherwise there is a 'fork' on f5) **7 ♕b2+ ♘b3.** 7 ... ♔a5 8 ♘c4+ leads to an elementary mate. But now with a brilliant queen sacrifice the king is deflected to the fatal square.

8 ♕a3+!! ♔xa3 9 ♘c2X.

A.Petrov, 1863

White mates in 4 moves

The mechanism of the combination is simple, rather it is a scheme: **1 ♘b3+ ♔a2 2 ♖d1!**, and the blocking in of the king is unavoidable – **3 ♖a1+ ♗xa1 4 ♘c1X.**

An echo of the study of the first Russian master came to us after a hundred years.

Tomovic – Sokolov (1961): **1 ♖e5+?** (1 ♖a8) **1 ... ♔f2! 2 ♖e8** (the rook sacrifice can only delay mate) **2 ... ♖h1+ 3 ♗xh1 ♘f1X.**

The knight makes a highly successful team with pawns. When attacking the castled position it is necessary to keep in mind such mating finishes:

The scheme of the tactical operation carried out in one of these attacking finishes against the kingside castled position is conveniently traced to the ending of a game Kolvich – Koch (1959).

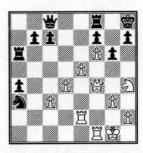

1 ♕h6 ♖g8 2 ♘f3 (threatening 3 ♘g5) **2 ... ♕f8**, and none the less – **3 ♘g5!** Black resigned (3 ... ♕xh6 4 ♘xf7X).

Note the elements of the combination: 1 ♕h6 – drawing the rook to g8 with the aim of blocking in the enemy king; 3 ♘g5! – deflecting the black queen from its defence of the f7 square. Let's also draw attention to the pawn wedge on f6, taking away from the king its only free square.

The same combination may be accompanied by various tactical nuances.

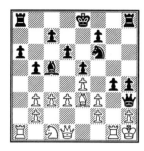

In the game Weiss – Schallopp (1883) after **1 ... &xe3 2 fxe3 gxf3** White, trying to defend against numerous threats, played **3 ₩f1**, on which followed the already familiar to us thrust **3 ... ♘g4** with an immediate result. The feature of the position lies in the fact that White cannot ransom the exchange: after 4 ♖xg4 the queen on f1 is left unprotected.

With a pawn wedge on h6 (h3) mating finishes retain a familiar pattern – as before, the main role is assigned to the knight, changing only the direction of the attack, while the scheme of the tactical operations is marked by great variety.

Perez – Chaude de Silans (1958): **1 ♖xf7!** A blow, realising the pin along the 6th rank, based on yet another variation: 1 ... ₩xf7 2 ₩xd8+ ₩g8 3 ₩f6+.

1 ... ₩e5+ 2 f4 ₩d6 3 ₩b2+ ₩d4 4 ♖f8+ &g8 5 ♘g5! Here it is, zest! Exploiting the pinned bishop g8, White

threatens mate on f7, and against this there is no defence.

Belyavsky – NN (1975): **1 ♖xe6!** ₩xc4. On 1 ... dxe6 Belyavsky gives this variation: 2 &xe6+ ♖f7 3 ₩xd4 &f8 4 &xf7 ₩xf7 5 ♘d6, and White wins.

2 ♖xg6+! &h8 3 ♘d6 ₩d5 4 ♖g8+! ♖xg8 5 ₩xd4+! ₩xd4 6 ♘f7X.

Both combinations are quite complicated in their arrangement. But the general idea, the routes of the white pieces, is standard, as indeed are the typical devices used in the attack: movement of the knight to an attacking position, blocking in the enemy king and deflecting the queen from the critical f7 square.

Let's look at one more tactical mechanism, leading to a similar mating picture.

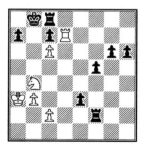

Janowski – NN (1900): **1 ♘a6+ &a8 2 ♘xc7+ &b8** (not possible, of course, is 2 ... ♖xc7 3 ♖d8+) **3 ♘a6+ &a8.**

Draw? No! Janowski has already seen the familiar mating position and prepares it with a quiet move.

4 ♖b7! Black resigned in view of the inevitable finish 5 ♖b8+! ♖xb8 6 ♘c7X.

The same mechanism was put into operation by P.Romanovsky (White) in a game against his brother A.Romanovsky (1907), true, not without help from a close relative.

1 ♕h6 ♘h5. Losing immediately is 1 ... ♘e6 2 ♘e7+ ♔h8 3 ♖c2 with the threat of 4 ♕xh7+ or simply 4 ♖h2 (in case of 4 ... e4).

2 ♕xh5! gxh5? (2 ... ♔h8 3 ♕h6 ♖g8 4 ♖c2 g5 5 ♖h2) **3 ♖g1+ ♔h8 4 ♘h6!**, and Black resigned, since there is no defence against 5 ♖g8+ ♖xg8 6 ♘xf7X.

But where is the 'brother's help'? It was shown already on the 2ⁿᵈ move. Instead of 2 ... gxh5? leading to a draw was the surprising counter-sacrifice of the queen: 2 ... ♕xc3! Now if 3 ♖xc3 gxh5 White will not be able to construct the mating mechanism (4 ♘h6+ ♔h8 5 ♖c1 ♖ad8 6 ♖g1 ♖d7). To avoid worse White would have to resort to perpetual check after 3 ♕h6 ♕xf3+ 4 ♔g1 ♕g4+ 5 ♔h1 etc. (the king cannot step either to h2, or on the

f-file because of ♕g4-f4+ with an exchange of queens).

Certain patterns and a series of other mating situations, arising from a joint knight and pawn attack, can be identified. In the endgame, for example, when the kings are led directly to their few remaining troops, the knight often forces the surrender of the enemy in the last line of fire.

We use two studies by way of example.

W.Speckmann, 1956

White mates in 4 moves

1 ♘b7 ♘c4 2 ♘c5 With the intention of occupying the critical e4 square, from where it simultaneously observes two end points – d6 and f6.

2 ... ♘d6 3 ♘a6! Now Black cannot cover the c7 square, since the b5 pawn gets in the way of the knight, and on the next move White delivers mate.

A.Marzeil, 1934

White mates in 6 moves

Also here the knight must choose the optimal route, so that in the shortest possible time it can get to one of the three squares – c4, c6 or b7.

1 ♘g3 ♗e7 2 ♘e4 ♗b4 3 ♘g5!.

Now the bishop needs to think carefully where to go. However, like Buridan's ass between a bundle of hay and a pail of water, he cannot make a choice: (a) 3 ... ♗f8 4 ♘e6 ♗e7 5 ♘d4 (with the continuation 5 ... ♗c5 6 ♘c6X); (b) 3 ... ♗d6 4 ♘f3 ♗e5 5 ♘d2; (c) 3 ... ♗d2 4 ♘f7 ♗f4 5 ♘d8.

Let the bishop ponder, it wants so much, but we somehow know that the knight will get where it needs to go in timely fashion.

Note: in both cases, the black king was stalemated on the edge of the board and the white knight had freedom to manoeuvre. This is an important condition for successful mating attacks not only in composed studies but also in practical play.

NN – Richter (1938): **1 ... ♔f1! 2 ♖xh3 ♘g4!**. White resigned.

Udovcic – Nedeljkovic (1957): **1 ... ♔g1!** White resigned.

Sometimes the threat of mate leads to the gain of material or forced transfer to a winning endgame.

Vukic – Zinn (1969). Black played **1 ... h5?** and after **2 ♘d3!** laid down his arms, since the threat of mate on f2 can be parried only at the cost of a bishop.

It what seems a completely harmless position, Flesch against Farago (1973) played **1 ... ♔g1!**, and it suddenly became clear that there was no defence against the manoeuvre ♘f5-g3-h1-f2X, since after **2 ♗xf5** (2 g4 ♘g3 3 gxh5 gxh5 4 ♗g6 ♘h1 5 ♗xh5 ♘f2X) the pawn ending is also lost: **2 ... gxf5 3 g3** (3 g4 fxg4+ 4 fxg4 f3) **3 ... ♔f2! 4 g4 fxg4+ 5 fxg4 ♔e2**, and White resigned.

Well-known is the legend of Dilaram – beloved wife of a Muslim prince, who was such a passionate chess player, that, having lost his fortune, made *her* his last bet. And lamentably this game was almost over for him, as can be seen from the bleak position of the white king.

'Dilaram's Mate', 12ᵗʰ century

However Dilaram, closely following the game and apparently understanding chess better than her hapless husband, exclaimed: "Sacrifice both rooks and

save your wife!" And though women's liberation in those dark days was still not heard of, the lord nevertheless heeded the advice.

1 ♖h8+ ♔xh8 2 ♗f5+ (*According to the old Arab rules the bishop could move only three squares along the diagonal, and if a piece stood in its path then it could jump over it, but not take it.*) **2 ... ♖h2 3 ♖xh2+ ♔g8 4 ♖h8+ ♔xh8 5 g7+ ♔g8 6 ♘h6X**

The mechanism of the combination, employed by I.Zaitsev in a game against Bobolovich (1960), is in no way reminiscent of 'Dilaram's mate', but the final position is very similar. In any case, he had less worry about winning than the husband of the beautiful Muslim.

1 ♘f5 ♘d2+ 2 ♔g1 ♗xf2+ 3 ♔h1 ♖g8 4 ♕g7+! ♖xg7 5 hxg7+ ♔g8 6 ♘h6X

81. Position by P.Stamma, 1737

White to move

250 years ago, just like today.

82. Matsukevich – Tuchek, 1979

White to move

Today, just like 250 years ago ...

83. Klir – Reder, 1938

White to move

Aren't there too many pieces crowding the long diagonal?

84. Koch – Stuber, 1934

White to move

There is a pin on the knight e6, but is it durable?

85. NN – NN

White to move

How to bring the knight f3 into battle?

86. Lubensky – Makarov, 1963

Black to move

And he played cunningly – 1 ... b6 2 cxb6 axb6, expecting 3 ♕xb6. What happened next?

87. Eik – Derremo, 1970

Black to move

Who, where and why?

88. Ermenkov – Karapchansky, 1975

White to move

1 f4 exf4?, and now ...

89 Rugiadnin – Jakobsen, 1962

Black to move

In and out of the cadre.

90. Bairamov – Gik, 1968

Black to move

Pulling the string tight ...

91. Najdorf – Larsen, 1968

Black to move

Without fear or doubt.

92. Pokoevchik – Zhaina, 1977

White to move

When a king goes into battle ...

93. Shereshevsky – Buslaev, 1973

White to move

1 ♘g5? ♘d3 and Black wins. But if he thinks about it thoroughly ...

94. Botvinnik – Alexander, 1946

White to move

Triple attack.

95. Jansson – Ivarson, 1973

White to move

1 ♘e7+ ♔h5? – suicide.

96. Vadasz – Lukacs, 1977

Black to move

All on one.

97. Dartov – Kogan, 1977

Black to move

A novel with a sequel.

98. Study by A.Galitsky, 1900

White mates in 3 moves

Zugzwang – for some a friend, for others an enemy ...

99 Study by A.Petrov, 1985

White mates in 5 moves

Willy-nilly ...

102. U.Belyankin, 1950

White to move and win

Lured into the corner!

100. S.Loyd, 1885

White mates in 3 moves

The fewer, the better.

103. Ending of study by M.Liburkin, 1935

White to move and win

A surprising resource.

101. A.Troitsky, 1898

White to move and win

Standard but amazing and striking.

104. A.Herbstman, 1934

White to move and win

Not quantity, but quality.

105. O.Blathy, 1922

White to move and win

Only one pawn against the whole set of pieces – have you ever seen anything like it?

106. K.Jaenisch, 1850

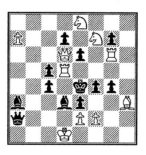

Smothered mate in 10 moves

An unusual study: White commences and gives 'smothered matc' in 10 moves. Namely 'smothered' and no other!

* * * *

"Possession of the advantage carries the obligation to attack, otherwise there is the threat of losing that advantage."

W.Steinitz

"Many players try to attack when their pieces are scattered over the whole board, without any interaction, and in the end they wonder what was their mistake."

J.Capablanca

"A true attack is carried out with many co-ordinated pieces and rarely just one or two."

F.Philidor

"An attack has chances of success only when the opponent's position is already weakened."

W.Steinitz

"One of my favourite annotations 'All the pieces are taking part in the attack!'."

B.Larsen

"In some positions combinations are as natural as a baby's smile."

R.Fine

"First it is necessary to study combinations, before trying to play positionally."

R.Reti

5. The Pawn

"A check to the king, a check to the queen, and the pawns have removed the king!" That's the last line of a poem by G. Agatov, written in the first years of the Russian Revolution. In those days chess kings were identified with real ones and insulted in every possible way.

> ... That Petya
> could dash
> To critique a world match
> "Neither is worth a thing –
> Capablanca and Alekhine
> both, oh my,
> evasive in the ring
> guarded their king ...
> ... and I
> won't stand for all of this –
> let a pawn eat monarchists!"

Vladimir Mayakovsky. *The Load at the Top*.

But to 'eat' the king with a pawn is not so simple. And not because it's made of wood. First of all, a lone infantryman does not have the capacity for this operation. Secondly, the king should be very belligerent and engage in hand to hand fighting, or else be seen as a complete scatterbrain, apathetically watching the approach of enemy infantry.

A king might support an attack with a pawn.

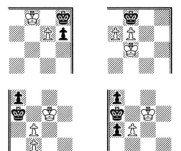

This study by P.Morphy is simple in construction and also elegant.

White mates in 2 moves

After **1 Za6!** Black falls into zugzwang, since his bishop cannot leave the b8 square because of 2 Zxa7X, while **1 ... bxa6** frees the way for the pawn – **2 b7X**.

E.Dvizov, 1965

White to move and win

1 ♔g6! Only this. Leading to a draw is 1 ♔f6? ♚g8! 2 g6 b3! 3 h6 b2 4 h7+ ♚h8 5 g7+ ♚xh7 6 ♔f7 b1=♛.

1 ... ♚g8. Other continuations also lose: 1 ... c3 2 ♔f7 c2 3 g6 c1=♛ 4 g7+ ♚h7 5 g8=♛+ ♚h6 6 ♛g6X or 1 ... b3 2 ♔f7 b2 3 g6 b1=♛ 4 g7+ ♚h7 5 g8=♛+ ♚h6 6 ♛g6+ ♛xg6+ 7 hxg6 c3 8 g7 c2 9 g8=♛ c1=♛ 10 ♛g6X.

2 h6 b3 3 h7+ ♚h8 4 ♚h6 b2 5 g6 b1=♛ 6 g7X.

A whole cycle of studies was initiated after a problem by R.Brown (1841).

White mates in 4 moves

1 ♚c4! b5+ 2 ♚c3 b4+ 3 ♚c4 (zugzwang) **3 ... b3 4 axb3X.**

In a further elaboration of this theme the white pawn on b2 was replaced by a black pawn on a3, while the blocking in of the enemy king was implemented with the help of various sacrifices.

G.Kasparian, 1929

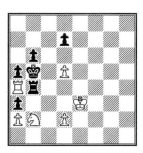

White to move and win

1 ♘d1!. It is interesting that 1 Zxb4+?? would even lead to defeat: 1 ... axb4 2 ♘d1 b3 3 axb3 ♚b4 4 ♘c3

♔xb3 etc.

**1 ... ♖xa4 2 ♘c3+ ♔b4 3 ♔d4! d6
4 ♘xa4 ♔xa4 5 ♔c4 b5+ 6 ♔c3 b4+
7 ♔c4 b3 8 axb3X.**

The mating finish ends with an echo
variation: **3 ... b5 4 ♘e4!** (here, hasty
and mistaken is the direct 4 ♘xa4?,
which leads to a draw after 4 ... bxa4!
5 ♔e5 ♔c4 6 ♔d6 ♔d4 7 d3 ♔c3
8 ♔xd7 ♔b2 9 ♔c7 ♔xa2 10 d6 ♔b1
11 d7 a2 12 d8=♕ a1=♕.) **4 ... d6
5 ♘c5! dxc5+ 6 ♔d3 c4+ 7 ♔d4 c3
8 dxc3X.**

A.Kakovin, 1940

White to move and win

White is a rook up but both his pieces
are under attack. The first two moves
are obvious.

1 ♖d8 ♗a5 2 ♖d5 The rook has
broken out into the open, indirectly
defending the knight a4. It seems that
it's all over but Black has surprising
counterplay.

2 ... bxa4! 3 ♖xa5 b5. Now the white
rook is imprisoned and should die.
However, by taking it, Black gets
into zugzwang, as in the study by
R.Brown.

4 ♔c3 ♔b7 5 ♔d4! (on 5 ♔b4? –
5 ... ♔b6 with mutual zugzwang and a
draw) **5 ... ♔b6 6 ♔d5 ♔xa5 7 ♔c5 b4
8 axb4X.**

Another mechanism to achieve
a similar finale is illustrated by a
well-known problem by S.Loyd.
'Charles XII at Bender (1859)'. He also
accompanied it with a funny story
about the chess exploits of the King of
Sweden, which led to unexpected
consequences in no way associated
with chess.

In 1713, Charles XII was besieged by
Turkish troops in the fortress of
Bender. In lulls between the fighting
the king amused himself by playing
chess with his minister K.Grotuzen.
One of their games reached this
position:

"You are checkmated in three
moves" announced Charles, who
played White.

But he didn't have time to do the
deed, as into the window flew a stray
Turkish bullet and knocked the white
knight off the board.

"The knight I will give you," – smiled the king – "and without it I announce checkmate in four moves."

Here (as befits the plot) another bullet came whistling through, and this time shot down the pawn on h2.

Then Charles thought and announced mate in five moves.

Though his minister was in an agitated state, the king did not let him go until he had come to a decision in each position. After this experience, the following day Grotuzen ran away from the fortress to the Turkish camp.

Let the conscience of the great chess humourist be a very free interpretation of the reasons for betrayal by the Swedish minister, and evidence of the chess humour of the war-like Charles, who, by his own admission, did not take off his boots for six years. But now we have greater interest in the chess content of Loyd's problem and it is exactly in line with our theme.

Mate in 3 moves: **1 ♖xg3** (threatening 2 ♖h3+ ♗h4 3 g4X) **1 ... ♗xg3 2 ♘f3 any 3 g4X**.

Mate in 4 moves: **1 hxg3 ♗e3 2 ♖g4 ♗g5 3 ♖h4+ ♗xh4 4 g4X**.

Mate in 5 moves: **1 ♖b7! ♗e3 2 ♖b1 ♗g5 3 ♖h1+ ♗h4 4 ♖h2! gxh2 5 g4X** or **1 ... ♗g1 2 ♖b1 ♗h2 3 ♖e1 ♔h4 4 ♔g6 and 5 ♖e4X**.

Only the last variation brings us the main tactical idea of the famous composer!

Yet another mechanism to achieve an analogous mating finish is illustrated by a famous study by O.Duras (1926).

Black has a great material advantage, moreover the threat of promoting the pawn on g2 hampers White's activities. None the less White wins because of the cramped position of the enemy king.

1 ♔c6! (threatening mate on a7) **1 ... a6 2 ♖xd5+ b5 3 ♖d4 g1=♕ 4 ♖a4+ bxa4 5 b4X**

Or **1 ... ♔a6 2 b4** (with the threat of 3 b5+ ♔a5 4 ♖xa7X) **2 ... b5 3 a4 bxa4 4 ♖xd5 g1=♕** with the inevitable finish – **5 ♖a5+ ♗xa5 6 b5X**.

We now show how ideas expressed in compositions are reflected in practical play.

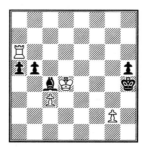

In the game Moldyarov – Samochanov (1974) a similar finish was prepared by a forcing manoeuvre of the rook and king.

Upon 1 ♖xa5?! ♔g3 Black's counterplay might give quite a lot of trouble. Therefore White switches – and very successfully – to the other flank: **1 ♖g6! a4 2 ♔e3 a3 3 ♔f4 a2 4 ♖g3!** (threatening mate) **4 ... ♗e6**. Now follows the familiar operation – **5 ♖h3+! ♗xh3 6 g3X**.

Quite often seen are these spectacular mating finishes, prompted by O.Duras' study:

In the following three examples, Duras' combination was repeated – the only difference being that the function of the king in the final mating pattern is taken by the rook.

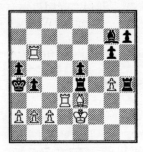

Shablinsky – Ushkal (1974): **1 ♖a3+! bxa3 2 b3X**.

Rubel – Usachi (1960): **1 ... ♕h4+!** White resigned.

This is the basic scheme, but here it is a combination with deflection and blocking.

Georgadze – Kuindzhi (1973): **1 ... ♕f2+!** (freeing the rook from the pin) **2 ♕xf2 ♖h5+! 3 ♗xh5 g5X**.

A pawn can deliver the concluding blow with support from a knight, bishop, and also another pawn.

First, two examples from the middlegame.

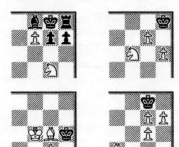

Roganov – Komarov (1944): **1 e6 ♕e7 2 ♕f7+ ♕xf7 3 exf7X**.

Hallstein – Janin (1916): **1 ... f3!** White resigned. The threat of 2 ... f2X (and incidentally also 2 ... ♕e3X) can be repulsed only at the cost of heavy material loss.

G.Zahodyakin, 1934

White to move and win

If 1 b3, then 1 ... ♔xc8 with a draw. Meanwhile Black is threatening to take the b2 pawn.

1 ♘b6+ ♔c6! The best defence. After 1 ... ♘xb6 2 ♗xb6 h4 White has time to neutralise the enemy pawn and defend his own: 3 ♔g6 h3 4 ♗g1 ♔c6 5 ♔g5 ♔b5 6 ♔g4 ♔b4 7 ♔xh3 ♔b3 8 ♗d4.

2 ♘xa4 ♔b5. Now White must lose one of his attacking pieces.

3 ♗c3! ♔xa4. There is no salvation in 3 ... h4 4 ♗f6 h3 5 ♘c3+ ♔c4, and then 6 ♘e2 h2 and 7 ♘g3.

4 ♔e6. By threatening to get into the square of the enemy pawn, White weaves a mating net.

4 ... h4 5 ♔d5! h3 6 ♔c4! h2 7 ♗b4 h1=♕ 8 b3X.

Upon a mass pawn advance a mating situation arises usually on the opponent's last line of defence.

I.Zaitsev – Bakulin (1964): **1 ... ♘c3+ 2 ♔a1 ♔f7 3 h7 ♔g7.** Zugzwang: the bishop does not have a single square along the d1-a4 diagonal, and White is in no position to prevent a decisive advance of the b-pawn.

4 ♗d3 b3! (4 ... cxd3?? 5 h8=♕+! ♔xh8 – stalemate). White resigned: 5 ... b2X is unstoppable.

In one variation from the game Vasyukov – Lukin (1972) the following position arose:

Here White intends the continuation 1 ♕g6! fxg6 2 hxg6 ♖xg7 3 fxg7+ ♔g8 4 h7X. The armada of pawns literally swamps the black king.

White found a beautiful solution in a game played in 1962 (the players are not known).

**1 ♕g5+!! ♗xg5 2 hxg5+ ♔h5
3 ♖h8!**, and Black resigned, since the
threat of 4. ♖xh7+ forces the capture of
the rook, after which the g3 pawn,
freed from the pin, delivers the decisive
blow – 3 ... ♕xh8 4 g4X.

In a game against Veroci (Black),
Gaprindashvili (1974) unfortunately
missed just such a rare chance.

In severe time trouble, the women's
world champion forced a draw by
perpetual check: **1 ♕g4+?** ♔h6
2 ♕g7+ ♔h5 **3 ♕g4+** etc. However
there was a forced win for White:
1 ♖xe5+!! (exposing the h4-d8
diagonal) **1 ... fxe5 2 g4+ ♔h4 3 ♕e7+**
(forcing the black queen to relinquish
its attack on the critical g3 square)
3 ... ♕g5 4 g3X.

A very typical situation is where a
pawn delivers mate not with a move
up the file but with the capture of an
enemy piece or pawn. Of course, in this
case all the squares around the king
must be either blocked or controlled by
the attacking pieces.

In the game, Mik.Tseitlin – Nei
(1975), the outcome of the battle was
decided by a direct threat.

1 ♕g3! Black resigned. The variation
2 ♕g6+ ♘xg6 3 hxg6X can only be
'exchanged' for something less
spectacular.

The same idea was presented in a
more refined form in the game Karpov
– Taimanov (1972).

1 ♕c1! (with the threat of **2 ♘g5+**
and **3 ♖xb3**) **1 ... ♕a2 2 ♘g5+ ♔h8
3 ♘xf7+ ♔h7 4 ♕g5 ♕b1+ 5 ♔h2**
Black resigned. As in the previous
example, there is no defence against
6 ♕g6+ ♕xg6 7 hxg6X.

Another mating finish was
constructed by Glazkov (Black) in a
game against Gorodetsky (1958).

1 ... 罩c3 2 奠b2 罩e1+ 3 查h2 包g3!
Threatening 4 ... 罩h1X, and after the
forced 4 fxg3 the pawn distinguishes
itself – 4 ... fxg3X.

And here are some examples of a
forced destruction of the king, obliged
to march to the place of his own
execution due to the sluggishness of his
courtiers.

Csom – Ghitescu (1970): **1 包e8+
查h6 2 奠f8+ 查h5 3 包g7+ 查h4**
(3 ... 查h6 4 包f5+ 查h5 5 g4X – is also
not bad) **4 查h2! 奠d8 5 f4!** Black
resigned: 6 g3X cannot be stopped.

A.Kazantsev, 1967 (ending of a study)

White to move and win

With a series of brilliant sacrifices
White 'smokes out' the opponent's
king from its refuge, forcing the enemy
pieces to block all its exits and
concluding with a blow by a 'sleepy'
pawn.

1 包g6+! fxg6 2 奠f6+! 魏xf6 3 查d5+
(the rook comes out of hiding) **3... 查g5
4 h4+ 查f5 5 g4+ hxg4 6 罩f4+! 奠xf4
7 e4X!**

L.Kubbel, 1925

White to move and win

1 罩g6 包f6 2 魏h6+ 查f7. The king
cannot step back to the 8th rank because
of the loss of the queen. This factor
forces him to go into the centre.

**3 罩xf6+! exf6 4 魏h7+ 查e6 5 f5+
查d6 6 c5+ 查d5** It seems that White's
attacking resources are exhausted,
but ...

7 魏g8+! 魏xg8 8 查d3! The game is
crowned with a modest king move.
Despite his enormous material
advantage, Black cannot prevent
9 c4X.

Of course, it is extremely rare for
such 'tricks' to succeed in tournament
practice, but of course they have
to be taken into account. In the next
game a forcing operation against
the white king leads to an unusual
finish.

NN – Soldatenkov (1928): **1 ... ♘e4+
2 ♔e2** (2 ♔f1 ♘d2+) **2 ... ♕d2+ 3 ♔f3
♕xf2+ 4 ♔xe4 ♕xg2+ 5 ♘f3 ♕g6+
6 ♔e5 ♕f6+ 7 ♔d6 ♕e7+ 8 ♔e5**
(8 ♔c7 ♘a6X) **8 ... d6+ 9 ♔e4 f5X!**,
'... and the pawn takes out the king!'

Triumph of the blockade! The
colourful 'still life with pawns' is
admirable.

As they say, don't be inventive just
for fun ...

* * * *

107. Spassky – Petrosian, 1967

White to move

The 'iron mask'.

108. Stahlberg – Becker, 1944

White to move

Is the king not too bold?

109 Durao – Catozzi, 1957

White to move

Who is attacking who?

110. Babrikowski – Muller, 1977

White to move

Chest out – and on towards the enemy!

111. Medina – Sanz, 1975

White to move

Don't wait a second ...

112. Bernstein – NN, 1909

Black to move

Nutcracker pawn.

113. Holmov – Tseshkovsky, 1978

White to move

The road to the scaffold

114. A.d'Orville, 1842

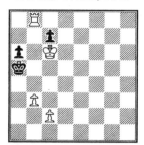

White mates in 4 moves

Whether he likes it or not!

115. K.Beyer, 1856

White mates in 9 moves

'Immortal'.

116. J.Betins, 1894

White to move and win

Slowly but surely.

117. I.Schindler, 1969

White to move and win

6. Two Rooks

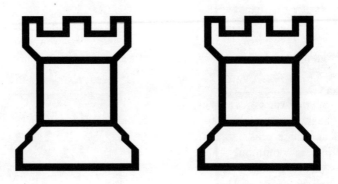

"Watch out, tanks!" This front-line signal sounds over the field of chess battle every time the rooks are striving to break through. By all the rules of war they can make deep raids, roundabout manoeuvres or advance in a column – depending on the tactical task they are set. The principal conditions for a successful attack are a quick assault and freedom from breaks in communication caused by enemy rooks.

> I am drawn to the expanse of squares,
> A signal for the rooks, "On your way!"
> And all that freedom that is dear to me –
> The position is open.
>
> Then, sweeping away the pawn structure
> (Let the enemy start to worry!).
> I can double on the file
> With the rook's sister.
>
> By now nothing will do:
> Everywhere there is danger ...
> And about the rabid rooks
> I will remain silent (for clarity).

That's how the 'rook theme' was resolved by candidate master Evgeny Ilyin, whose poetry was linked closely to chess.

How to checkmate the lone king with two rooks? This is perhaps one of the first tasks faced by the novice when getting to understand the ABC of chess. Chasing the poor king across the board, he finally has the joy of discovering the following final positions.

Either of the rooks can without prejudice be replaced with the queen.

A linear mate, as this final construction is commonly known, concludes many games both in the endgame and middlegame. This danger arises primarily in situations where heavy pieces have open lines, and the defending side's king can be forced back to the edge of the board.

Polugaevsky (White) won with a surprising manoeuvre against Szilagyi (1960).

1 ♖g1+ ♔h6. The king is driven to the edge file.

2 ♗f8+! The bishop is sacrificed in order to divert the black rook from the d-file.

2 ... ♖xf8 3 ♖d3! Black resigned: mate on h3 is unstoppable.

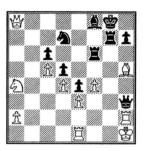

In the game Miles – Uhlmann (1975/76) Black had introduced his rooks to battle stations.

1 ... ♕xh2+! 2 ♔xh2 ♖h6 3 ♕e8 ♘f6! White resigned.

The encounter Silich – Rokhlin (1929) had a dramatic finish.

After **1 ♖f8+ ♔h7** a win for White seemed in no doubt, sufficient was 2 ♖xc8 ♗xf3+ 3 ♔h2 ♖g2+ 4 ♔h3, but even better was 2 ♕e4+ (with the continuation 2 ... ♗xe4 3 ♗xe4+ ♖gg6 4 ♗xg6+). White, however, played **2 ♗e4+?**, on which followed the thunderous reply **2 ... ♕f5!!**, and it was all over (3 ♖xf5 ♖xh4X or 3 ♗xc6 ♕h3X).

To create a linear mate in the middlegame, the enemy king's pawn cover must be destroyed. Most often this is achieved by blowing it up with a sacrifice (in Nimzowitsch's terminology).

When attacking the kingside castled position, the immediate target is often the h-pawn.

Ivanov – A.Petrosian (1978). Black parried the obvious threat of 2 ♕f6X by **1 ... ♕d4.** But there followed **2 ♕xh7+!**, and the sentence was carried out (2 ... ♔xh7 3 ♖h1+). However by now Black could not have avoided defeat. If 1 ... ♗g6, then 2 ♖xg6 hxg6 3 ♕xg6 with the same consequences.

Smrcka – Mikhel (1977): **1 ... ♗xh3!** White resigned (2 ♗xh3 ♕xh3+! 3 ♔xh3 ♖h6+).

Here we see a typical technical device. The g-file serves as a springboard for moving the rook to the h-file. This operation was also carried out in the game Sokolov – Osnos (1965).

1 ♖dg1. Deciding the outcome of the battle since the threat of 2 ♘xh7 ♕xh7 3 ♕xh7+ ♔xh7 4 ♖h3X is irresistible.
1 ... ♖e7 2 ♕h6 ♕e8.

It rarely happens that some idea or another occurs in a pure form. Thus the rook on f8 can be played to g8, but on this would follow 3 ♘f7+ and 4 ♖xg8X. In reply to 2 ... ♖fe8 there is a win after 3 ♘xh7 ♖xh7 4 ♕f6+. The move in the game allows White to carry out his original intention.

3 ♘xh7! Black resigned.

The transfer of the rooks towards the main attack can also be carried out on other open lines.

Tal – Gedevanishvili (1970): **1 ♘f6+! gxf6 2 ♗xh7+ ♔h8.**

The position is complicated by the fact that the white queen cannot leave the rook b1 undefended. Nevertheless on 2 ... ♔xh7 would have followed 3 ♕h5+ ♔g8 4 ♖bf1 (with the threat of 5 ♖h4, which also works after 4 ... ♕xc2) 4 ... ♘g6 5 exf6 with the unavoidable 6 ♕h6 and 7 ♕g7X.

3 ♖h4 ♔g7 4 ♕c1! ♘g8 (giving up the queen – 4 ... ♕xb1 5 ♕xb1 – would only prolong any resistance) **5 ♗xg8.** Black resigned (5 ... ♖xg8 6 ♕h6X or 5 ... ♔xg8 6 ♖g4+ ♔h7 7 ♖b3).

In this example the castled position was razed to the ground. Such operations nearly always have the support of heavy pieces.

Velimirovic – Gipslis (1971):
1 ♖xg5+! ♔h8 (1 ... ♗xg5 2 ♕xg5+
♔f7 3 ♕g7X) **2 ♕xh7+!** Black
resigned (2 ... ♔xh7 3 ♖h5X).

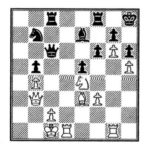

Adorjan – Ostojic (1970): **1 ♗xh6
♗xb4 2 ♗xg7+! ♔xg7 3 h6+ ♔xh6
4 g7 ♖g8 5 ♖g2!** Black resigned.

In combinations leading to the
destruction of the king's pawn cover it
is crucial to direct the heavy pieces
quickly towards the main direction of
the attack. And this is understandable:
the sacrificed pieces must be replaced
by reserves before the enemy has had
time to organise a defence.

(see next diagram)

In the game Pritkova – Sharova
(1955) after **1 ♖xh7+! ♔xh7 2 e3**
Black resigned, since White's next
move – 3 ♗d3+ gives him the
possibility, without loss of time, to
transfer his rook from d1 to the mating

square h1. Moroever, the same
objective can be achieved by 2 ♖d4.

A linear mate lies at the basis of the
combination made by Henkin (White)
against Masich (1957).

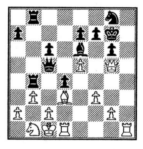

The two sides are conducting attacks
on opposite flanks. In such situations
success usually comes to the one who
first breaks through the enemy defence.

1 ♖h8!. The tactical justification of
this strange move is served by the
variation 1 ... ♔xh8 2 ♗xg6! fxg6
(2 ... ♔g7 3 ♗h7+!) 3 ♕xg6, and mate
with the rook on h1 is unanswerable.
At the same time White intends to
strengthen the attack by doubling
rooks, which forces the opponent
immediately to play his trump card.

1 ... ♗xb3! Now Black, for his part,
creates the threat of 2 ... ♗xc2, and in
the event of 2 axb3 ♖xb3 he obtains
serious counter-chances.

2 ♕h4! White first constructs a mating net (3 ♕h7+). Black must go over to defence.

2 ... ♕xe5 3 axb3, and White realised his advantage.

With a paradoxical king manoeuvre Black prepared a decisive redeployment of the rook in the game Vostin – Karlsson (1973).

1 ... ♔f7(!?).

There arises the threat of 2 ... ♘f4+ 3 gxf4 ♖h8X. But White can take with his knight on d6, even with check and a fork! Let's try: 2 ♘xd6+ ♔e7. Black's queen is 'untouchable' because of the same jump ♘h5-f4+. On 3 ♘f5+ Black replies 3 ... ♖xf5, maintaining all the threats. There remains 3 ♕e3, but then 3 ... ♘f4+ 4 ♕xf4 ♖h7+ 5 ♕h4+ (5 ♔g2 ♕e2X) 5 ... ♖xh4+ and 6 ... ♔xd6.

White chooses another variation: **2 ♘xe5+ ♔e7** (again playing for 'beauty', but why not simply 2 ... dxe5 ?) **3 ♕xb5** (he could prolong resistance by 3 ♘c6+ ♖xc6 4 ♕e3) **3 ... ♘f4+ 4 gxf4 ♖h8X.**

However, as in the words of the song, "Beauty to me is useless." In the diagram position Black achieves victory with the modest move 1 ... ♖f6!

with the same ideas, but with less expenditure of 'grey matter' ...

In the cases considered, the 'punitive' rook had to be moved to the place of execution without delay. In the following example, taken from the game Spassky – Nikolaevsky (1963), this operation lasted for several moves.

Black to move. In order to weaken the mailed fist of the white pieces with exchanges, Y.Nikolaevsky played **1 ... ♘xe3**, reckoning on 2 ♕xe3? ♗xe5 3 ♖xe5 ♗d5. B.Spassky, however, thought up a piece sacrifice, wrecking the opponent's king's flank.

2 ♘xf6+! gxf6 3 ♕xe3 fxe5 4 ♕xe5 h6 (the only defence against 5 ♖g5+) **5 ♖f6 ♔h7.**

Again the only move, though it will not save him. White threatened 6 ♖h6+. On 5 ... ♘d5 possible was 6 ♕g3+ ♔h7 7 ♗d3+, while after 5 ... ♗d5 White wins by means of 6 ♖xh6 f6 7 ♕g3+ ♔f7 8 ♖h7+ ♔e8 9 ♖e1+ ♗e6. In these variations the power and range of the heavy pieces is strikingly displayed.

6 ♖df1 (White ties his opponent to the defence of the f7 square, preparing the entry of the other rook to an attacking position) **6 ... ♗d5** (while now the queen, with tempo, transfers to the g-file, in order to cut off the king on the edge of the board) **7 ♕f5+ ♔g7 8 ♕g4+ ♔h7** (and, finally, the last sacrifice and a decisive manoeuvre) **9 ♖xh6+ ♔xh6 10 ♖f5**. Black resigned.

The main direction of the attack can run not only along the file, but also the rank.

Palatnik – Sveshnikov (1976): **1 ♖d8+! ♔h7 2 ♕f5+ g6 3 ♕xf7+ ♕g7 4 ♖e7!** Black resigned.

Up to here we have seen how the linear mate comes on the edge of the board. Quite frankly, a linear mate in the centre is a unique event. It happened in the game Kogan – Kotenko (1972), played by correspondence.

Black's position is extraordinarily dangerous. But the white queen is attacked, and Black is counting on exploiting the time necessary for its retreat. However a surprise awaits him.

1 ♘xe6! ♕xe6. No good is 1 ... fxe6 2 ♕g6+ ♔e7 3 ♖he1 ♕b6, while after 1 ... hxg4 2 ♘c7+ ♔e7 3 ♘7d5+ White wins back the queen with satisfaction.

2 ♕d4! The black queen is under attack and he threatens mate on d8. There is one defence – 2 ... ♘c6, but now White carries out a spectacular final operation.

3 ♕d7+!. Black resigned. After 3 ... ♕xd7 4 ♗xd7+ ♔e7 5 ♗xc6 ♗xc6 6 ♖he1+ he delivers a linear mate in the centre!

In 1914 at the international tournament in Petersburg, S.Tarrasch sacrificed two bishops and gained a beautiful victory.

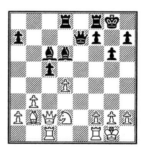

1 ... ♗xh2+! 2 ♔xh2 ♕h4+ 3 ♔g1 ♗xg2!

Only two moves ago the white king remained in blissful ignorance, but now is in a distressed state. 4 ... ♕h1X is threatened and in the event of 4 ♔xg2 ♕g4+ 5 ♔h2 ♖d5 matters are concluded with a linear mate. Nimzowitsch tries to lead his king out of the danger zone, but the black pieces relentlessly pursue it all over the board.

4 f3 ♖fe8 5 ♘e4 ♕h1+ 6 ♔f2 ♗xf1 7 d5 (7 ♔xf1 ♕h2+ winning the queen) **7 ... f5 8 ♕c3 ♕g2+ 9 ♔e3 ♖xe4+!**

10 fxe4 f4+ 11 ♔xf4 ♖f8+ 12 ♔e5 ♕h2+ 13 ♔e6 ♖e8+. White resigned (14 ♔d7 ♗b5X).

You can imagine S.Tarrasch's frustration when the tournament committee did not award him the first brilliancy prize. At the closing banquet the vexed grandmaster appealed to GM. Lasker:

"Tell me, doctor, is it not true that my combination against Nimzowitsch is very beautiful?"

" Not only beautiful, – said the world champion – but extremely rare. Such combinations are met once in 25 years ... "

Those present took Lasker's hint: exactly 25 years previously he had first given up two bishops at the altar of the attack. Tarrasch's combination, despite its spectacular effect, was not original, whereas beauty is always unique.

Let's see the original – the ending of the game Em.Lasker – Bauer (1889).

1 ♘h5 ♘xh5?. Allowing White to carry out a famous combination. However let's not blame Bauer. The tactical operation, devised by Lasker, at the time was still unknown.

2 ♗xh7+! ♔xh7 3 ♕xh5+ ♔g8 4 ♗xg7!. Black must also 'eat' this bishop, although his appetite is already spoiled. Mate is threatened on h8, and if 4 ... f5, then 5 ♖f3 ♕e8 6 ♕h6 ♗f6 7 ♖g3 with a quick win.

4 ... ♔xg7. Now, when the pawn cover of the king has been demolished, the heavy pieces are brought up for the breakthrough.

5 ♕g4+. Cutting off the king on the edge file, in order to prevent its escape.

5 ... ♔h7 6 ♖f3. The rook is ready to deliver the final blow from h3. He has to give up the queen.

6 ... e5 7 ♖h3+ ♕h6 8 ♖xh6+ ♔xh6. It seems that Black has sufficient material equivalent for the queen, but Lasker completes the combination with one more blow.

9 ♕d7! Black resigned: he loses one of the bishops.

Lasker's combination has become a typical tactical device but is rarely seen in high class competitions. However in 1973, in the higher league of the USSR championship, G.Kusmin did manage to realise Lasker's idea in a pure form. His opponent was E.Sveshnikov (Black).

The 'Lasker bishops' have trained their sights on the opponent's king's flank. However, played at once, the combination loses strength: after 1 ♗xh7+!? ♔xh7 2 ♕h5+ ♔g8 3 ♗xg7 ♔xg7 4 ♕g4+ ♔h8 5 ♖f3 Black has the defence – 5 ... ♘xf4 6 ♖xf4 f5. Therefore it is necessary to deflect the knight from the d5 square.

1 ♘b6! ♘xb6 (mission accomplished, now – all according to the famous pattern) **2 ♗xh7+ ♔xh7 3 ♕h5+ ♔g8 4 ♗xg7 ♔xg7 5 ♕g4+ ♔h8 6 ♖f3.** Black resigned.

In the final position White is three pieces down, but the threat of mate on h3 is irresistible.

Here are another pair of rampaging bishops, but in a different format.

Mohring – Finsch (1961). Black's position, quite frankly, is poor. For example, a decisive attack is offered by 1 ♗f6 g6 2 ♕g5 ♖fc8 3 ♖e4 etc. However White finds a forced decision, inspired by Lasker's combination.

1 ♗xh7+! ♔xh7 2 ♗f6! gxf6. It is not difficult to convince oneself that this is the only defence against mate. But 'the king is the goal!'

3 ♕h4+ ♔g8 4 ♕g3+! ♔h7 5 ♖e4.

The point of the last two checks lies in the fact that not only did they cut off the king along the g-file, but also brought the queen to a square where it does not restrict the manoeuvrability of the rook along the fourth rank. Black resigned.

The sacrifices of the bishops can also be made in another order, as happened in the game Knutter – Rodewald (1962).

If 1 ... ♗xh2+ 2 ♔xh2 ♗xg2, then White can refuse the second sacrifice – 3 ♕d3 and defend. It is not necessary to start with that bishop.

1 ... ♗xg2! 2 ♔xg2 ♕g4+ 3 ♔h1 ♕f3+ 4 ♔g1 (now the other bishop enters the fray) **4 ... ♗xh2+! 5 ♔xh2 ♖d5.** White resigned.

The following famous game was played a century ago by international master Edward Lasker.

Dutch Defence
Ed. Lasker – Thomas 1911

1 d4 f5 2 ♘f3 e6 3 ♘c3 ♘f6 4 ♗g5 ♗e7 5 ♗xf6 ♗xf6 6 e4 fxe4 7 ♘xe4 b6 8 ♘e5 0-0 9 ♗d3 ♗b7 10 ♕h5 ♕e7

We will not find fault with Black's play. We mention only that his last move leads to defeat, necessary was 10 ... ♗xe5, after which 11 ♘f6+ is no good because of 11 ... ♖xf6. But Sir George Thomas' mistake proves fatal – it gives the opportunity for a grandiose combination, completed with a rare mating finish.

11 ♕xh7+!! ♚xh7 12 ♘xf6+ ♚h6 13 ♘eg4+ ♚g5 14 h4+. A quicker way to his objective is 14 f4+ ♚h4 (14 ... ♚xf4 15 g3+ ♚f3 16 0-0X) 15 g3+ ♚h3 16 ♗f1+ ♗g2 17 ♘f2X.

14 ... ♚f4 15 g3+ ♚f3 16 ♗e2+ ♚g2 17 ♖h2+ ♚g1. Incredible but true. A total of seven moves ago the black king was in his residence on g8, surrounded by servants, but now, in splendid isolation, he is perishing in the rear of the enemy.

18 ♔d2X! A matter of taste. Also possible is 18 0-0-0X.

"If Edward Lasker had in his life only played this one game – remarked former world champion M.Botvinnik – it would have been sufficient to immortalise his name".

(Because of the numerous discrepancies published, and still being published to this day, in books and magazines all over the world, it is necessary to provide some clarification.

In his book, published in London in 1952, Ed.Lasker gave these opening moves: 1 d4 f5 2 ♘f3 e6 3 ♘c3 ♘f6.

The last (mating) move was, according to Ed.Lasker, not 18 0-0-0X, but 18 ♔d2X.

Furthermore Lasker wrote: "This was not played in a tournament but was a so-called 5-minute game. This way of timing a game was very popular in the London chess club in 1911".

So the game was played not in 1912, but in 1911.)

Any more players who get their mate by castling edited should be offered 'compensation'.

This position arose in a game played by P.Morphy against an unknown amateur in 1858. The reader may be puzzled: what happened to the rook a1? Well, it was not there from the very start. Morphy gave a rook odds, and, judging by the strange location of the enemy king, rightly so.

1 ♕g4+ ♚d3 2 ♕e2+ ♚c2 3 d3+ ♚xc1 (there is also no salvation in 3 ... ♚b1 4 0-0 ♚xa2 5 ♕c2) **4 0-0X!**.

A normal linear mate – albeit from the department of chess humour ...

In study compositions the linear mate is usually constructed with the help of subtle rook manoeuvres.

W.Holzhausen, 1921

White mates in 3 moves

1 Rc7! (threatening mate on g8 and covering the h2 – b8 diagonal, so as not to give the bishop the possibility of participating in the defence via the f4 square) **1 ... Kb8 2 Re7!** (and now preventing defence via the g5 and a3 squares) **2 ... any 3 Rg8X.**

G.Ernst, 1911

White mates in 7 moves

The rook manoeuvres are very typical: by creating the threat of mate from both sides, White increases his radius of activity and tears away from the 'adhesive' king.

1 Rg1 Kh2 2 R5g2+ Kh3 3 Rg7 Kh2 4 R1g4 Kh3 5 R4g5 Kh4 6 Rg1, and mate on the next move.

In studies a linear mate is most often used as a threat.

L.Prokes, 1948

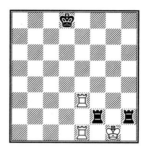

White to move and win

We begin of course with a check. But which one? There is no win by 1 Rd3+? Kc7 2 Rc1+ Kb6 3 Rb3+ Ka5 4 Ra1+ Ra2 5 Ra3+ Rxa3 6 Rxa3+ Kb4.

Leading to his objective is **1 Rd1+! Kc7 2 Rc3+ Kb6 3 Rb1+ Rb2 4 Rb3+ Rxb3 5 Rxb3+.**

Because of their range and special 'linear' properties, the heavy pieces are extremely dangerous when they break through into the enemy rear. In these cases, mating finishes may take different forms.

The simplest method of diverting an enemy piece from defence of the back rank is illustrated by a position from the game Barcza – Tarnowski (1950).

1 ... ♕f3+! 2 ♖xf3 ♖b1+ with mate in two moves.

It is interesting that both players did not notice this elementary possibility. Black played 1 ... ♖g3? and in the end even suffered defeat.

Deflecting pieces and pawns from defence of rear squares lays at the heart of many combinations.

In the game Essen – Rindell (1955) the path for the black rooks is blocked by the g2 pawn. However it is possible to deflect it with a queen sacrifice: **1 ... ♕xh3+! 2 gxh3 ♖g1+ 3 ♔h2 ♘xf3+ 4 ♖exf3 ♖8g2X.**

The blow **1 ... ♕xg2+ 2 ♖xg2 ♖d1+,**

occurring in the game Kubert-Mard (1957), is not difficult to find but a similar sacrifice, albeit in a more complicated situation, was overlooked even by grandmaster W.Uhlmann in an encounter with Dely (1962).

In this position, playing White, Uhlmann decided to force home a win with a standard tactical device: **1 ♖xg7? ♖xg7 2 ♗xf6**, assuming that after 2 ... ♖eg8 3 ♗xg7+ ♖xg7 4 ♕d8+ he mates his opponent, along the lines we are currently exploring. One can imagine the amazement of the grandmaster when he himself was mated in the same way!

2 ... ♕g2+! 3 ♖xg2 ♖e1+, and White had to resign. Though the rook on g7 is bound hand and foot, his 'sister' does not merely provide moral support. Apparently Uhlmann was under the impression it was it was 'pinned to death', but it proved to be not quite so lifeless.

A beautiful deflecting sacrifice ended the encounter Panno – Bravo (1975).

1 ... ♛e2!, and White resigned, since after 2 ♖dxe2 ♖f1+ 3 ♖xf1 ♘xe2+ he is mated on the f1 square, while after 2 ♘f6+ ♖xf6 3 exf6 ♛xd2 he remains a piece down. Also no help is 2 ♖ed1 in view of 2 ... ♛xd1+ 3 ♖xd1 ♘e2+.

A classical example of two rooks at work on the 8th rank is illustrated by the game Alekhine-Colle (1925).

1 ♛xd7! ♖xd7 2 ♖e8+ ♔h7 3 ♖cc8 ♖d8 4 ♖exd8. Black resigned.

Of course you noticed that the g6 pawn and the queen on g5 block his own king, preventing it from escaping? This factor frrequently is a motive for a combination, since the direction of attack can run not only along the rank but also the file.

In this position from the game Crawford – Tucker (1960) White tried to seize the initiative by **1 ♖ad1**, but the daunting reply **1 ... ♛h7!** prompted an immediate surrender. After 2 ♗xh7 ♖cxh7 the white king, surrounded by 'personal protection', falls under the blows of the opponent's connected rooks.

The capture of the back rank can be achieved by an immediate elimination of enemy pieces, defending the rear.

Lombardy – Kramer (1957): **1 ♗c6!** White wins the exchange, since not possible is **1 ... ♛xc6** because of **2 ♛xf8+! ♔xf8 3 ♖e8X**; also 1 ... ♛xa3 leads to material loss after 2 ♖xa3.

(The game actually went: 1 ... ♗c8 2 ♗xd7 ♛xd7 3 ♖d3 ♛c7 4 ♛d6. Black resigned.)

As a preventive measure we will show two identical tactical oversights at a higher level, which had an impact on grandmaster R.Holmov.

Simagin – Holmov (1966): **1 ♗xc7?** **♘g4+!** White resigned. (2 hxg4 ♖h6+ 3 ♔g1 ♖d1X).

Seven years later ...

Estevez – Holmov (1973): **1 ... ♖e6? 2 ♘g5+!**. Black resigned (2 ... hxg5 3 ♕h5X).

Often the final operation is preceded by a complicated introduction to the play, as was the case, for example, in the game Gislasson – Boey (1956).

Black's pieces are actively placed, but for the time being there are no real threats. On 1 ... ♖g6? White replies 2 ♕d5, maintaining equality (2 ... ♖e4 3 ♕d8+).

1 ... ♖e4! Exploiting the pin on the 3rd rank (♕b3), Black makes a play for the most vulnerable point in the opponent's position – the f4 pawn. It cannot be defended: 2 ♖c4 ♖g6.

2 ♔g1 ♕e3+ 3 ♔h1 ♖xf4. Threatening mate on the 1st rank, while White's pieces on the queen's flank cannot come to his assistance.

4 ♖g1 (the very moment has arrived when it is the gun that does the talking...) **4 ... ♕xg1+! 5 ♔xg1 ♖g6+ 6 ♔h1 ♖f1X**.

In the game Arakelov – Litvinov (1959) the 8th rank is accessible to the white rooks.

But what to do after **1 ♖d8+ ♔h7** ?

It turns out that here lies a hidden combination based on a pin: **2 ♖h8+!** (the king is lured to the a1-h8 diagonal, on which the white bishop is operating) **2 ... ♔xh8 3 ♕xh6+ ♔g8 4 ♖d8+**, and mate on the next move.

In especially favourable circumstances, driving the king to the edge of the board and creating mating situations comes about without material cost.

Schmid – Hoffmann (1958): **1 ♖h6+ ♔e7 2 ♖g7+ ♔d8** (leading to the loss of a rook is 2 ... ♖f7 3 ♖xf7+ ♔xf7 4 ♖xh7+) **3 ♖d6+ ♔c8 4 ♖g8+**. Black resigned.

Thus the dislocation of enemy troops can be a basis to infiltrate the opponent's rear on the 7th (2nd) rank. Reaching this rank can be very profitable in terms of both small and large prey. The following position illustrates the ravenous appetite of doubled rooks on the 7th rank.

On the move, White exploits the threat of mate to capture all six of Black's pawns!

1 Ïxg7+ êh8. Trying to hide the king on the other flank could be even more costly: 1 ... êf8 2 Ïxh7 êe8 3 Ïxc7 êd8 4 Ïcg7, and mate on the following move.

2 Ïxh7+ êg8 3 Ïdg7+ êf8 4 Ïxc7 êg8 5 Ïcg7+ êf8 6 Ïxb7. The repetitive manoeuvres of the white rook are reminiscent of the swing of a pendulum, but each time the degree of oscillation increases, and reduces the number of black pawns.

6 ... êg8 7 Ïbg7+ êf8 8 Ïxg3 Ïxa2. At last Black has the opportunity to do something. Incidentally it is still not too late for White to lose: 9 Ïxc3? Ïa1+ 10 êb2 Ï8a2X.

However White played **9 Ïh8+ êe7 10 Ïxa8 Ïxa8 11 Ïxc3**, and won easily.

But if in the original position it were Black to move, then after 1 ... Ïxa2 White's initiative is good enough only for perpetual check.

Szabo (White) exploited the devastating power of doubled rooks against Duckstein (1957).

1 Ïxh7+ êg8 2 Ïcg7+ êf8 3 Ïxa7! (not just to win a pawn but in order to remove the rook with tempo, creating the threat of mate simultaneously from a8 and h8) **3 ... êg8 4 Ïhg7+ êh8** (4 ... êf8 5 Ïgf7+! Ïxf7 6 Ëh8X) **5 Ïgf7!** Black resigned: he loses a rook or gets mated.

Direct mating finishes on the 7th (2nd) rank usually look like this:

This is achieved by various tactical means, with some of which we will now familiarise ourselves.

In the game Morphy – Maurian (1866) the 7th rank resembles a desert: all life has already been extinguished from it. In order to achieve a mating finish, it is necessary to divert the black rook to the f8 square. This task falls upon the shoulders of the knight.

1 ≡g7+ ♔h8 2 ♘f8! The threat of 3 ♘g6X forces Black to capture the stalking knight, but then his own rook blocks the king's path to safety.

2 ... ≡xf8 3 ≡h7+ ♔g8 4 ≡cg7X.

The ending of the game Alekhine – Yates (1922) might serve as another example of the enforced blockade of an enemy king.

1 ♘d7! (with the unambiguous threat of ♘f6+) **1 ... ♔h8 2 ♘f6 ≡gf8 3 ≡xg7 ≡xf6 4 ♔e5!**, forcing the rook to return to f8 and block the king. Black resigned.

There was a very good mating construction in the game Hartston – Whiteley (1974).

1 ♕g8+ ≡f8 2 ♕g6+! Black resigned (2 ... ♕xg6 3 ≡exe7+ ♔d8 4 ≡bd7X).

Cherepkov (Black) against Bannik (1961) created a mating attack with a decisive manoeuvre of the queen and rooks.

1 ... ≡g5+ 2 ≡g2 (otherwise 2 ♔h2 ≡h5+) **2 ... ♕c5+ 3 ♕f2.** If 3 ♔h1, then 3 ... ≡h5+ 4 ≡h2 ≡ee5!, and White will not avoid defeat.

3 ... ≡e2! An excellent blow! All of Black's pieces are under fire, but none of them can be captured. The main variation leads to a thematic mate: **4 ♕xc5 ≡gxg2+ 5 ♔h1 ≡h2+ 6 ♔g1 ≡eg2X.**

White played on through inertia, 4 ≡xg5, but after 4 ... ♕xg5+ he laid down his arms.

Often other pieces give the 'green light' to the rooks by sacrificing themselves.

In the game Czerniak – Vasiliev (1971), White had to act without delay in view of the threat of mate on g2.

1 ♘g6+! fxg6 (after 1 ... ♔g8 2 ♘e7+ he loses the queen) **2 ♕xh7+!**

&xh7 3 ♖xg7+ &h8 4 ♖h7+ &g8 5 ♖ag7X.

The occupation of the penultimate rank by heavy pieces almost always gives the attacking side a decisive advantage. But the opponent should be vigilant for the safety of his rear, and allow such a possibility only in a hopeless situation. So it is necessary to obstruct his forces. Here are two famous games played by Capablanca, in which he managed to win using the same tactical idea.

This position arose in the encounter Nimzowitsch – Capablanca (1927). One black rook is already hanging around the 2nd rank, but what about the other one? A deflecting sacrifice comes to his assistance.

1 ... e5! 2 ♗xe5 ♖dd2

The task is fulfilled, and White's situation suddenly becomes pitiful. If 3 ♕f1, then 3 ... ♕d5! 4 ♗d4 ♕h5! (with the threat of 5 ... ♖xf2 6 ♕xf2 ♖xf2 7 &xf2 ♕xh2+) 5 h4 ♕f3 and 6 ... ♖xf2. Black wins beautifully after 3 ♖f1 ♕xe3! 4 ♗f4 ♖xf2! 5 ♗xe3 ♖g2+ 6 &h1 ♖xh2+ 7 &g1 ♖cg2X.

3 ♕b7. Nimzowitsch defends the g2 square, intending to give up his queen as dearly as possible.

3 ... ♖xf2 4 g4 ♕e6 5 ♗g3 ♖xh2!. A new sacrifice finally demolishes the king's pawn cover. 6 ♗xh2 is not

possible because of 6 ... ♕xg4+ 7 &h1 ♕h3 with mate.

6 ♕f3 ♖hg2+ 7 ♕xg2 ♖xg2+ 8 &xg2 ♕xg4, and Black realised his advantage.

Also here the black pieces are conducted by Capablanca, but this time his opponent was Alatortsev (1935). As in the previous position, one of the rooks is already on the 2nd rank. It seems that the other rook cannot provide further assistance, since the b6 pawn is attacked. However Black has a tactical blow available.

1 ... ♖xf2! With an explosive sacrifice Black lays bare the 2nd rank for invasion by the second rook. On 2 &xf2 follows 2 ... ♖c2+ 3 &e1 ♕xg2 with unavoidable mate (4 ♕b8+ &g7 5 ♕e5+ f6).

2 ♕g3 (equivalent to capitulation, but by now there was no defence) **2 ... ♖e2.** White resigned.

The same idea lies at the basis of the combination played by Chigorin (Black) against Pollock (1889).

1 ... ♗xh3! 2 gxh3. The sacrifice must be accepted, since Black threatened 2 ... ♖e4 and 3 ... ♕g4+.

2 ... ♖8xe3! The second sacrifice completely disorganises the defence. On 3 fxe3 would of course follow 3 ... ♕xh3.

3 ♖ce1 ♕xh3 4 ♖xe2 ♖xe2 5 ♖b1 ♖e4. White resigned (6 ♖b4 ♖e1X).

In the game Botvinnik – Euwe (1948) still not one of the white pieces has penetrated to the 7th rank. If White retreats the attacked knight, then Black obtains time to castle and escape immediate danger. Botvinnik, leaving the knight under attack, breaks through with his heavy pieces into the opponent's camp.

1 ♕g3! fxe5 2 ♕g7 ♖f8 3 ♖c7. The operation is completed, Black can resign with a clear conscience, since 3 ... ♕d6 4 ♖xb7 d3 5 ♖a7 ♕d8 6 ♕xh7 is hopeless.

3 ... ♕xc7 4 ♕xc7 ♗d5 5 ♕xe5 and soon Euwe laid down his arms.

In many positions capture of the 7th (2nd) rank is the main tactical task. And for this objective the attacking side is prepared to give up material.

Original means were employed to get heavy pieces to the 7th rank in the game Skulener – Taborov (1975).

1 ♕h4! ♗xe3. The knight has been sacrificed, what to do now? If 2 ♖g7, then 2 ... h6, and Black can still hold (3 ♕g4 ♗g5).

2 ♕g4 ♗h6 3 ♕h5! ♗xd2. The sacrifice of a second knight allows the white queen to draw closer to the f7 pawn.

4 ♖g7 h6 5 ♕xf7. Black resigned.

Euwe (White) carried out a brilliant combination in a game against Speyer (1924).

1 ♖xe7! The rook noisily invades the 7th rank. 1 ... ♔xe7 is not possible because of 2 ♗a3+ ♔e8 3 ♕e1+ ♘e4 4 ♖c7 ♖d7 5 ♖xd7 ♕xd7 6 ♘xe4.

1 ... ♗xf3 2 ♗a3!! ♕a6!. Ask a question, get an answer. Both opponents are equal to the occasion, this is the best defence, whereas 2 ... ♗xd1 3 ♖e3+ ♔g8 4 ♖xd3 ♖e8 5 ♖xd1 or 2 ... ♖d6 3 ♖e3 ♕xe3 4 ♘xf3! leaves no hope for Black.

3 ♖cc7!. After 3 ♕xf3? ♕xa3 4 ♖cc7 ♕xe7 Black defends himself. Now, however, the white rooks, penetrating

combinational paths on the cherished rank, mercilessly torment their victim.

3 ... ♕xa3 4 ♖xf7+ ♔e8 5 ♕e1+. Black resigned.

An important role in an attack on the king is played by the pawns. They restrict its living space, cutting off the neighbouring squares and creating outposts for attacking pieces.

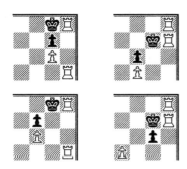

We begin our study of how to create this mating formation with the game Alekhine – Hulscher (1933), which has become a classic example.

The move 1 g6?, threatening mate on h8, is presently unfavourable because of 1 ... ♕xg6 2 ♕c4+ (with the aim of forcing Black to block the f7 square) 2 ... d5, and White achieves nothing. But if he eliminates this defence, then the advance of the g-pawn will decide the outcome of the battle.

1 ♘e5!! With the knight sacrifice the d6 pawn is diverted from the d-file. Upon 1 ... g6 Black is mated in two moves (2 ♖h8+ ♔g7 3 ♖1h7X), while if 1 ... ♕xe5 2 ♕xe5 dxe5 then 3 g6 leads to mate. **1 ... dxe5 2 g6.** Black resigned (2 ... ♕xg6 3 ♕c4+).

There was a spectacular final attack in the game Bloel – Wegener (1956).

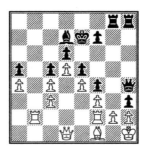

1 ... ♕g3! The queen must be taken, otherwise there follows **2 ... ♕xh2+! 3 ♔xh2 hxg2+ 4 ♔g1 ♖h1X.**

(The game continued: 2 hxg3 hxg2+ 3 ♔g1 ♖h1+ 4 ♔xg2 ♖gh8 5 gxf4 exf4. White resigned).

An advanced pawn also supports an attack by the rook against an uncastled king.

Bykov – Klaman (1963). The opponents have still not emerged from the opening, but already a skirmish is taking place. Black's kingside is in a 'primitive state' and in such cases it is important that the attacking side brings its main forces into action at once.

1 ♗b5! (an excellent move, after which events unfold by force) **1 ... ♗xb5 2 ♖hd1** (but now a storm is brewing) **2 ... ♘d5 3 ♘xd5** (with the 'mild threat' of 4 ♘c7+) **3 ... f6 4 e6 ♔d8 5 ♗f4.** Black resigned.

In the game Szabo – Bakonyi (1951) the pawn wedge was hammered into the castled position with the help of a sacrifice, containing a strong threat.

1 ♕f6! Black resigned. The threat of mate forces the acceptance of the sacrifice, but after **1 ... ♗xf6 2 gxf6** (2 exf6) arises a new mating situation, corresponding to that which we have just examined.

Also from the 5th rank the pawn proves helpful to the attacking pieces, cutting off the enemy king's flight squares.

Karlsson – Ilushenko (1972): **1 ♕f7+ ♔h8 2 ♗c3 ♗xc3 3 ♕f8+ ♕xf8 4 ♖xf8+ ♔g7 5 ♖hf1 ♗d2+ 6 ♔b1.** Black resigned.

In the game Pakulla – Hartmann (1957) the e4 pawn has a decisive say.

1 ... ♖xh2! 2 ♗xg5. Realising that the rook cannot be captured at once because of 2 ... ♖h8+ 3 ♔g2 ♕h6, White places his hopes on this intermediate move, so that after a queen move he can defend against checks on the h-file with a bishop on h4. But the queen is not forced to move. **2 ... ♖dh8.** White resigned.

The combination of Turykina (White) against Mitina (1974) depends on the pawn wedge on e5.

1 ♘f8! ♔xf8 **2 ♕xh6!** ♔e8 **3 ♕h8+!** ♗f8 (3 ... ♗xh8 4 ♖g8+ ♖f8 5 ♗g6X) **4 ♕xf8+ ♖xf8 5 ♗g6+ ♖f7 6 ♗xf7+ ♔xf7 7 ♖g7+ ♔f8 8 ♖g8+ ♔f7 9 ♖1g7X.**

Upon an attack with heavy pieces along adjacent ranks and files, a far advanced pawn is likewise capable of creating a mating formation, by restricting the enemy king and supporting the rook.

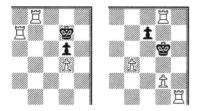

In the game Goglidze – Botvinnik (1935) Black exploits the weakness of the 1st and 2nd ranks, and likewise the pawn wedge on e4, for a decisive combination.

1 ... ♖ab8! (the rook, with tempo, is introduced to an attacking position) **2 ♕d6 ♕xf1+! 3 ♔xf1 ♖c1+**, and mate on the next move.

Karpov – Mecking (1972/73). The raid of the 'Brazilian cruiser' on f4 proves fatal.

1 ♖1h3! Cutting off the king's escape route: 1 ... ♔g5 2 ♖g7+ ♔f4 3 ♖f3X or 1 ... ♔xg4 2 ♖h1!, and to repulse the threat of 3 ♖g7+ would incur significant material loss.

1 ... ♗d4 (It seems that Mecking did not suspect a thing ...) **2 ♖g7!**, and

Black resigned, since it is impossible to avert 3 ♖f3X.

Rook activity along the 7th (2nd) rank is particularly effective when the rook is also supported by a bishop pawn.

Here are examples taken from major tournament practice.

Larsen – Petrosian (1958). To prevent mate on f8, Black played **1 ... ♘d6**. There followed **2 ♖h7+ ♔g8 3 h6! ♘e8 4 ♖hf7!**, and Black resigned, since there is the threat of 5 h7+ ♔h8 6 ♖f8X, and on 4 ... ♘d6 White continues 5 ♖g7+ ♔h8 6 ♖h7+ ♔g8 7 ♖ag7+ ♔f8 8 ♖h8X.

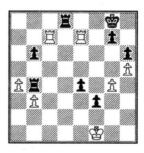

Botvinnik – Levenfish (1937). Despite the dangerous passed pawns, White is insured against loss: he

always retains the possibility of perpetual check. This factor induces Botvinnik to exploit his last chance, which is surprisingly crowned with success.

1 g5! ℤd1+? Now Black loses. Leading to a draw is 1 ... e3 (threatening mate from d1), and if 2 ℤxe3, then 2 ... ℤh4.

2 ♔f2 ℤd2+ 3 ♔e1 ℤe2+ 4 ♔f1.

There are no more checks, while the threat of 5 ℤc8+ ♔h7 6 g6X can only be averted in one way.

4 ... hxg5 5 ℤxg7+, and Black resigned, since on any move follows 6 h6 with mate according to the well-known pattern.

The bishop pawn also serves as a good support point for operations by the rooks along the penultimate rank.

In the game Romanishin – Savon (1975) after **1 ... ℤf2+ 2 ♔g1 ℤxg2+** White acknowledged defeat in view of the variation 3 ♔f1 ℤcf2+ 4 ♔e1 ℤa2 5 ♔f1 f3 6 ℤc3 ℤxh2 7 ♔g1 ℤag2+ 8 ♔f1 ℤh1X.

* * * *

118. Shumov – Winawer, 1875

White to move

On 1 ♕xa7 Black could exchange queens – 1 ... ♕c5+. So what did he do?

119 Konyagina – Nakhimovskaya, 1963

Black to move

The rook f6 is pinned and for the present cannot take part in the attack. Will this be for a long time?

120. Gunnar – Jonas, 1960

White to move

An operation on a 'staircase'.

121. Domuls – Staerman, 1972

White to move

How to get at the king?

122. Lematchko – Popova, 1970

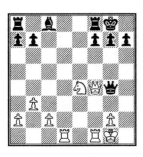

White to move

Both straight ...

123. Geller – Debarnot, 1976

White to move

... and diagonally.

124. Shagalovich – Levin, 1950

White to move

Discomfort on Black's kingside ...

125. Westerhagen – Schmaus, 1956

White to move

Who emerges from the ambush?

126. Chigorin – Lebedev, 1901

White to move

The horse is still in the stable ...

129 Adams – Candet, 1961

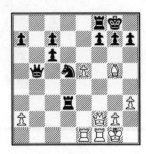

White to move

Geometrical motif.

127. Strekalovsky – Sabinin, 1974

White to move

No sacrifice necessary.

130. Kusmin – Krivonosov, 1974

White to move

Who is heading where?

128. Zaitseva – Muslimova, 1973

White to move

Trouble in store – a bad king.

131. Poetzsch – Blatek, 1960

Black to move

1 ... ♘h4 and everything is 'hanging' ...

132. Alekhine – Borochow, 1932

White to move

Without sight of the board, but seeing everything.

133. Jansa – Tukmakov, 1977

Black to move

Quietly and simply.

134. Smyslov – Flohr, 1949

White to move

Both left and right ...

135. Butnorus – Panchenko, 1975

Black to move

Against all expectations.

136. Lapshin – Kosov, 1975

Black to move

1 ... ♖xe3 and mate ... for who?

137. Cordovil – Garcia, 1970

White to move

What is the hindrance?

138. Ilchenko –Zhuzhina, 1971

Black to move

Women chessplayers know everything!

139 Padevsky – Belkadi, 1962

Black to move

'The Devil's wheel.'

140. Boleslavsky – Bondarevsky, 1941

White to move

1 ♖xh5. But is it good?

141. Lilienthal – Johannesen, 1976

White to move

On a circular route.

142. Ageichenko – Shilov, 1970

White to move

The commander-in-chief's reserves.

143. Kislov – Beribesov, 1971

White to move

Along a well-trodden track.

144. Rittner – Carbonnel (?)

White to move

Mate by correspondence.

145. Barkhatov – Koslov, 1971

White to move

Slowly but surely.

146. Torre – Pahrhuber, 1969

White to move

The hour of the rook.

147. Gragger – Brucker, 1976

Black to move

Encirclement of the blockade.

148. Portisch – Hubner, 1978

Black to move

Separately and together.

149 Estevez – Anderson, 1977

Black to move

Battering ram and cavalry.

150. Muller – Kohler, 1967

Black to move

1 ... 0-0 – out of the frying pan into the fire.

151. Alekhine – Drewitt, 1923

White to move

An old song.

152. Abrosimov – Kirpichnikov, 1969

Black to move

1 ... g4 (in order to drive the rook off the f-file). However ...

153. Spielmann – Schrossel, 1912

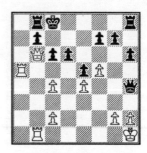

White to move

Into the attack on the b7 square. But how?

154. Schroeder – Kunel, 1963

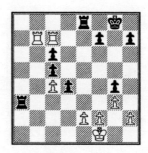

Black to move

Such terrifying rooks on the 7th rank.

155. Grigorian – Seredenko, 1972

Black to move

1 ... f3? But 2 ♖f4. How can he do better?

156. Timoshchenko – Michalchishin, 1973

White to move

With no respite ...

157. L.Kubbel, 1941

White mates in 2 moves

At the crossroads.

158. C.Kipping, 1911

White mates in 3 moves

Getting out of harm's way.

159 W.Speckmann, 1969

White mates in 4 moves

Outwitting the knight.

160. F.Palatz, 1934

White mates in 5 moves

Step by step.

161. H.Rinck, 1916

White to move and win

The imprisoned queen.

162. A.Mandler, E.Konig, 1924   163. H.Rinck, 1925/26

White to move and win   *White to move and win*

The adhesive king.   The denouement, as in a novel.

*   *   *   *

"Every cramped position carries the germ of defeat"

S.Tarrasch

"A very important method against a cramped position is to avoid any exchanges that do not give you any benefit in return."

R.Reti

"In open positions, it is quite natural to infuse life in the pieces quickly and because of this here it is very important to develop the pieces as quickly as possible and bring them into play without loss of time"

R.Reti

"An overwhelming position in the centre confers the right to start active operations on the flank."

A.Nimzowitsch

"I consider the flank attack an integral part of the game. It rarely leads to a worsening of the position. If the attack is beaten off, there always remains a mass of possibilities to take the struggle to other parts of the front."

B.Larsen

"In a good position everyone is capable of playing well, but it is necessary to have the ability to play well in a bad position."

Em.Lasker

"A logically played game, completed by a beautiful combination – that is my chess ideal."

V.Simagin

7. Rook and Bishop

At the beginning of the battle each chess army has two rooks and two bishops. But if rooks are similar to each other like Siamese twins, the bishops, despite their superficial resemblance, 'mow' in different areas. Rooks are ready to cooperate with bishops. These pieces have a wide range of action and the ability to strike from a distance. And while co-operation is based on principles of mutual benefit and equality, the rook always has to reckon with the fact some bishops will go forward into an offensive position. And because opposite coloured bishops are striking different targets, then the direction of the attack is largely determined by their position.

Rooks need open lines, the bishop – free diagonals. Therefore, the greatest activity for both these pieces develops in positions not restricted by pawn chains. Operating on opposite sides, they place the enemy king in a vice, cutting him off from neighbouring squares, and target a whole range of squares along the main avenues of attack.

The final blow might be delivered by any of the attacking pieces, but more often this will be the rook: under the protection of the bishop, it enters without ceremony into direct contact with the enemy king.

When the castled position is weakened by the advance of the g-pawn, the rook, supported by the bishop on the 'highway,' often delivers the final blow along the h-file.

In the game Vilen – Strom (1933) the bishop on d4 dominates the main thoroughfare, while the rook is lurking on the h-file.

1 ♗xe4 dxe4 2 ♕h5!

He cannot take the queen because of 3 ♖g3+ with mate on the following move. Black replied **2 ... ♗h4**, hoping after 3 ♕xh4 f5 to organise a defence. But now it is quite easy to find the concluding blow: **3 ♕xh7+! ♔xh7 4 ♖xh4+ ♔g8 5 ♖h8X**.

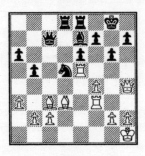

Ravinsky – Petryaev (1962). Here the same mechanism comes into play. Though the long diagonal is closed, the rooks are halfway to their objective and the spring is rapidly unwinding: **1 ♕xh7+ ♔xh7 2 ♖h5+ ♔g8 3 ♖h8X**.

Here the freeing of lines (in the present case diagonals) was achieved in a forcing way. This method might be repeated.

Spielmann – Honlinger (1929): **1 ♘e7+ ♕xe7 2 ♕xh7+ ♔xh7 3 ♖h5+ ♔g8 4 ♖h8X**.

In both examples an important role in the transfer of the rook was played by the bishop d3 – it pins the g6 pawn. In the game Gutop – Roshal (1963) another pawn becomes the object of the pin.

1 ... ♕xd5! After the forced **2 ♗xd5 ♗xd5** White is in no position to avert mate with the rook on h1. The f2 pawn is nailed to a 'pillory'.

Yet another typical means of freeing a diagonal is a pawn break.

Larsen – Andersson (1971): **1 d5!**
cxd5 2 ♕f6 ♕d8 3 ♕h8+! Black
resigned (3 ... ♔xh8 4 ♖xh5+ ♔g8
5 ♖h8X).

In the mechanism of this
combination the king is lured to a poor
diagonal, upon which the transfer of
the rook is accomplished with the help
of a double check.

With opposing bishops on the
diagonal it is necessary to reckon on
their X-Ray properties. The bishop, as
with all linear pieces, has an indirect
influence on the rear squares through
its 'antipodes'.

Trayanov – Consulting players
(1936): **1 ♘e4!** At first sight an
impulsive thrust, pursuing an
elementary aim – deflection of the
knight g5 from its defence of the h7
square. In fact, White takes aim at
another target and the attempt to
distract the knight is used as an
additional threat.

1 ... dxe4? (or 1 ... e5) **2 ♕h8+!**
♗xh8 3 ♖xh8X. The bishop b2 shoots
right through its black rival!

In a game against Malevinsky
(1969), Rytov (White) only needed one
move to 'irradiate' the enemy king's
position.

1 ♗f6!, and Black resigned, since
1 ... ♗xf6 is not possible because of
2 ♕h7+ and 2 ... ♔f8 3 ♕xf7X, but
otherwise the threat of mate on h8
cannot be averted (1 ... ♗h6 2 ♕xh6
♘xh6 3 ♖xh6).

In the last variation a mating finish
was inevitable, mainly because Black,
despite having the turn to move, cannot
close the long diagonal. With the
bishop on f6 (f3) the diagonal is
noticeably shortened and in fact ceases
to be 'long'. Such a situation often
allows the attacking side to invest a
great deal of material and even provide
the enemy with a few tempi.

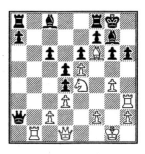

Mileika – Seledkin (1971): **1 ♕c1!**
(the direct threat is 2 ♖a1, and the
masked one...).

1 ... dxe4 2 ♕xh6! Black resigned.

In reply to **1 ... ②f4+?** Blackburne against Schwarz (1881) sacrificed a queen and a rook to produce the same scheme on the board: **2 ♕xf4! ♗xf4 3 ♖xh5! gxh5 4 ♖xh5.** Black resigned. Mate on h8 can only be delayed.

In order to occupy the f6 square with the bishop Gaprindashvili (White) against Vujanovic (1975) gave her opponent what seemed dangerous counterplay.

Black expected the attacked knight to move away. But suddenly ...

1 ♗xg7!! ♕xc3+. Of course, 1 ... ♔xg7 is not possible because of 2 ♕h6+, while upon 1 ... bxc3+ White replies, as in the game, 2 ♔b1!.

2 ♔b1! ♕xd2 3 ♗xf6! The objective is achieved. The threat of mate on h8 can only be prevented by serious material loss. (3 ... ♕xd1+ 4 ♖xd1 ♔f8 5 ♖h1 ♗h3 6 ♖xh3 ♔e8 7 ♖h8+ ♔d7 8 ♖h7 ♖f8 9 ♗g7, and Black resigned).

The 'normal' path of the bishop to its destination is via the g5 square.

Santasiere – Blumin (1939): **1 ♗xh6! g6** (1 ... gxh6 2 ♕g4) **2 ♕g5 ♕e7** (2 ... ♗xh6 3 ♖h3) **3 ♖h3 ♔g8 4 ♕f4 ♕c5 5 ♗g5 ♖d4 6 ♗f6 ♗g7 7 ♕h6.** Black resigned.

In the game Bruntse – Huert (1973) White's queen's bishop is still in a 'cage'. But its time will soon come.

1 f5! exf5 2 ♕h7+ ♔f8 3 ♕xg7+!. Black resigned in view of the forced variation 3 ... ♔xg7 4 ♗h6+ ♔h8 5 ♗g5+ ♔g8 6 ♗f6.

In all the examples the rook delivers the final blow by a frontal attack on the h-file. However it can happen that the rook penetrates the king's fortress by a detour – along the back rank.

(See next diagram)

Rek – Sternberg (1957): **1 ♖d8+ ♔h7 2 ♗xf6!** Black resigned (2 ... ♕xc7 3 ♖xh8X).

The back rank is subject to particular danger when there is a bishop on h6 (h3). From this square the bishop successfully complements or supports the rook in the attack.

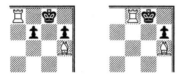

The tactical device of deflecting pieces, overloaded with restricting chess troubles, is a faithful companion of many combinations.

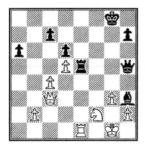

Lederman – Pytel (1977): **1 ... ♕f3.** White resigned. The queen is deflected from its defence of the rook e1.

Karstens – Ulrich (1932). White's last move (1 ♕f3-f4) was interpreted by Black as a blunder. By taking the bishop – **1 ... ♘xd3??**, he was attacked by the full complement of heavy pieces. However the 'trident' was defective: **2 ♕f6!** Black resigned. The e7 pawn, removing one mating threat, is forced to allow an enemy spy into its rear.

In the game Koltanowski – Garcia (1959) White succeeded by repeatedly deflecting the queen from critical squares.

1 ♗a4 b5 2 ♗xb5 ♕xb5 3 ♕xf6 ♕e5 4 ♖ae1! Black resigned.

In all three examples the threat of mate on g7 (g2) is combined with similar threats along the back rank.

In the following position, taken from the game Wikman – Kanko (1973), White attacked the 8th rank on all fronts.

1 ♖d1! This move places Black in a hopeless position. The threat is 2 ♖xc7

131

♕xc7 3 ♕e8+. 1 ... ♕xe6 is not possible because of 2 ♖d8+, while on 1 ... ♗b7 follows 2 ♖xb7. If 1 ... ♗f5 2 ♖xc7 ♗xe6, then 3 ♖xc8+ ♗xc8 4 ♖d8+.

The main variation is **1 ... ♗c6 2 ♖xc7 ♕xe6** (2 ... ♕xc7 3 ♕xc6 ♕xc6 4 ♖d8+). **3 ♖xc6! ♕e8 4 ♖cd6**, and **5 ♖d8** is unstoppable. White wins back the queen and is left a piece ahead. Therefore Black resigned.

Another attacking mechanism, based on the 'X-ray' of one's own heavy pieces, is illustrated by the game Janak – Urbanec (1976).

1 ♖e2! Black resigned.

If we conduct this operation to the end (1 ... ♗g7 2 ♖e8+ ♖xe8 3 ♖xe8+ ♗f8 4 ♖xf8X), then the final position differs from the previous one only by its final chord: the rook captures the enemy bishop on the f8 square. Such situations arise when the opponent has a fianchettoed bishop.

Kunnerman – NN (1934). In reply to **1 ... ♕xb2** White went **2 ♕f6!** (the immediate sacrifice 2 ♖xe5 ♖xe5 3 ♕f6 leads to a draw after 3 ... ♕b1+ 4 ♔g2 ♕e4+ 5 ♔g1 ♕e1+ etc.).

Of course the queen cannot be taken because of 3 ♖e8X. But now White wants to eliminate the bishop on e5, thereby removing the defence of the g7 square.

Black played **2 ... ♕xc3?**, increasing the number of 'X-rays' on the long diagonal (3 ♖xe5 ♕xe5). But there followed a stunning blow **3 ♕g7+!!** (the black bishop will go back to being fianchettoed!), and the game ended: **3 ... ♗xg7 4 ♖e8+**.

Nevertheless there was a surprising defence for Black! Instead of 2 ... ♕xc3? he could offer a counter-sacrifice of the queen – 2 ... ♕c1!, which after 3 ♕xe5 ♕xh6 guarantees him against defeat.

The attacking bishop might also be on the second echelon.

Radulov – Cuellar (1973): **1 ♕e2!** ♘xf3+ Since, one way or the other, the queen will be deflected from defence of the rook c8, Black tries to open up the enemy king in order to obtain counterplay.

2 ♘xf3 ♕xe2 3 ♖xc8+ ♗f8 4 ♗h6 (the mating position has been created, and the white king easily escapes from the checks) **4 ... ♕d1+ 5 ♔f2 ♕c2+ 6 ♖xc2.** Black resigned.

The same construction lay at the basis of the counter-operation undertaken by Tal (White) against Boensch (1969).

1 ... ♖xc3? To 'trap' Tal is tempting isn't it?) **2 ♖d8+ ♗f8 3 ♗f4!** (and to 'fall' for it is simple enough for Tal). Black resigned. The threat of 4. ♗h6 can be averted only at the cost of a piece (3 ... ♕a5 4 ♖xf8+ ♔xf8 5 ♕xc3).

When the bishop is on a short diagonal the main direction of the attack often becomes the f-file.

In the game Ujtelky – Alster (1957) White tried to oust his dangerous neighbour on h3 with the move **1 ♕h5?**, but after **1 ... ♕b6+!** he resigned at once: the rook on b1 is deflected from its defence of the 1st rank.

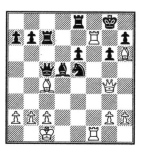

Tseshkovsky – Korensky (1972): **1 ♕d4!** The black queen cannot leave the a3-f8 diagonal in view of the mate on f8, also not possible is 1 ... ♘xf7 because of 2 ♕g7X. On **1 ... ♗xc4** White won easily after **2 ♕xc5 ♖xf7 3 ♖e1**.

Sometimes efforts are aimed at deflecting pieces closing the diagonal of the bishop. For this purpose heavy sacrifices of material may be made.

Chigorin – NN (1874): **1 ♗c4+ ♕xc4 2 ♕e8+! ♘xe8 3 ♖f8X.**

A complex struggle for the f8 square unfolded in the game Muller – NN (1937).

1 ♖bf1 ♖f7. The best defence. If 1 ... ♘f7, then 2 ♖xg6+, while on 1 ... ♘e6 follows, of course, 2 ♕xe6+.

2 ♕d7! The familiar theme of deflection: 2 ... ♖xd7 is not possible because of 3 ♖f8+.

2 ... ♖ef8 3 ♕e7! Black resigned: There is no satisfactory defence against 4 ♕xf8+, e.g. if 3 ... ♘e6 4 ♖xf7 ♖xf7 5 ♕e8+ ♖f8 6 ♕xf8+ ♘xf8 7 ♖xf8X. A characteristic 'X-ray' operation of the white rooks along the f-file: the rook f1 fires at the f8 square through both its own and the enemy's pieces.

Let's become acquainted with a few more tactical devices to move the rook and bishop up to attacking positions.

Richardson – Delmar (1887): **1 ♘f6+! gxf6 2 ♕f8+! ♔xf8 3 ♗h6+ ♔g8 4 ♖e8X**.

Novozhenin – Panfilov (1975): **1 ♕h6+! gxh6 2 ♖xf6+**. Black resigned (2 ... ♔g7 3 ♗xh6+ ♔g8 4 ♖f8X).

In the next position, from the game Vasyukov – Rech, nobody would think that in a few moves the white rooks

will break into the enemy rear and together with the bishop h6 threaten mate on f8.

1 ♘f5 exf5 2 ♘d5 ♕b7 3 exf5 Opening the e-file, the bishop on e7 finds itself under threat, moreover 4 f6 is menaced.

3 ... ♗h4 (With tempo Black repulses two threats, but a third comes into operation) **4 ♖xe8! ♗xg3 5 ♘f6+! gxf6 6 ♖xf8X**.

(In the game 2 ... f4 3 ♗xf4 ♖xb3 4 cxb3 was played, and White won; we gave the main variation of the combination thought up by White.)

In the previous examples the bishop came to a favourable position on the c1-h6 (c8-h3) diagonal. However he could also utilise other lines of communication.

Quite frankly, in the game Petzold – Kreschmar (1963), Black's position is not brilliant. Nevertheless he should not lose in one move – **1 ... g6?** **2 ♕e8+! ♖xe8 3 ♖xe8+ ♔g7 4 ♗f8+ ♔g8 5 ♗xh6X**.

The same zigzag was successfully made by the bishop in the encounter Kroning – Strerud (1963).

1 ♕f6! ♖dxd7 2 ♕d8+! ♖xd8 3 ♖xd8+ ♔g7 4 ♗f8+ ♔g8 5 ♗h6X

Such an artful bishop manoeuvre, forcing the king to the edge of the board with one touch, very often goes unnoticed.

On the short diagonal the bishop participates in the creation of mating positions and in an attack along the h-file.

It is easy to see that the outlines of these schemes are similar to the previous ones – it is as if they have been rotated by 90 degrees. However, the ways of achieving them are unique. Here are two combinations with the typical mechanism.

Santasiere – Adams (1926): **1 ♕xh7+! ♔xh7 2 ♖h5+ ♔g7 3 ♗h6+ ♔h7 4 ♗f8X**.

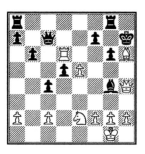

Duras – Olland (1907): **1 ♗f8+ ♗h5 2 ♕xh5+ gxh5 3 ♖h6X**.

Note the poor position of the black rook, as well as the typical tactic – a discovered check with the bishop. When attacking along the g-file, the final blow can be delivered by both a rook and a bishop, without entering into direct contact with the opponent's king.

The primary concern of the attacker becomes the introduction of mating pieces to an attacking position and the destruction of the royal guard.

Zhuravlev – Romanov (1952): **1 ♕g7+!** The bishop e5 'outshines' its counterpart on f6. Black resigned (1 ... ♗xg7 2 ♗xg7+ ♔g8 3 ♗f6+, and mate on the following move). Of course also 1 ♖xf6 wins.

Nikolaevsky – Elistratov (1961): **1 ♘e5!** Black resigned. 1 ... fxe5 is practically forced, but this leads to mate in two moves.

Farago – Rigo (1976): The extra rook dulled White's senses. Upon 1 ... ♖g4+? he expected to repel the raider with a cool retreat of the king to h1. And Black did actually play 'there', but, alas, not with that piece ...

1 ... ♕g4+! White resigned, without allowing the black bishop to a draw a 'magic triangle' – 2 ♗xg4 ♖xg4+ 3 ♔h1 ♗g2+ 4 ♔g1 ♗f3X.

In the game Bronstein – Kotov (1946) Black made an attempt to

exchange queens with the move **1 ... ♘d7?**. However the blow **2 ♗h6!** forced him to resign immediately: 2 ... ♘xe5 3 ♗xg7+ ♔g8 4 ♗xe5+ ♗g5 5 ♖xg5X.

The opening of lines is achieved not only by a direct destruction of the g-pawn, as in the previous example, but also its deflection, which likewise will be attended by sacrifices of different values.

Nimzowitsch – Nielsen (1928). The bishop e5, taking an active part in the attack, must be retained: **1 ♖d7 ♖ad8 2 ♖xd6! ♖xd6**.

Now on 3 ♖g4? Black has the defence 3 ... f6. But Nimzowitsch had already seen a spectacular finish: **3 ♕f6!** Black resigned. On 3 ... gxf6 (deflection!) follows 4 ♖g4+ ♔h8 5 ♗xf6X.

Neuman – Bergman (1913): **1 ♕xf6! gxf6** (1 ... ♖xd1 2 ♕xg7+! ♔xg7 3 ♗e5+ ♔h6 4 ♗g7+ ♔h5 5 ♗e2+) **2 ♗h4+ ♔h8 3 ♗xf6X**.

Baljon – Hun Yun Wal (1974): **1 ♕h6!** Black resigned.

M.Taimanov (White) carried out a splendid mating attack in a simultaneous exhibition (1964).

Smyslov – Euwe (1953): **1 ♗xe5!** **♖xe5 2 ♕xe5** (the black queen is deflected from defence of the c6 square) **2 ... ♕xe5 3 ♗xc6+ ♔b8 4 ♖b7+ ♔a8 5 ♖b5X.**

The opposing bishops on the long diagonal and rook on the 7th rank suggest a tactical motif, but realising it requires a perfectly combinational ear.

1 ♗c4! ♕xc4 2 ♖xg7+!. It becomes clear why the queen was deflected to c4. Now Black cannot take the rook g7 because of 3 ♗xe5+.

2 ... ♔h8 3 ♗xe5! The queen is also sacrificed but White creates the mechanism for a discovered check.

3 ... ♕xc2 4 ♖f8+! Another sacrifice, deflecting the rook from the e8 square, where it attacks the bishop on e5, which is designed to deliver the concluding blow.

4 ... ♖xf8 5 ♖xg6+, and mate on the following move.

A similar mating finish could arise on the queen's flank and even on a major highway.

Fischer finished elegantly in a speed game against Fine (1963): **1 ♖fe1+ ♔d8** (nothing is changed by 1 ... ♗xe1 2 ♖xe1+) **2 ♕g3!** Black resigned, since on 2 ... ♕xg3 follows 3 ♗f6X. Also on other moves, the queen loses control of the critical f6 square.

The threat of mate on the g-file is often associated with similar threats along the 8th (1st) ranks.

In the game Winawer – NN (1896) White had a pleasant choice between 1 ♕g5+ and 1 ♖e8+. Winawer preferred to start with the queen.

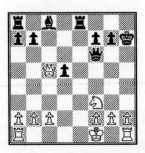

Kirdetzof – Kann (1918): **1 ... ♕xf3! 2 gxf3 ♗h3+ 3 ♔g1 ♖e6 4 ♕c7**, so as to defend against 4 ... ♖g6+ with the move 5 ♕g3. More stubborn was 4 ♕d4 ♖g6+ 5 ♕g4, though also in this case after 5 ... ♖e8! 6 ♕xg6+ ♔xg6 7 f4 ♖e2 Black has a great positional advantage.

4 ... ♖ae8! White resigned. 5 ... ♖e1+ can only be parried by 5 ♕c3, but then the rook mates from the g6 square.

This position is from the game Janowski – Marshall (1912). Black carries out a mating combination, the main role in which is assigned to the rook and bishop.

1 ... ♕xf3! 2 cxb4. It is clear that he cannot take the queen because of 2 gxf3 ♗h3+ 3 ♔g1 ♖e1+ 4 ♗f1 ♖xf1X, but 2 h3 deserves consideration.

2 ... ♘c6! 3 ♗b2. As before, the queen is invulnerable. 3 ♗e3 is no good in view of 3 ... ♗h3! 4 gxh3 ♕xh1+.

3 ... ♘xb4! 4 ♗xh7+ ♔h8 5 gxf3 ♗h3+ 6 ♔g1 ♘c2 7 ♗xc2 ♖e2 8 ♖c1 ♖ae8 9 ♗c3. It seems that White has avoided immediate dangers, retaining a material advantage, but his king cannot get out of the mating net.

9 ... ♖xc2! 10 ♖xc2 ♖e6!, and mate with the rook on g6 cannot be averted. (This possibility was missed by F.Marshall, though he still won the game by 9 ... ♖8e3 10 ♗b4 ♖xf3 11 ♗d1 ♖f6).

Of course, you noticed that in all the last examples the king of the injured side was in a 'half-castled' state. He somehow reached out for the rook, but did not have time to jump over it. This dormant rook was also the main culprit in the death of his monarch.

An attack by the rook on the last rank might be secured by a pin.

Most often the final blow by the rook is preceded by a sacrifice on f7 (f2). Here is the scheme of the operation:

Harms – Cooper (1947): **1 ♕xf7+ ♖xf7 2 ♖e8X**. The pin along the diagonal paralyses the black rook, it becomes a silent witness to the catastrophe.

A similar finish, but in a somewhat different format, was seen in the game Schwarz – Tarrasch (1883).

1 ... ♗c5+ 2 ♔h1 ♘f2+ 3 ♖xf2 ♕d1+ 4 ♘g1 ♕xg1+ (4 ... ♗xf2 was also sufficient) **5 ♔xg1 ♖d1X**.

Tarrasch once sarcastically remarked that some chess players appreciate the beauty of a combination with the sacrifice of 'corpulent' pieces. The 'fattest' piece is the queen, and, say what you will, queen sacrifices make an extremely attractive impression. They appeal not only to novices, but also seasoned veterans. Once master Panov discussed creativity. "I'm interested to know" – not without malice maitre P.Romanovsky asked – "how many queens have you sacrificed in your whole life?"

Vasily Nikolayevich Panov, who was never noted for restraint, but always – wit, got angry and said: "What good is it that you yourself have sacrificed tens of lousy queens! Half of them you just blundered!" This not very polite argument, contested in the heat of

controversy, is not too far from the truth. Without encroaching on the noteworthy chess legacy of the two warring disputants, we present the case, as they say, 'for quite a different story'.

Many of you will probably know the sensational Ruy Lopez game Capablanca – Marshall (1918), where after the moves 1 e4 e5 2 ♘f3 ♘c6 3 ♗b5 a6 4 ♗a4 ♘f6 5 0-0 ♗e7 6 ♖e1 b5 7 ♗b3 0-0 8 c3 the American champion first demonstrated his famous attack: 8 ... d5 9 exd5 ♘xd5 10 ♘xe5 ♘xe5 11 ♖xe5 ♘f6 12 ♖e1 ♗d6 13 h3 ♘g4 14 ♕f3 ♕h4 15 d4 ♘xf2.

Capablanca laid a cunning trap for his opponent, and played 16 ♖e2.

But here L.Steiner in a game against Helling (1928), hypnotised by the possibility of a 'brilliant' queen sacrifice, landed right in the trap.

16 ♕xf2? White's calculation was based on the variation 16 ... ♗g3 17 ♕xf7+ ♖xf7 18 ♖e8X. However there followed **16 ... ♗h2+! 17 ♔f1**, and only now – **17 ... ♗g3**.

Assuming that the situation had not changed, Steiner played his intended defence – **18 ♕xf7+??**, not noticing that the rook takes the queen with check!

So it is with easy but necessary caution, that we return 'to our sheep.' Operations based on a pin are not always so obvious, here is one that is more disguised.

In reply to **1 ♖d5?** Blomberg (Black) against Danielsson (1967) prepared a queen sacrifice with the introductory move **1 ... ♖ae8!!** and carried it out after **2 ♕f1 ♕xf2+ 3 ♕xf2 ♖e1X**.

Also pretty good, even by the most stringent standards, is the combination made by Ljubojevic (Black) in a game against Larsen (1975).

1 ... ♕h4! 2 ♕xe5 ♕f2! and White resigned without waiting for the spectacular, even if simple, finish – **3 ♖g1 ♕xg2+ 4 ♖xg2 ♖c1+**.

"The h-file has many sacrifices on its conscience", said S.Tartakower, author of many famous chess aphorisms. We have already convinced ourselves of the validity of such an accusation, and we will convince ourselves of it time and again in the future. The file

'without a conscience' becomes the main military line of communication in positions where the bishop, operating on the a2-g8 (g1-a7) diagonal, cuts off an enemy king's way of escape.

If an h-pawn, covering the king after short castling, has still not moved, the first task of the attacker is to destroy it or divert it from the file. Very often, this goal is achieved by a sacrifice of the knight on g6 (g3).

Hocking – Bennett (1962): **1 ... ♕xe4!** (first eliminating the knight and deflecting the queen, covering the critical g3 square) **2 ♕xe4 ♘g3+!** (the h2 pawn is diverted from the edge file) **3 hxg3** (now the way is open) **3 ... ♖h5X**.

NN – Stoner (1929): **1 ... 🗗xh2+! 2 🖺xh2 ♘g3+! 3 🖺xg3 ♕h8+ 4 🖺h2 ♕xh2+! 5 🖺xh2 🗗h8+**, and mate on the following move.

Alekhine – Supico (1924). At first glance, there is no hint of a similar mating finish, but Alekhine was capable of finding the most hidden possibilities in positions.

1 ♕g6!! Under fire from enemy batteries! In view of the threat of 2 ♕xg7X (1 ... 🗗g8 2 ♕xh7+ 🖺xh7 3 🗗h3X) the sacrifice must be accepted.

1 ... fxg6 2 ♘xg6+ hxg6. White consistently opens the a2-g8 diagonal and the h-file. From a sharp position the game has arrived at a simple mating pattern. Such a transformation is typical of many, even very complicated, combinations.

3 🗗h3+ ♕h4 4 🗗xh4X.

The same tactical elements were exploited by Kaiszauri against Sznapik (1970):

1 ♘g6+!. Black resigned. Both variations lead to mate: 1 ... 🖺g8 2 ♕xh7+ 🖺xh7 3 🗗h3+ and 1 ... fxg6 2 ♕xh7+ 🖺xh7 3 🗗h3+.

Let's look at a few methods of bringing up mating pieces to an attacking position. Here anything goes.

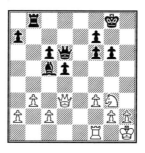

Alapin – Schiffers (1902): **1 ... ♕xg3! 2 hxg3 🖺g7!**, and White, despite having the move, cannot close the diagonal of the bishop on c5.

In the two following examples characteristic tactical methods are employed.

Anderssen – Lange (1859): **1 ... 🖺c5+ 2 🖺h1 ♘g3+! 3 hxg3 ♕g5 4 🗗f5**. The only defence against mate on h6. But now Black opens the h-file with a typical pawn attack.

4 ... h5! 5 gxh5 (5 🗗xg5 hxg4+) **5 ... ♕xf5 6 g4 ♕f2 7 g3 ♕xg3 8 ♕f1 ♕xg4**. White resigned.

Kovacs – Ornstein (1976): **1 ♗c4!**
♕g6 (the queen is riveted to defence of
the g7 square; if 1 ... ♕d7, then 2 ♖ad1)
2 ♕xg6 hxg6 3 ♖f3. Black resigned.

A remarkable combination was seen
in a game by N.Rossolimo, who had rich
chess imagination.

NN – Rossolimo (1957): **1 ... ♖d1!!**
This splendid move contains several
tactical ideas: deflection (the rook b1 –
after which the queen on b2 is left
unprotected), interference (by breaking
the communication between the white
rooks, he threatens 2 ... ♕xf1+),
discovering an attack and a pin (the
bishop a7 is introduced into the battle,
the f2 square is subjected to attack).
There is no defence.

2 ♗xb7+ ♔b8 3 c4 (3 ♕xb5 ♗xf2+
4 ♔h2 ♖h8+, the same thing also
follows on 3 ♖fxd1) **3 ... ♖xf2 4 ♔h2**
(4 ♕xf2 ♕xb1 or 4 cxb5 ♖fxf1+ 5 ♔h2
♖h1X) **4 ... ♕h5+**.

It happens that a bishop can
temporarily assume the duties of a

queen but the scheme of operations
remains standard.

Uhlmann – Mariotti (1976): **1 ♘f4**.
Black resigned (1 ... ♕e7 or 1 ... ♕c7 –
2 ♘g6+ hxg6 3 ♖h4X). Here the queen
denies the king the g8 square.

The same situation arose in the game
Karpov – Taimanov (1977).

1 ... ♖a1 2 ♖b1 ♘g3+! (or 2 ♕e2!?)
White resigned. Why? You see, after
3 hxg3 not one of Black's pieces can
deliver a blow on the h-file. However:
3 ... ♖a8!, and mate is inevitable.
Such treacherous retreats are often
overlooked, and it even escaped the
attention of the world champion.

Like a hockey player, pressed against
the side of the ice rink and surrounded
by players, the king feels uncomfortable
in such situations:

The final blow is delivered by the rook, while the bishop is assured its immunity.

When attacking along the file, efforts are made to destroy or divert the g-pawn.

Kramer – Rooster (1926): **1 ♕h6!** The basic idea is 1 ... gxh6 2 ♖g8+ ♖xg8 3 ♖xg8X, and the associated 1 ... ♖g8 2 ♕xh7+ ♔xh7 3 ♖h3X. Besides this there is the simple threat to take on g7 with the rook. Therefore Black resigned.

Against Chaplinsky (1950) Krutikhin managed to deflect the g-pawn in another way.

1 ♘h5! gxh5 2 ♖g1! Black resigned.

Hartlaub – Testa (1913): **1 ♕d4** (an introductory move, after which events unfold at a blistering pace. But in fact even quicker is 1 ♖xg6 hxg6 2 ♕c3) **1 ... ♘e5 2 ♖xg7+! ♔xg7 3 ♖g1+ ♔h8** (3 ... ♔f6 4 ♕h4+ also leads to a quick mate) **4 ♕xe5+ dxe5 5 ♗xe5+.**

Black resigned, without waiting for the concluding blow: 5 ... f6 6 ♗xf6+! ♖xf6 7 ♖g8X.

In a position from the game Jung – Barden nothing portended a quick denouement, but meanwhile White is already on the edge of defeat. The explosive sacrifice – **1 ... ♗xg2+!** was decisive.

White resigned in view of the variation: 2 ♔xg2 ♕a8+ 3 f3 (3 ♔g1 ♖g6+ or 3 ♔h3 ♕f3+ 4 ♔h4) 3 ... ♖g6+ 4 ♔h1 (4 ♔h3 ♕c8+ 5 ♔h4 ♗d8+) 4 ... ♕xf3+! 5 ♖xf3 ♖g1X.

A rook on the penultimate rank is always a source of increased danger when, in collaboration with a bishop, it successfully attacks the h7 (h2) square.

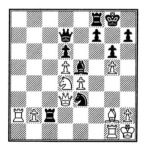

Karosene – Skegina (1968): **1 ... ♕h3!
2 ♘f3 ♖xg2 3 ♕xe3 ♕xh2+** White resigned.

Hemper – Good (1963): **1 ♘xg5+!
hxg5 2 ♗e4+ ♔h6 3 ♖h8+! ♗xh8
4 ♖h7X.**

In the game Wageheim – Janzelis (1898) the white rook does not have time to go to e7 because of mate on g2. But is it not possible to march on with tempo?

1 ♕h7+! ♔xh7 (the queen is sent off the pitch for a foul, but the keeper has been lured out of the goal ...)

2 ♖e7+ ♔h8 3 ♖h7X.

Upon queenside castling or with the king placed on f8 (f1) the joint attack of rook and bishop might lead to these mating finishes.

Here, as we see, the main direction of the attack becomes the central files.

Here is an operation, based on a pin.

Volchok – Kreslavsky (1970): **1 ♗e7!** Black resigned.

In the game Drijksna – Strautins (1968) Black deflected one of the enemy rooks with a queen sacrifice – **1 ... ♕c2+! 2 ♖xc2**, and then freed the d-file for his rooks – **2 ... ♘b3+!**, bringing the game to a clear mating picture.

Fridrich – Bantelon (1967): **1 ♘d7+!** Firstly opening the e-file, on which the white rooks can operate.

1 ... ♗xd7 2 ♕xc8+! Now the a4-e8 diagonal is freed for the bishop and at the same time the rook defending the 8th rank is eliminated.

2 ... ♗xc8 3 ♖e8X

The bishop can support a rook also from another diagonal.

Gligoric – Larsen (1973): **1 ♘xd7 ♗xd7 2 ♕c5+!** Black resigned (2 ... ♕xc5 3 ♖b8X).

Estrada – Gligoric (1962): **1 ... ♖xd6! 2 ♕xd6 ♖d8.** White resigned (3 ♕xe7 ♖d1X).

Mate with rook and bishop according to the pattern we have been considering is also seen against a king stuck in the centre.

Chess practice has seen hundreds of games, ending with the following textbook combination. It is usually well concealed and requires some experience to find it.

Maczuski – Kolisch (1864): **1 ♕d8+! ♔xd8 2 ♗g5+ ♔e8 3 ♖d8X.**

Let's note the tactical elements of the combination: 1 ♕d8+! – luring away the opponent's jeopardised king; 2 ♗g5+ – a discovered, in the present case double, check. These two methods are typical for this kind of operation.

Schulten – Horwitz (1846): **1 ... ♕f1+! 2 ♔xf1 ♗d3+ 3 ♔e1 ♖f1X.**

A combination by Dadian (1894) shows a slightly more complicated freeing of a line.

1 ♘c7+! ♘xc7 2 ♕d8+ ♔xd8 3 ♗g5+ ♔e8 4 ♖d8X.

The final mating position may look different.

145

Reti – Tartakower (1910): **1 ♕d8+ ♔xd8 2 ♗g5+ ♔e8 3 ♖d8X**.

The construction 2 ♗g5+ – 3 ♖d8X works smoothly in many combinations against a king stuck in the centre.

It is safe to say that the 'conscience' of the d-file is also weighed down to quite an extent.

Freeing the file and eliminating or deflecting pieces defending the critical d8 square – these tactical methods are the basis of all combinations of our theme.

Morphy finished his famous game beautifully against consulting 'Allies' – the Duke of Brunswick and Count Isuard (1858).

Ufnal – Banach (1964): **1 ♘xc7+! ♖xc7 2 ♕xc6+ bxc6 3 ♖d8X**.

Mackenzie – NN (1891): **1 ♖xe5+! dxe5 2 ♕xe5+ ♕xe5 3 ♗c6+ ♖xc6 4 ♖d8X**.

A swift attack, where there are alternate mating threats by different pairs of rooks and bishops, was conducted by Nimzowitsch against Alapin (1912).

1 ♗xd7+ ♘xd7 2 ♕b8+! ♘xb8 3 ♖d8X.

And here are some instructive variants, in which the theme of deflecting pieces comes through most vividly.

1 ♗f6! Played with the direct threat of 2 ♕d8+. He can only defend against this in one way – by taking the troublesome bishop. No good are either 1 ... ♗e7, or 1 ... ♗e6 because of

2 ♗xc6+ bxc6 3 ♕d8+.
1 ... ♕xf6 2 ♖he1+ ♗e7. There is nothing better: 2 ... ♗e6 3 ♕d7X; 2 ... ♘e7 3 ♕d8X; 2 ... ♕e7 3 ♗xc6+ bxc6 4 ♕d8X.
3 ♗xc6+ ♔f8 4 ♕d8+! ♗xd8 5 ♖e8X.
The rooks can also exploit other lines of communication.

Ponomarev – Demidov (1976): **1 ♕xd7+! ♖xd7 2 ♖b8ı ♗d8 3 ♗f6.** Black resigned.
In one of the variations from the game Spassky – Tal, played in the international tournament in Tallinn (1973), this position might have been reached:

Though it is his move, White must lose one of his rooks. If he tries to sell it more dearly and plays **1 ♖xh6+,** then after **1 ... gxh6** arises a peculiar position where every move of the rook leads to mate: 2 0-0 ♖g8X or 2 ♖f1 ♗f3 with the inevitable 3 a4 ♖d1X. It is clear that 2 f3 ♗xf3 3 ♖g1 ♖d1+ 4 ♔f2 ♖xg1 5 ♔xg1 gives Black an easy win.

Less frequently seen in tournament practice is a mating finish by rook and bishop of the 'epaulette' variety.

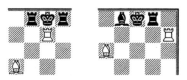

The cramped position of the black king was decisively exploited by Bogoljubow against an unknown opponent in a simultaneous display (1935).

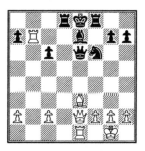

1 ♗c5! ♕xe2 2 ♖xe7+ ♕xe7 3 ♖xe7X.
In this tactical operation we are shown a particularly striking example of the 'X-ray' by the rook on e1.

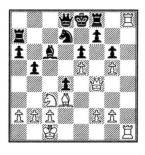

Seidman – Mrazek (1936): **1 ♕xf7+! ♔xf7 2 ♖1h7+ ♔e8 3 ♗xg6X.**
Here the final blow is delivered by the bishop, as the pin does not allow the rook f8 to come to the help of its king.
There are very diverse mating finales when pawns are also involved.

Here is the mechanism in action.

Wagenfuhrer – NN (1945): **1 ♕xh7+ ♔xh7 2 ♖h4X**

A queen sacrifice opens the h-file, the rook delivers a blow, while the bishop and f5 pawn cut off the enemy king from its neighbouring squares.

Skuja – Rosenberg (1962): **1 ♕xf8+!** (with this sacrifice White simultaneously removes two defenders of the h7 square) **1 ... ♖xf8 2 ♖xh7+ ♔xh7 3 ♖h1+ ♗h3 4 ♖xh3X.**

Kozlovskaya – Cardoso (1971): **1 ♕xh7+! ♘xh7 2 ♖xh7+ ♔xh7 3 ♖h3+ ♕h5** (3 ... ♔g6 4 ♗h5+ ♔h6 5 ♗xf7X) **4 ♗xh5.** Black resigned.

And here are two original plots:

The combination made by Tal (White) against Suetin (1969) is based on the first final position.

1 ♕xe5! (the knight, defending the f7 square, must be eliminated) **1 ... dxe5 2 exf7+.** Black resigned. 2 ... ♔d7(d8) leads to rapid defeat after 3 ♗f5+, while upon 2 ... ♔f8 3 ♗h6X arises the mating picture, shown in the diagram.

Blocking in the enemy king led to an economical finish in the game Trapl – Marszalek (1961).

1 ♗e6! ♕xe6 2 ♖f8+ ♘xf8 3 ♖xf8+ ♔d7 4 ♖d8X

When a passed pawn, supported by rooks and bishops, is far advanced, a mating net is often woven at the final frontier.

This situation is expressed in these twin problems by W.Pauly (1911) – mate in 3 moves.

1 0-0-0 ♘d3+ 2 ♖xd3

Now the threat of mate along the 8th rank can be prevented only by castling – **2 ... 0-0**. But then **3 ♖g3X**.

Here both sides have lost the right to castle, therefore **1 ♖xh6** with these variations: **1 ... ♘xh6 2 ♖e2** and **3 ♖e8X; 1 ... ♘xf2+ 2 ♔c2** and **3 ♖h8X; 1 ... ♘e3+ 2 ♔c1**.

And here is an example from tournament practice.

Padevsky – Polugaevsky (1970): **1 ♖xd5! exd5 2 e6**. Black resigned. Mate on h8 is threatened, while after 2 ... fxe6 the rook on a7 is lost.

A similar picture might also arise in the middlegame.

Ribakov – Sveshnikov (1974): **1 ♖xd6! ♕xd6 2 ♗xf6 ♕e7 3 ♕h8+ ♗xh8 4 ♖xh8X** (In the game Black declined the rook sacrifice with the move 1 ... ♕e7, which obviously also did not save him from defeat).

Lodz – Smit (1971/72): **1 ♖xg7+! ♔xg7 2 ♘e6+ ♗xe6 3 ♗d4+ ♔g8** (3 ... ♖f6 4 dxe6) **4 ♕h6 ♔f7 5 dxe6+ ♔e8 6 ♕xf8+! ♔xf8 7 ♖h1**. Black resigned.

164. S.Andersson – Knutsson, 1974

Black to move

Old as the world.

165. Matulovic – Asfari, 1972

White to move

A trifle, but neat nevertheless.

166. Montel – Serano, 1962

White to move

1 ♗d1. And now your move!

167. Szilagyi – Madarasz, 1971

White to move

On two fronts.

168. Pritchett – Maluf, 1972

White to move

First, the prelude ...

169 Gligoric – Rosenstein, 1963

White to move

Go right through.

170. Onderka – NN, 1958

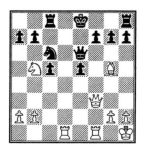

White to move

A blow, then another blow ...

171. Zukertort – Andersen, 1865

White to move

It can also happen to the greats ...

172. Zaichik – Chekhov, 1977

White to move

Like a fish in a net ...

173. Knaak – Doda, 1976

White to move

The straw that broke the camel's back.

174. Wagner – Schepps, 1954

Black to move

Today and every day.

175. Stefanov – Gerensky, 1959

White to move

A dangerous turning.

176. Butnorus – Gutman, 1974

White to move

Looking for a change of place ...

177. Vilerte – Kostina, 1972

Black to move

It never rains but it pours.

178. Antonuk – Zak, 1978

Black to move

A powder keg.

179 Begun – Baliev, 1975

White to move

In the corner of the ring.

180. Dely – Grags, 1953

White to move

Cocking the gun.

181. Zeidler – Wexler, 1972

White to move

When the guard is taken out.

182. Chigorin – Znosko-Borovsky, 1903

White to move

Don't overlook the mate on c2!

183. Euwe – Loman 1923

Black to move

And why not take the knight on d4?

184. Rosenthal – NN, 1873

White to move

Carbon copy.

185. Kubicek – Privara, 1976

White to move

Mass circulation.

186. Ivkov – Tomovic, 1958

White to move

1 ♗e3? ♗c4! But what was correct?

187. Freiberg – Dahlin, 1976

White to move

Fully automatic.

188. Ostropolsky – Ivanovsky, 1949

White to move

Breaking and entering.

189 Golz – Borowski, 1972

White to move

The general is taken prisoner!

190. Selivanovsky – Jaroshevsky, 1958

White to move

The road to nowhere.

191. Komov – Haritonov, 1973

White to move

On course for mate.

192. Oberle – Pfister, 1958

Black to move

A topsy turvy 'epaulette'

193. Bungan – Groul, 1933

Black to move

And who wins?

194. Kostel – Rada, 1932

White to move

Body check.

195. Aitken – Keffler, 1955

Black to move

In turn.

196. Schneider – Braun, 1974

Black to move

1 ... ♗e7 is prose. But what if it's poetry?

197. Belov – Osachuk, 1965

White to move

Like a machine gun.

198. Tseshkovsky – Gufeld, 1975

Black to move

Two queens are no hindrance.

199 Evans – Bisguier, 1958

White to move

A pin is good, but a counter-pin is better.

200. Koshevoi – Ruinsky, 1972

Black to move

1 ... ♘e4. Where to move the bishop?

201. Maura – Rocha, 1955

Black to move

And another pin?

202. Koltanowsky – Krause, 1957

Black to move

1 ... ♕c6. All that glitters is not gold.

203. Meyer – Meck, 1932

White to move

Not only exchanges.

204. Konevich – Levin, 1924

Black to move

From both flanks.

205. Muller – Dimmer, 1958

Black to move

'Give everything, hold nothing back.'

206. Anderssen – Harrwitz, 1848

White to move

In Anderssen style.

207. Johansson – Ekenberg, 1976

Black to move

A picnic on the side of the road.

208. M.Tseitlin – Kusmin, 1975

White to move

1 ♖e5 ♕c2, and then as in a story (a blitz game).

209 Markov – Luzganov, 1963

Black to move

Once again the epaulette – it will be the 'general' this time.

210. Aleksandrov – S.Zaitsev, 1974

White to move

Running around like a squirrel in a cage.

211. Amrein – Lummar, 1955

Black to move

A surprise is imminent.

212. Haisert – Stark, 1973

Black to move

1 ♖xd4. How to recapture?

213. Richter – NN, 1957

White to move

Three blows as a warning.

214. Estrin – Obukhovsky, 1971

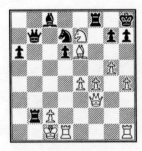

White to move

Disposition and displacement.

215. W.Speckmann, 1968

White mates in 2 moves

At right angles.

216. W.Speckmann, 1952

White mates in 4 moves

Off with the blanket.

217. F.Palatz, 1932

White mates in 5 moves

Operation 'pendulum'.

218. *T.Nissl, 1910*

219. *I.Tero, 1944*

White mates in 6 moves

Bishop-dodger.

White to move and win

Not stalemate, but mate.

* * * *

"What is the secret of victory?" – Em. Lasker was asked
"Anticipate the crisis in the game." – said the chess sage.

"How does Tal win?" – D.Bronstein was asked.
"Very simple," – said the grandmaster, – "he places his pieces in the centre and then sacrifices them somewhere."

"What is better: to attack or counterattack?" – T.Petrosian was asked.
"Better is to win!" – was the reply.

"How many moves ahead do you calculate variations?" – S.Tartakower was asked. "Two moves. But then these are two good moves!" – replied the grandmaster.

"Who attacks, leads" – said Chigorin.
"Who defends, discovers" – said Steinitz.

"You cannot play for a win if you are in the mood for a draw."

A.Karpov

"I do not play in chess, I fight in chess. Therefore I readily combine the tactical with the strategical, the fantastic with the scientific, the combinational with the positional, since I am trying to satisfy the requirements of the given position."

A.Alekhine

"Chess truth lies far more in ideas than in variations."

R.Reti

8. Rook and Knight

The rules concerning the moves of rook and knight (in contrast to the queen and bishop) over the course of many years of chess history have not changed. These truly old friends have preserved all the fighting capacity conferred on them by the unknown inventor of chess. The tricky jumps of the knight and the ramming blows of the rook are not only consistent with the names of the pieces, but also fit harmoniously into the complex image of the chess battle. If a rook and a bishop usually require considerable space for a successful attack, the rook and a knight can work together on a relatively small area of the board. This is due to the specific move of the knight, capable of delivering blows or supporting a rook in the overall hurly-burly of battle. But we should not forget that for the final thrust the rook needs at least a half-open line, on which it can smoothly enter the residence of the enemy king. Once upon a time the rook and a knight were the most powerful pieces. It is no coincidence that very old chess problems (Mansuby from the East) often end in mating positions constructed with this glorious battle chariot.

Here are two ancient mating finishes. The rook and knight take away all free squares from the enemy king without the help of 'outsiders'. Ways of achieving this position are very diverse. Let's start with the simplest, but perhaps the most surprising.

This, of course, is not a game, but a composed position, since it is hard to imagine how chessplayers could get into such a predicament. Yet the position is not chosen by chance. It clearly illustrates the interaction of rook and knight in the attack on the king. After **1 ♘f6!** the whole complement of black pieces cannot prevent mate on h7.

This coordination is based on the well-known mechanism of perpetual check, which often serves as a means of salvation for a 'shipwreck'.

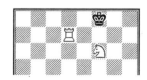

1 ♘h7+ ♚e8 2 ♘f6+ ♚f8 3 ♘h7+ ♚g8 4 ♘f6+, and the king, under pain of death, (4 ... ♚h8 5 ♖h7X) is obliged to return to f8.

To create a mating situation in the corner of the board the rook must operate on a rank clear of pieces, and a knight without any fear of being prevented from taking 'the oblique opposition' in relation to the king.

Levchenkov – Mileika (1976): **1 ♖a8+ ♚b7 2 ♖d7+! ♚xa8 3 ♘c6**. Black resigned.

The jump of the knight to f3 in the game Ugolitsev – Ashikin (1976) is prevented by the white queen. **1 ... ♛e1!** (deflection) is decisive **2 ♛xe1 ♘f3+ 3 ♚h1 ♖xh2X**.

The freeing of ranks and movement of pieces to the battle front is achieved in various ways.

Stahlberg – Keres (1936): **1 ... ⧄f3!** The g2 pawn is diverted from the 2nd rank. Mate is threatened on h2. If **2 g3**, then 2 ... ♖d2. The same would follow on 2 gxf3. White resigned.

In the game Urseanu – Anastasiad (1949) the black f7 pawn, defended by the queen on a2, blocks the way of the rook. Incidentally, we note that White cannot favourably exploit the mechanism of discovered check on the long diagonal, as his queen is under attack from the rook on d8. The study-like move **1 ♗d5!** cuts the Gordian knot. The double interference (interrupting the radius of action of the queen a2 and the rook d8) disorganises the defence. There followed **1 ... ♖xd5 2 ♖xf7!**, and Black resigned.

In this position from the game Stern – Golke (1956) not one of White's pieces has yet reached the firing line. It is very instructive to trace how skilfully the mating attack is prepared.

1 ♗e7! Again, interception. The black queen is excluded from defence

of the f7 square, with an attack on the rook f8. **1 ... ⧄xe7 2 ♖xf7 ♖xf7 3 ♖xf7**. Now not only 4 ♖xe7 is threatened, but also 4 ⧄f6+.

3 ... ♛a4 4 ⧄f6+ ♚h8. White needs a total of four moves, in order to bring the rook and knight to an attacking position. There remains only the elimination of the bishop g7. **5 ♛h6+!** (deflection) **5 ... ♗xh6 6 ♖h7X**.

Parma – Damjanovic (1960): **1 ... ♖xg2! 2 ♚xg2 ♛g6+ 3 ♚h1 ♖xf2 4 ♖g1 ⧄f3!** White resigned.

White's task in the game Samter – Strin (1964) is to bring the knight f4 to f6, where it increases the attack to the maximum. White decides on a queen sacrifice.

1 ♛xb6! ♛xb6 2 ⧄d5 (the knight with tempo transfers to f6, and Black's position will be destroyed) **2 ... ♛a5**. There is no salvation in 2 ... ♗c5 3 ⧄f6! ♛xb3+ 4 ♗b2, and then in the game or 2 ... ♛xf2 3 ♖xf2 ♗c5 4 ♖g7 ⧄e6 5 ♖fg2.

3 ♘f6 ♘e6 4 ♖g7! The rook cannot be captured, and the h7 pawn cannot be defended. Therefore Black resigned.

The united attack of rook and knight on the h7 (h2) square can happen not only via the 7th (2nd) rank, but also along the h-file.

Salov – Sermiksis (1976). Is everything defended? No, not everything ... **1 ♕xf8+!** Black resigned.

Rossolimo – Reissman (1967): **1 ♗xd5 cxd5 2 ♘f6+ ♔h8 3 ♕g6!** This spectacular move is based on the variations 3 ... fxg6 4 ♘xg6+ hxg6 5 ♖h3X and 3 ... gxf6 4 ♕xf6+ ♘g7 5 ♖g3 ♖g8 6 ♘xf7+. In both cases the rook is transferred from the queen's flank to the kingside.

3 ... ♕c2 (defending against the immediate threat 4 ♕xh7X) **4 ♖h3!** Black resigned. After the forced 4 ... ♕xg6 5 ♘xg6+ fxg6, mate is delivered by the rook 6 ♖xh7X.

Let's look at the means of achieving a position in which the rook delivers the decisive blow on the g8 (g1) square.

Larsen (Black) skilfully wove a mating net against Taimanov (1967) when the Leningrad grandmaster carelessly wandered with his king into the enemy's rear: **1 ... ♘g4!** (cutting off the king's way of retreat) **2 ♖d1 ♖g5+ 3 ♔h8 ♘f6** (constructing the mechanism) **4 ♗a4+ ♔e7.** White resigned.

In the game Koltanowski – Halsey (1959) it seems that Black controls the g-file, however the rook g7 is tied to the defence of the h7 square: **1 ♖g3! ♕xc2 2 ♕h6 ♖ag8 3 ♕xh7+! ♖xh7 4 ♖xg8X.**

In the game Reiner – Steinitz (1860) mate with the rook on g1 is prevented by the white rook on g4. The first world champion removes the barrier with a double offer of the queen: **1 ... ♕h4! 2 ♖g2 ♕xh2+ 3 ♖xh2 ♖g1X**.

One of the ways to open the g-file is demonstrated by the ending of the game Winter – Colle (1930).

1 ... ♘f3! Of course, though this move does not contain any immediate threat, the knight cannot be taken (2 gxf3 ♕g5). However Black had already prepared a decisive manoeuvre.

2 d5 (trying to close the diagonal of the bishop b7 and thereby reduce the pressure) **2 ... ♕h4!**. As in the previous example, White creates a threat against the h2 square, but his main objective is to open the g-file.

3 h3 ♕xh3+! 4 gxh3 ♖g1X.

The black rook carried out a roundabout manoeuvre to set up a mating position in the game Orlov – Chistiakov (1935).

1 ... ♘e5! 2 ♖xd6 ♘f3+ 3 ♔h1 ♖xg3! 4 hxg3 ♖g2! White resigned,

mate on g1 or h2 (if the knight flees from f1) is unavoidable.

Upon an attack on the long castled position, the direction of the main blow is delivered on the b-file. Here many tactical methods, which we have looked at above, come into play.

Porral – Burgalat (1945): **1 ... ♘c3! 2 ♖c1 ♕xa3+! 3 bxa3 ♘c2+ 4 ♖xc2 ♖b1X**.

The two following mating schemes are also characteristic for positions where the king is placed in the corner of the board.

The rook delivers a blow on the same square as in the previous examples, while the knight is assured its immunity.

Monk – NN (1914): **1 ♘c7+ ♔a7 2 ♕xa6+! bxa6 3 ♘b5+ ♔a8 4 ♖a7X**.

A double check allows the knight to remain at the forefront of the attack.

And here is an example of a frontal assault.

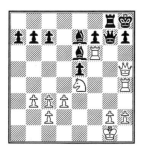

Orev – Rashev (1976): **1 ♘g5**. Black resigned: the h7 square cannot be held.

A final attack may be preceded by a blockade of the opponent's king. Usually this is combined with other tactical elements, most often the diversion of enemy pieces from defence of critical squares.

Fuchs – Harel (1959): **1 ♗g8!** Any capture on g8 by an enemy piece leads to mate: 1 ... ♔xg8 2 ♘f7+, 1 ... ♘xg8 2 ♕xh7+ ♕xh7 3 ♖xh7X, 1 ... ♖xg8 2 ♕xf6+ ♕xf6 3 ♖xh7X. Black replied **1 ... ♘g4**, but resigned after **2 ♕g6!**.

The rook's path to the enemy king may also be along the back rank.

After the 'long' move **1 ... ♖c1!** in the game Dijks – Miles (1973) White found himself in an original zugzwang (2 ♖xc1 is bad because of 2 ... ♘xg3+). The reply **2 ♗xf3** led to mate – **2 ... ♕g1+** ('X-ray') **3 ♖xg1 ♖xg1X**.

A similar mating finish also occurs in other unpleasant 'living conditions' of an enemy king.

Pollock – Allies (1893): **1 ♕d7+!** **♗xd7 2 ♘d6+ ♔d8 3 ♘f7+ ♔c8 4 ♖e8+! ♗xe8 5 ♖d8X**.

A beautiful combination. The double deflection of Black's light-squared bishop from the critical d and e-files is very effective.

Upon an attack along the 8th (1st) rank, the knight can also support the rook from other squares.

In the game Lutikov – Gorniak (1972) White completed the attack with the united force of the two pieces.

1 ♘xe6! Of course, the queen is untouchable because of 2 ♖f8X. In the meantime mate is threatened on the next move.

1 ... h5? (?). An escape for the king should be provided by the more modest advance 1 ... h6, though even in this case after 2 ♘xg7 ♖xe5 3 ♘xe8 ♖xe8 4 ♖f6 White obtains a winning rook endgame. Now, however, A.Lutikov decides the outcome of the battle by a forcing manoeuvre.

2 ♕xg7+ ♘xg7 3 ♖f8+ ♔h7 4 ♘g5+ ♔h6 5 ♘f7+. Black resigned: 6 ♖h8X can be averted by the exchange sacrifice 5 ... ♖xf7 6 ♖xf7, which is tantamount to capitulation.

Wetger – Heimberg (1956). After 1 ... exd5? White surprisingly replied 2 ♘g6!, whereupon the game was over:

2 ... ♕xe4 is not possible because of 3 ♖f8X, while on 2 ... ♕d8 follows 3 ♕e7, and as before the threats are irresistible.

The most frequently seen mechanism is the following tactical operation.

Kogan – Fuster (1937): 1 ♕xh7+! ♔xh7 2 ♖h5+ ♔g8 3 ♘g6 ♗xd4+ 4 ♔h1 Black resigned. Mate with the rook on h8 is unanswerable.

The same idea was exploited in the game List – Mannheimer (1930).

White's position seems critical. He is two pawns down, moreover his knight on d5 is about to perish. A surprising counter-blow dramatically changes the picture of the battle.

1 ♘xf4! (the pin proves to be illusory) 1 ... ♕xd4 (if 1 ... ♕xf4, then 2 ♖h1+ ♔g8 3 ♕xd8) 2 ♖h1+ ♔g8 3 ♘g6! Black resigned.

Let's switch our attention to the bishop on b3 – the main 'witness for the prosecution'. The pin on the f7 pawn enables the knight to remain on the g6 square for as long as needed in order to achieve checkmate. 3 ... ♘c3+ 4 bxc3 ♛h4 5 ♖xh4 and 6 ♖h8X.

If the knight takes away all loopholes of escape from the enemy king, then the rook can deliver the final blow at a 'respectful' distance.

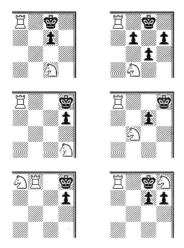

In these constructions the motif of the combination is the weakness of the 8th (1st) rank.

The Georgian Prince Dadian was a great chess lover. In 1898 he won a game with a simple but elegant combination against an opponent who wanted to remain anonymous.

The desperate situation of the white king prompts the solution: **1 ... ♘g3+! 2 ♖xg3 ♖xg1+ 3 ♔xg1 ♖e1X.**

Vidmar – Euwe (1929). The threat of mate on h2 cannot be repulsed, but, as S.Tartakower said, "chess is the tragedy of a single tempo". White starts, and ...

1 ♖e8+ ♗f8 (1 ... ♔h7 2 ♛d3+) **2 ♖xf8+! ♔xf8 3 ♘f5+ ♔g8 4 ♛f8+!** Black resigned (4 ... ♔xf8 5 ♖d8X).

The Yugoslav grandmaster utilised a rich arsenal of tacical weapons.

Unexpected dangers may lie in wait for a careless player even at the beginning of the game.

Hoffman – Forder (1927): **1 ♘xd5!** (the motive is the undefended rook on c8) **1 ... ♘c2 2 ♘b4!** Black resigned.

In certain situations, it is enough to maintain the knight at its post for a few moments, to give the rook time to help.

E. del Rio, 1750

1 ♕d6+ ♔a8 2 ♕c6! ♕c8 (2 ... ♗xc6 3 ♖d8+) **3 ♖d8**, and one of two mating finishes is unavoidable.

Durka – Yablonsky (1977): **1 ♘f5 ♖e8?** Also bad was 1 ... gxf5 2 ♖d8+ ♔g7 3 ♖g8+ ♔xg8 4 ♕xf6 but 1 ... ♖e2+! 2 ♔xf3 (2 ♔f1 gxf5 3 ♖d8+ ♔g7 4 ♖g8+ ♔xg8 5 ♕xf6 ♗g4) 2 ... ♖e8 3 ♕d3 gxf5 4 ♖d5 ♖e4, seems to save the game.

2 ♖d8! Black resigned. As in the position by Del Rio, he faces the same unpleasant choices.

Wielfond – Baratz (1955): **1 ... ♘f3+ 2 ♔h1** (if 2 gxf3, then 2 ... ♕g3+

3 ♔h1 ♕xh3+ 4 ♔g1 ♗xf2+! 5 ♖xf2 ♖e1+ or 5 ♔xf2 ♕h2X). **2 ... ♕xf2!**. White resigned (3 ♖xf2? ♖e1+).

Kasper – Grotke (1977): **1 ♕f7+ ♔h8 2 ♘e8! ♗xh6 3 ♕xf8+**. Black resigned.

Ivanov – Mashin (1971). How to save the knight g4? Only in this way: **1 ♘f6! ♕xe2 2 ♘g8+ ♔e8 3 ♘c7+ ♔f8 4 ♖d8X**. A surprising finish! Once again the pin proved illusory.

Michalchishin – Kozlov (1974): **1 ♘d5!** A typical sacrifice, the aim of which is the deflection of the e6 pawn and occupation of the f5 square. Now Black should play 1 ... ♗xd5, rejecting the dubious gift, but White's combination is masked and Kozlov doesn't unravel it.

1 ... exd5? 2 ♘f5 ♕d8 3 ♗xc5!. It is necessary to eliminate this knight so that it cannot travel via the e6 square to defend the king's flank.

3 ... ♔h8. Only here did Black see that capturing on c5 with the rook or either pawn leads to a forced mate. For example: 3 ... dxc5 4 ♕h6 g6 5 ♖h3 ♖e8 6 ♕xh7+ ♔f8 7 ♕h8+! ♗xh8 8 ♖xh8X, and we have the familiar finish.

4 ♗xd6 dxe4 5 ♕h5! Black resigned.

A similar finish concludes the attack on the h- (or a-) file.

The only difference is in the means of conducting attacks and the mechanisms of the tactical operations.

In the game Komov – Sydor (1952) Black lured the king to the h2 square in order to exploit the mechanism of double check and bring his knight to an attacking position.

1 ... ♖h1+! 2 ♔xh1 ♕h7+ 3 ♔g1 ♕h2+! 4 ♔xh2 ♘f3+ 5 ♔h1 ♖h8X.

Semashov – Zhuravlev (1968): **1 ... ♘e4.** This move clearly was not a surprise for White, who had placed his hopes on the counter-reply – **2 ♘d5.** However after the exchange of queens – **2 ... ♖xf3 3 ♘xc7** Black drove the opponent's king into the corner with two checks – **3 ... ♗xg5+ 4 ♔b1 ♘c3+! 5 ♔a1**, after which arose a mating situation – **5 ... ♖a4X.**

1 ♘e7+ ♔h8 2 ♕xh7+! ♔xh7 3 ♖h1X.

Let's recall the mechanism of this standard operation: the knight drives the enemy king to the edge file, one of the heavy pieces is sacrificed on the h7 (h2) square, the other delivers a decisive blow on the h-file.

(See next diagram)

Gottschall – NN (1901): **1 ♖df1! ♕xc4** (1 ... ♕e8 2 ♖xf8+ ♕xf8 3 ♘g6X) **2 ♘g6+ ♔g8 3 ♘e7+ ♔h8 4 ♖xh7+ ♔xh7 5 ♖h1X.**

In the game Leonhardt – Englund (1908) the outcome of the struggle was decided by just one threat.

First Black brings his knight to an offensive position **1 ... ♘e2+ 2 ♔h1**, and then with the move **2 ... ♔e7!** opens the 8th rank for transfer of the rook b8 to the h-file. It is not hard to convince oneself that there is no defence against the threat of 3 ... ♖xh2+. The bishop b7 pins the g2 pawn, and in the event of 3 h3 the rook mates on this square.

The transfer of the rook to the edge file can be carried out on any free rank. Sometimes the rank must be freed by the use of force.

Abrosimov – Ambainis (1975): **1 ♖1xd4 exd4 2 ♕xh7+**. Black resigned.

And to conclude – two beautiful combinations spanning a whole century.

Golmayo – Loyd (1867): **1 ... ♖a1+!!** A radical solution ... But the great chess composer had already seen the brilliant finale.

2 ♖xa1 ♕g5+ 3 ♔b1 ♘d2+ 4 ♔c1 ♘b3+ 5 ♔b1 ♕c1+! (the 'smothered mate' theme!) **6 ♖xc1 ♘d2+ 7 ♔a2** (finally) **7 ... ♖a8+**. White resigned. The rook was lured to a1, in order to deny the king this square and free the a-file for the final chord.

Here the white pieces are conducted by Tal against an unknown opponent in a simultaneous exhibition (1974).

1 ♗xh7+! ♔xh7 2 ♖h3+ ♔g8. The bishop has been sacrificed but how to continue the assault? On 3 ♕h5? follows 3 ... f6, and there appears to be nothing real.

3 ♘f5! One more piece is included in the attack, but it seems Black now has a good defence.

3 ... ♕g5. Preventing the thrust of the enemy queen to h5, but ...

4 ♕h5! Black resigned. If 4 ... f6, then 5 ♘e7X ("I like this mate more", – said M.Tal), while after 4 ... ♕xh5 it comes down to familiar finale: 5 ♘e7+ ♔h7 6 ♖xh5X.

Also these finishes are closely aligned to those we have looked at:

Here it is the knight that is the last point of contact, while the rook cuts off the enemy king's path of escape. In these cases, the rook operates on the g or h-files and the knight deals the final blow on the e7 (e2) or f7 (f2) squares. To complete the operation it is necessary that all the squares around the opponent's king have been blockaded. One way of blockading was seen in a simultaneous game by P.Romanovsky (1936).

1 ♕f8+! ♖xf8 (1 ... ♔xf8 2 ♖h8X) **2 ♘e7X.**

In the game Mandolfo – Kolisch (1859) the white king is already wearing a 'straitjacket', but how to free the e2 square for the knight d4? Well, the other knight comes to his assistance, reaching the square with the help of an ingenious manoeuvre linked to a beautiful queen sacrifice.

1 ... ♘e4!! **2 ♗xd8.** If 2 dxe4, then 2 ... ♕xg5, and the threat of 3 ... ♕h4 is decisive (nothing is changed by 3 exd5 0-0-0).

2 ... ♘g3! White to move is a queen ahead, he can even discover check with his knight e5, and yet he is lost since mate with the knight (either!) on e2 (or the rook on b1) is unstoppable.

In all the cases we have looked at, the h-file was free of enemy pieces, and rook dominated it as it wished. We are already familiar with the means of eliminating obstacles placed in our way by the enemy.

After the careless **1 ... ♘xh2?** in the game Bernstein – Seidman (1959) White replied **2 ♘fe5!**, and in view of the threat 3 ♖h4 Black was left with nothing else than **2 ... ♕xe2**. There followed **3 ♕xh7+! ♔xh7 4 ♖h4+ ♔g8 5 ♘e7X**.

Marshall (Black) ended his game against Levitsky (1912) with a perfectly paradoxical move.

Black is a piece ahead, but his queen and rook are under fire. Moreover White threatens at an opportune moment to go over to a counterattack (♖c5-c7). It is hard to believe that in this position White did not make another move ...

1 ... ♕g3!! White resigned: 2 hxg3 ♘e2X; 2 fxg3 ♘e2+ 3 ♔h1 ♖xf1X; 2 ♕e5 ♘e2+ 3 ♔xe2 ♕xh2X; 2 ♕xg3 ♘e2+ 3 ♔h1 ♘xg3+ 4 ♔g1 ♘xf1, and with an extra piece Black wins easily.

An elementary mechanism of the combination, frequently met in chess practice, is illustrated by the game Johner – Haan (1934).

To defend against the mate on g7, Black played **1 ... ♗f6**, but trouble came from the other side: **2 ♕g8+** (the rook is deflected from its defence of the f7 square) **2 ... ♖xg8 3 ♘f7X**.

Poutiainen – Szabo (1975): **1 ... ♗xg2+! 2 ♔xg2 ♖g8 3 ♔h1** (3 hxg4 ♖xg4+ 4 ♔f1 ♕g3) **3 ... ♕h2+!** (and here the bishop is deflected from defence of the f2 square) **4 ♗xh2 ♘f2X**.

Combinations, ending in a similar mating pattern, are far from always being so clear.

In the game Suta – Sutei (1953) Black has a great material advantage. Moreover the g-file is under his total control, while the threat of mate limits the opponent's activity. Nevertheless White has a remarkable combinational opportunity, based on certain features of the position.

Above all, we note the cramped position of the black king. It is easy to see that the knight d6 is ready to inflict a decisive blow on f7, if this square were not defended by the queen. And so there emerges the idea of diverting the queen.

1 ♖g5! Not too difficult a move, since the variations 1 ... ♕xg5 and 2 ♘xf7X or 1 ... ♕xe4 2 ♘xf7X can be seen with the naked eye. However White must reckon on a stronger retort.

1 ... ♕xf6. It seems that Black's attack has been repulsed, but White carries out his plan to the end, for a second time distracting the enemy queen from defence of critical squares.

2 ♕d4!! A stunning blow! The cooperation of the white pieces has reached its ideal.

2 ... ♖g6 3 ♖xg6! Black resigned (3 ... ♕xd4 4 ♘xf7X).

When the king's subjects get in his way, picturesque mating patterns can arise.

In the game Popert – Cochrane (1841) the role of court jester was played by the knight g1.

1 ... ♕xf2+! 2 ♖xf2 ♖xf2+ **3 ♔h1 ♘g3X.**

Also in this position, taken from the game Neiner – Weiszinger (1955), the knight g1 appreciably cramps his king.

1 ... ♕xe3! 2 fxe3 ♘g3+ **3 ♔h2 ♘xf1+ 4 ♔h1 ♘g3+ 5 ♔h2.** Perpetual check? No. Black has eliminated all the king's defenders and now produces a decisive, forcing manoeuvre. **5 ... ♘e4+ 6 g3** (6 ♔h1 ♘f2X) **6 ... ♖f2+ 7 ♔h1 ♘xg3X.**

The same shortcoming, but in the position of the black king, can be detected in the game Muller – Reithoffer (1937).

Here the clumsy assistant of the king proves to be the bishop f8.

1 ♕xf6! Black resigned, since on 1 ... gxf6 follows 2 ♘xf6X, and 1 ... ♔xd7 does not save him because of 2 ♕xf7+ ♗e7 3 ♖d1+.

Not only in the corner, but also on the centre files, the limited mobility of the king might serve as a motif for a combinational solution to the position.

Above all be forewarned of the dangers of a double check by rook and knight which usually leads to big trouble.

Consultants – Rellstab (1933): **1 ... ♖xd4+! 2 cxd4 ♕e1+!** (a similar enticement of the king to an attacking file to those we are already familiar with from the last chapter) **3 ♔xe1 ♘f3+ 4 ♔d1 ♖e1X**.

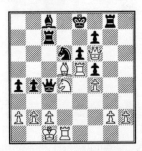

The attempt to exchange queens, undertaken by Mukhin (Black) in a game against Katalymov (1976), led to the same situation.

1 ... ♘e4 (reckoning on 2 ♗xc4 ♘xf6) **2 ♗xe4 fxe4 3 ♕d8+!**. Black resigned. After 3 ... ♔xd8 the double check – 4 ♘c6+ leads to mate on the next move (4 ... ♔e8 5 ♖d8X).

In the game Sokolov – Ruzhinkov (1967) Black, with his last move h7-h6, wants to destroy the mechanism for double check that White has created. His hopes were apparently based on the b2-pawn – about to promote to a new queen ...

Alas, the struggle ended in three moves: **1 ♖xb7+! hxg5 2 ♘c6+ ♔e8 3 ♖e7X**.

Sarkula – Kalugari (1965). Here, after the excellent move **1 ♗f4!**, the c7 square proved critical: **1 ... ♗xd1 2 ♘c7+ ♔d8 3 ♘ce6+ ♔e8 4 ♘xg7+ ♔d8 5 ♘5e6+ ♔c8 6 ♖c7X**.

When the king is in a cramped position the rook and knight succeed in creating a final picturesque 'epaulette mate'.

The tactical method of blockading the king is illustrated by a position of La Bourdonnais (1833).

1 ♘e6+ ♔e8 2 ♕d8+! ♗xd8 3 ♖f8+ ♖xf8 4 ♘g7X.

In the game Mecking – Rocha (1964) the 'epaulette' of the black king was attached to the edge rank.

1 ♖b1+ ♔a7 (1 ... ♔c8 2 ♕d7X) 2 ♕d4+! ♕xd4 3 ♘xc6X.

And again the black king had to make the intricate journey to the place of his 'award' in the game Karpov – Holdosz (1973).

1 ♘xe5! ♕xe2 2 ♖f7+ ♔h6 3 ♖h8+

♔g5 4 ♖g8+ ♔h4 (4 ... ♔h6 5 ♖g6X) 5 ♘g6+ ♔g5 (4 ... ♔h6 5 ♖g6X) 6 ♘xe7+ ♔h4 7 ♘f5X.

And here is one of the most surprising mating finishes which have ever been met in tournament practice.

Feldman – Oman (1956): 1 ♘f5 ♖d8? 2 ♕e3 ♖xd1? 3 ♕h6+ ♔e8 4 ♘g7+ ♔f8 5 ♘xe6+ ♔e8.

Here White spoilt the 'song': 6 ♘g7+ ♔f8 7 ♘h5+ ♔e8 8 ♘xf6X. Meanwhile after 6 ♕f8+!! ♗xf8 he could have delivered a splendid mate with the move 7 ♘g7X! (or 7 ♘c7X).

Both mating pieces are under attack, Black has an enormous advantage in material. But this is just such a case where mind prevails over matter!

We have already convinced ourselves of the fact that pieces with different playing features combine successfully in an attack on the king. It is possible to say the same about the fighting trio – knight, rook and pawn.

When defended by a pawn, the knight can occupy a menacing outpost if it is placed in the close vicinity of the king.

In this position from the game Rudik – Holikov (1969) it is enough for the black rook to occupy the second rank to threaten an unstoppable mate on h2. Therefore it is necessary to deflect the white queen from its control of the c2 square.

1 ... ♕xa3! 2 f6+ ♔h8 3 ♕e2 ♕c1 4 ♖f1 ♖c2!, and White resigned, since after 5 ♖xc1 ♖xe2 6 ♖h1 ♘f2+ he loses the exchange.

Gutop's combination against Kuindzhi (1977) also led to the capture of the penultimate rank.

1 ♕h5 g6 (1 ... h6 2 ♕xe8+) **2 ♕xh7+! ♖xh7 3 ♖xe8+ ♔g7 4 ♖1e7+ ♔h6 5 ♖xh7X.**

Smyslov – Benko (1969): **1 ♘g5+ ♔f6.**

Upon 1 ... ♔f8 2 ♖f7+ and 3 ♖f6 Black loses a pawn. On 1 ... ♔g8 possible was 2 ♖c6 ♘b2 3 ♔f3 with the same result. Nevertheless Black should choose one of these variations. P.Benko assumed that the move 2 f4, creating a mating threat, was not possible because of the pin. But this is only momentarily ...

2 ♔f1! (by freeing himself from the pin with tempo, White wins the game) **2 ... ♖e5 3 f4 ♖xg5** (the only move to avert an immediate mate) **4 fxg5+**, and soon Black resigned.

When the pawn is advanced to the 6th (3rd) rank, it can serve as a support for the rook. In these cases capitulation is forced by the knight or rook, depending on the circumstances.

Bronstein – Geller (1961): **1 ♕g6!** With a queen sacrifice White deflects the f7 pawn from the 7ᵗʰ rank, allowing the rook and knight to continue their dialogue with the black king (1 ... fxg6 2 ♖xg7+ ♔h8 and 3 ♘xg6X). Black resigned.

Radovsky – Karlsson (1977): Here a rook sacrifice leads to the objective – **1 ... ♖xf3!**, opening up the 2ⁿᵈ rank. White resigned. After 2 gxf3 ♖h2 there is the threat of 3 ... ♘e2X, and if 3 ♖d1, then 3 ... ♘xf3+ 4 ♔f1 ♖f2X.

Bach – Boto (1975): Black offered an exchange of queens and in any case had hoped to get rid of the unpleasant 'interlocutor' on h6. An unexpected sacrifice upsets his calculations.

1 ♖g6! fxg6 (1 ... ♕e5 2 ♖g7) **2 hxg6 ♖f7 3 ♕f8+! ♖xf8 4 ♖xh7+ ♔g8 5 ♘h6X**

In positions of an endgame type, as well as the given mating finishes the following must also be taken into account:

In the game Hamann – Bednarksi (1971) White threatened to get a new queen.

Black has available a perpetual check (1 ... ♘h2+ 2 ♔e1 ♘f3+ 3 ♔f1 ♘h2+ 4 ♔g1 ♘f3+ etc.). However, exploiting the fact that the newly appearing queen will have no checks, he manages to construct a mating net.

1 ... h4! 2 gxh4 (2 g4 h3 3 a8=♕ h2) **2 ... g4! 3 a8=♕ g3**, and mate with the pawn on g2 is inevitable. **4 ♕xc6 g2X.**

This position is from the game Hamann – Gligoric (1972). Again the Danish player was suffering and indeed almost in the same situation.

To obtain a mating attack it is necessary to include the knight. However the direct way – 1 ... ♘e5 does not achieve its objective because of 2 ♖e4, and if 2 ... f3? (2 ... ♘d3 3 d7), then 3 ♖xe3. Gligoric changes the order of the moves.

1 ... f3! 2 gxf3 (2 ♖a1 fxg2+ 3 ♔g1 ♘e5) **2 ... ♘e5 3 ♖e4 ♖f2+ 4 ♔e1 ♘d3+ 5 ♔d1 ♖d2X**

With quite modest resources, Smyslov (White) created an irresistible attack against Penrose (1954).

1 g6! The familiar method. Upon 1 ... fxg6 the last obstacle is cleared from the 7th and the black king perishes: 2 h7+ ♔h8 3 ♘xg6X.

1 ... ♘d8 2 ♘d7! ♖e8+ 3 ♔d5. Black resigned. The threat is 4 ♘f6+, and on 3 ... ♖e6 follows 4 ♖a8! ♖xg6 5 ♖xd8+ ♔h7 6 ♘f8+.

If, in the game Keres – Foltys (1950), Black manages to take the g6 pawn, he could still put up a successful defence. Therefore Keres played **1 ♘f5!**, sacrificing the distant passed pawn for an attack. After **1 ... ♖xa5 2 ♖e1** White already threatens to win the game by 3 g7+ ♔f7 4 ♖e8. In reply to **2 ... ♖a7** there followed **3 ♗d6+**, and Black resigned, since after 3 ... ♔g8 he gets mated – 4 ♖e8X.

The king can also perish on the edge file.

Such situations arise mostly in the endgame, but if the king violates the rules of traffic safety at the chess crossroads, it can be 'detained' even in the middlegame.

In the next two examples the black king is driven by force to the edge of the board and caught in a mating net.

Belinkov – Lapenis (1968): **1 ♗a6+ ♔b8 2 ♖b6+ ♔a7 3 ♖b7+!** Black resigned (3 ... ♔xa6 4 ♘c5+ ♔a5 5 b4X).

Christoffel – Muller (1965): **1 a5+
♔xa5 2 ♖b7 ♘b5 3 ♖a3+! ♘xa3
4 b4+ ♔a4 5 ♘c5X**.

Bellon – S.Garcia (1976). Here the
white king is already on the edge of the
board, but there are still many holes in
the mating net. The Cuban grandmaster
darns these with one flick of the wrist.

1 ... ♖g2! The manoeuvre involves a
fork – 2 ♔xg2 ♘e3+. White resigned;
the threat of 2 ... ♘f4X costs him too
much:

Supporting a rook and knight with
the king is even better than a pawn. It
might not only serve as a support for
his pieces, but also it takes away an
even greater number of squares from
the enemy king.

As a rule, endings with a rook and
knight against rook end in a draw, but
there are exceptions. The success of an
attack depends on whether or not the
king can defend himself against the
attack of the enemy rook.

In the game Chistiakov –
Kremenetzky (1968) White won with
the move **1 ♘g6**, because if 1 ... ♖g3+
the king hides from the checks behind
the h5 pawn: 2 ♔h6. If it were not for
this pawn, the white rook would have
pursued him from the rear until 'he was
blue in the face'.

In the game followed **1 ... ♖f3
2 ♔h6!** (threatening mate, in the first
instance on g7) **2 ... ♖f7 3 ♖d8+**. Black
resigned.

Pismenny – Bangiev (1975). Here
the white king hides from the checks
behind his own knight: **1 ♔g6 ♖g4+ 2
♔f6 ♖b4 3 ♘h6+**. Black resigned:
after 3 ... ♔h8 4 ♔g6 the rook is now
denied the g4 square.

A beautiful mating position with very modest resources was constructed by Rotlewi against Fahrni (1911).

1 ♔f7 ♔h6 (1 ... ♖h1 2 ♘d5 ♔h6 3 ♘f6) **2 ♔g8!** Black resigned. He can avoid the mate on g6 only at the cost of a whole rook. But if Black did not have the pawn he would achieve a draw: 2 ... ♖g1 3 ♖xg1 – stalemate!

In 1969 M.Tal (Black) played against young readers of *Pioneers Pravda*. After a fine brawl (as you can judge by the strange position of the pieces for an endgame) play arrived at a very picturesque position:

Tal continued **1 ... ♘g3+ 2 ♔h6 ♘f5+ 3 ♔xh7 ♖g7+ 4 ♔h8 ♖g8+ 5 ♔h7 ♖g7+ 6 ♔h8** with perpetual check and a draw.

A forced way to win was found by the Moscow schoolboy Vadim Brodsky:

1 ... ♘f4+ 2 ♔h6 (2 ♔h4 h5, and mate with the rook on g4 3 ... ♖g4X) **2 ... ♖g6+ 3 ♔xh7 ♖g7+ 4 ♔h6** (4 ♔h8 ♘g6X) **4 ... ♔g8!**, and before us we have a copy of the mating pattern from the previous game.

"The ex-world champion did not want to win against a pioneer!" – was Vadim's last word on the 'merciful' (or 'blind'?) Rigan grandmaster.

* * * *

220. Bronstein – Vasyukov, 1973

White to move

Position from a blitz match. White, playing for the flag to fall, indulged in some hocus-pocus. What?

221. Barcza – Bronstein, 1949

White to move

Yet another Bronstein joke. White decided to exchange queens – 1 ♕xf5 and ...

222. Katalimov – Kolpakov, 1975

White to move

The back rank again!

223. Buckenstrom – Nilsson, 1963

White to move

In three jumps.

224. Tartakower – Schlechter, 1908

Black to move

Mutual aid.

225. Garcia – Soribas, 1965

Black to move

Destroying the foundations.

226. Von Rein – Klish, 1963

White to move

Sweep away all the barriers ...

227. Geur – Olafsson, 1953

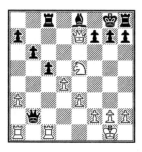

Black to move

1 ... cxd4. Mate along the first rank?

228. Rodriguez – Olafsson, 1978

Black to move

25 years later ...

229 Reiner – Kouatly, 1977

Black to move

Still not the end of the day ...

230. Farbo – Panno, 1962

Black to move

A house with no walls – or 'Perkovsky's box'

231. Chistiakov – Kogan, 1933

Black to move

A surprising encounter.

232. Meo – Giustolisi, 1959

Black to move

Where it is, there it will be ripped wide open.

233. Chigorin – Schiffers, 1878

White to move

Redundant queen and premier queen.

234. Fischer – Sanchez, 1959

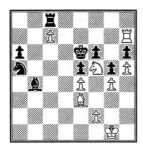

White to move

Duel of the bishops.

235. Sharke – Neindauer, 1938

White to move

Which check do you prefer ... ?

236. Kupreichik – Tseshkovsky, 1976

White to move

... and here?

237. Wilhelm – Meyer, 1977

Black to move

Changing of the guard.

238. Rusakov – Kalinkin, 1963

White to move

Restrained and injured.

239 P.Stamma, 1737

White to move and win

Seize a lucky moment!

240. Kamishov – Sokolsky, 1938

White to move

1 ♘g4. What next?

241. Stark – NN, 1962

White to move

What happened to the queen?

242. Polvin – Kreijik, 1954

Black to move

Time waits for no one, 2 ♘f8+ is threatened with perpetual check. The best defence is attack.

243. Mustonen – Sorakuannas, 1968

White to move

And here it's even more terrible ...

244. Kan-Bannik, 1952

White to move

In broad daylight.

245. Tal – Radulov, 1977

White to move

1 ♖d5 ♗f6 2 ♔f4(?) ♗d4 3 ♘e2+ ♔d2 4 ♘xd4 and White won. But what if there is no torture?

246. *Axenberg – Brondum, 1977*

White to move

A fianchettoed queen? She will not remain seated in her sledge!

247. *Kalabort – Balbe, 1971*

White to move

The seventh seal ...

248. *Timman – Debarnot, 1972*

Black to move

A discovered check ... But is it worth it?

249 *Yates – Alekhine, 1927*

Black to move

Disconnecting the queen ...

250. *Shashin – Ivanov, 1977*

White to move

Visible from the side ...

251. *Keene – Quinteros, 1975*

Black to move

1 ... ♘g4 2 ♗xg7 ♖xg7? Rectify the mistake.

252. Tarrasch – Chigorin, 1893

Black to move

'Nothing stands in the way of youth!'

253. Kuzmin – Smyslov, 1978

Black to move

The fewer the pawns, the greater the chances of a draw. 1 ... h4 2 ♘c4 hxg3. No good fortune in pawns!

254. Reshevsky – Ivanovic, 1976

Black to move

The guard perishes but he does not give up!

255. Daskalov – Padevsky, 1970

White to move

On board!

256. Kristol – Morozova, 1969

White to move

1 ♕f4? – 1 ... ♕xd5, 1 ♕e4? – 1 ... cxd5. Is that how it is?

257. Salvioli – NN, 1915

White to move

Both times on the same square.

258. Tot – Sigetti, 1946

White to move

'A rude guest.'

259 Stulfinga – Grahn, 1974

Black to move

Slaughter house.

260. Kogan – Petryaev, 1969

Black to move

One step forward, one step back.

261. Marshall – NN, 1912

White to move

American rhythm.

262. Torldalen – Bernstein, 1975

White to move

1 ♖f8 is parried by 1 ... ♘d5+. 1 ♘c4+ ♘xc4 2 ♖f8 is good. But even better ...

263. Van den Eiden – Prashak, 1974

White to move

In the steel pincers ...

264. Ornstein – Kinnmark, 1972

White to move

Powerless queen.

267. Em.Lasker – Schiffers, 1896

White to move

March to the right – a rook is lost. March to the left ...

265. Bondarevsky – Ufimtsev, 1936

White to move

How studies are created.

268. Karpov – Korchnoi, 1978

White to move

The champion's first victory in a world title match ...

266. Engel – NN, 1949

White to move

Three finishes.

269 Korchnoi – Karpov, 1978

White to move

... and his fourth.

270. L.Kubbel, 1939

White to move and win

On a swing.

272. V.Korolkov 1950

White to move and win

Playing hide and seek.

271. H.Lommer 1968

White to move and win

Rotation.

273. A.Mandler 1927

White to move and win

His own worst enemy.

274. G.Kasparian, 1936

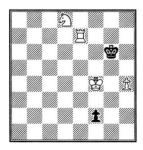

White to move and win

Leap into an abyss.

9. Two Bishops

Two bishops are deservedly regarded as a powerful offensive weapon. The advantage of the two bishops is often called the 'minor exchange'. But not everyone is aware of why the 'minor exchange' often leads to a great advantage. Usually they say that the bishop has a longer range than the knight. That's true. But, you know, one bishop has a longer range than one knight, but both pieces on the chess price list have the same value. The fact is that the two bishops are more than doubly stronger than one. This seemingly paradoxical statement is understandable when one considers that the bishops move along squares of different colours.

Two light-squared or two dark-squared bishops are exactly twice as strong as one. But simple arithmetic is not appropriate for a pair of opposite coloured bishops, because their range is much wider.

The bishop gains particular strength in open positions, when its mobility is not hampered by pawn chains. Smooth moving and well-disguised, bishops are able to strike from a long distance at any object, while controlling a wide area of the battle and firing at a large number of squares.

If a pair of bishops is operating on adjacent diagonals, mating situations can arise in the corner or on the edge of the board.

When blown by the wind along diagonals leading to the king, the bishops enter the zone of operations with great speed.

In the game Henkin – Maltsev (1953) the light-squared bishop has already 'stolen' a highway. White's task now is to capture the dark-squared diagonal. But the d4 and e5 squares are controlled by enemy pieces. How to deflect them from defence?

1 ♘d7! ♖xd7 2 ♖xd7 ♗xd7.

Now both the critical squares are defended only by the knight c6, but it is not up to the task.

3 ♕d4+! ♘xd4 4 ♗e5+ Black resigned.

Safarov – Bukhman (1977). Also here the struggle is conducted on the long diagonal. The h6 pawn creates additional threats: Black cannot allow the enemy rook to the 8th rank.

1 ♖e6! ♕d4 (1 ... ♗xg5 2 ♗c3+ ♗f6 3 ♗xf6+ ♖xf6 4 ♖e8+ or 1 ... ♕xe6 2 ♗xe6 ♗xg5 3 ♗c3+) **2 ♕xf6+!** Black resigned: 2 ... ♕xf6 3 ♖xf6 ♖xf6 4 ♗c3 ♘d7 5 ♗f7! leads to a quick mate.

Often the place of a missing bishop is taken by the queen, opening up lethal fire along the diagonal. The co-ordination of the queen and bishop in diagonal attacks, as we have already repeatedly seen, assumes a universal character.

Domuls – Skonda (1977): **1 ♖e8+!** The black queen is deflected from its defence of the bishop f6. But this is also interference (after 1 ... ♗xe8 2 ♕f8X).

And on 1 ... ♕xe8 comes 2 ♕xf6X.

Ludolf – Kots (1962). Any check by the queen on the a1-h8 diagonal will be fatal. The c3 and e5 squares are covered by black pieces, the sphere of activity of which intersects on the d8 square. And it is precisely at this point that White delivers a diversionary attack.

1 ♖d8! The problem is solved: either the rook loses control over the c3 square, or the queen over e5. Black resigned.

If the main road to the king is impeded by a pawn then it can be blown up by an attacking piece. Most mines are placed under the h6 (h3) or f6 (f3) squares.

Kostin – Sokolov (1975): **1 ♗c4+ ♔h8 2 ♖xh6! gxh6 3 ♖xf8+! ♖xf8 4 ♗b2+.** Black resigned as it's mate in two moves. With the sacrifice of two rooks White opened the long diagonal and eliminated its last defender – the bishop f8.

In reply to **1 ... ♖ad8** Marmou against Reichenbach (1961) cleared the diagonal with a queen sacrifice –

2 ♕xf6! gxf6 3 ♗xf6X.

Ignatiev – Rosenberg (1971): Black's position is of course lost, and he grabs his last chance – **1 ... ♖h6** (with the faint hope of 2 ♖f2?? ♖e1+ 3 ♖f1 ♕xh2X). But White is not thinking about defending. **2 ♕xh6!** (after 2 ... ♕xh6 3 f6 gxf6 4 ♗xf6+ the outlay is more than compensated) **2 ... ♕xf1+** (while here this is already the last chance – 3 ♔xf1 ♖e1+ 4 ♔xe1 – stalemate; however, 4 ♔f2 ♖e2+ 5 ♗xe2 destroys the idea) **3 ♗xf1.** Black resigned.

An attack by raging bishops on adjacent diagonals can overwhelm a king not only on the corner squares.

It seems that in the game Bayer – Gelner (1956) the black castle is solidly defended. However, White blows up the fortress walls with two powerful volleys.

1 ♖xh6+! gxh6 (if 1 ... ♔xh6, then 2 ♕g5+ ♔h7 3 ♕h4+ ♔g6 4 f5X) **2 ♕g8+! ♘xg8 3 ♗f5X.**

In a quiet position Volz (Black) against Muller (1940) was tempted by the cheap bait – **1 ... ♘xe4?** The lightning strike **2 ♕e6+! fxe6 3 ♗h5+** led to a familiar pattern.

In the following example, the final mating construction is made possible by a pin.

Alterman – Figler (1977): **1 ♕xd7+!** Black resigned (1 ... ♕xd7 2 ♖xb8+ ♕d8 3 ♗b5X).

Here the bishops are attacking the enemy king from different sides, forming a ring of fire around it. Together with this, the king's way of escape is closed by his own pieces. Such a blockade is often the result of structural defects in the position. A classic example is the game Schulten – Boden (1860).

1 ... d5! 2 ♗xd5 ♕xc3+! 3 bxc3 ♗a3X.

These episodes mostly occur with long castling, when the c-pawn has already made a step forward, and the opponent's bishop is on the h2-b8 (b1-h7) diagonal, cutting off the king from the corner square.

In the game Canal – NN (1934), all of these conditions are present, but the a6 square, from which the bishop on e2 could inflict a decisive blow, is protected by the queen on a5.

The b7 pawn can be eliminated by a queen sacrifice on c6. But how to deflect the black queen?

1 axb4! ♕xa1+ 2 ♔d2 ♕xh1. There is no choice, all the squares on the a-file are under fire. But now arises a situation similar to the previous example, only with colours reversed. **3 ♕xc6+! bxc6 4 ♗a6X.** The mechanism of the final operation is typical for most combinations of our theme, no matter on which part of the board they occur.

Alekhine – Vasic (1931): The bishop on a3 stalemates the black king, while the g6 square is weakened by the advance h7-h6. This pre-requisite creates the conditions for a standard tactical operation: **1 ♕xe6+! fxe6 2 ♗g6X**.

Kellerman – Friedl (1955): **1 ... ♕f6+ 2 ♘f3?** (2 ♘f5 ♘e3) **2 ... ♗e3+ 3 ♔f1 ♕xf3+! 4 gxf3 ♗h3X**.

It takes two temperamental Italians to shun standard play and create a unique romantic study on this theme with the use of bright tactical colours.

Kofman – Filatov (1962). This position bears a striking resemblance to the previous one. If the white knight were not standing on the e-file, the outcome of the struggle would immediately be decided by a queen sacrifice on e6. So, the knight needs to be moved with tempo.

1 ♘xc6! bxc6 2 ♕xe6+ fxe6 3 ♗g6X.

Vaccoroni – Mazzocci (1891): **1 ♕g4+!! ♗xg4 2 ♖xh6+! gxh6 3 ♗f7X**. A complete celebration of the blockade!

However, Count Alberic O'Kelly de Galway – a grandmaster from the more 'cold blooded' Belgium – also had the right to nominate his own production for the brilliancy prize.

Ofstad – Uhlmann (1963): **1 ♕d6+ ♗e7** (hopeless is 1 ... ♘e7 2 ♗xg5) **2 ♖xe7 ♘xe7 3 ♕f6+! gxf6 4 ♗h6X**.

Devos – O'Kelly (1937). White played **1 ♘xd4** reckoning on 1 ... exd4?

2 ♕xd4 f6 3 fxe3, "But the Count of Saint-Germain, as poeticised in 'The Queen of Spades', was not a coward ... "
1 ... ♕xf2+!! 2 ♔xf2 ♘g4+ 3 ♔f3. The king did not want to return to his apartments for fear of a conspiracy. However, a coup is already underway.
3 ... e4+! 4 ♔xe4 ♘df6+ 5 ♔f3 ♘e5+ 6 ♔f2 ♘fg4+ 7 ♔g1 (he has to go back, but under escort) **7 ... ♗e3X**.

Also in these constructions either of the bishops might replace the queen and all its tricks. The choice is often a matter of taste.

Dus-Chotimirsky – Robine (1910): **1 ♘xf7! ♔xf7 2 d6+ ♔f8 3 ♕h5 ♕e8 4 ♖xf6+! gxf6 5 ♕xh6+** (sceptics would start with the bishop...) **5 ... ♖xh6 6 ♗xh6X**.

Balk – Barnes (1926): **1 ... ♘xc3! 2 bxc3 ♖xe3+! 3 fxe3 ♗g3+ 4 hxg3 ♕xg3X**. If the black pieces on the diagonal were placed the other way around, the campaign would be completed by the bishop.

Chulkov – Haveman (1947): **1 ♗h6 ♖e8** (playing the exchange down is also no picnic) **2 ♗xf7+! ♔xf7 3 ♕b3X**. Black's attention was apparently focused on the vertical intentions of the white queen, while she was in a diagonal mood ...

When the bishops are 'tete-à-tete' with the opponent's king, they will accept his surrender in any of the four corners of the chess kingdom.

The operation proceeds smoothly, it is only necessary to beware of stalemate. It is important to remember that the stalemate position occurs not only at the end of the operation, when the king has already been backed into a corner, but also in the intermediate stages.

1 ♗g2 ♔d4 2 ♗f2+ ♔e5 3 ♔h2 ♔f4 4 ♔h3 ♔e5 5 ♔g4. Zugzwang. Bishops, working shoulder to shoulder, cut off the king on the right side of the board, creating an insurmountable barrier. Black is forced to retreat.

5 ... ♔e6 6 ♗g3 ♔f6 7 ♗e4 ♔e6 8 ♔g5 ♔e7 9 ♗f5 ♔f7 10 ♗d6 ♔e8 11 ♔f6 ♔d8 12 ♗e6 (12 ♔f7? – stalemate) 12 ... ♔e8 13 ♗c7 (12 ♗e7+? – stalemate) 13 ... ♔f8 14 ♗d7 ♔g8 15 ♔g6 ♔f8

Finally – complete satisfaction: 16 ♗d6+ ♔g8 17 ♗e6+ ♔h8 18 ♗e5X

Chess players of all generations never cease to admire the wonderful combinations of the 19th century German master A.Anderssen. In this book you will repeatedly come across his creative work. The next game (1852), the ending of which we now give, was called the 'Immortal' by his contemporaries. Playing Black was the famous French master J.Dufresne, author of a popular chess manual.

In modern practice similar mating patterns are seen.

The opponents have conducted fierce attacks on the kings, and it is unclear who will be the first to reach his goal. Moreover, White is two pieces down after sacrificing them earlier. But Anderssen is to play, and he decides the outcome of the struggle with a spectacular combination.

1 ♖xe7! ♘xe7 2 ♕xd7! ♔xd7 3 ♗f5 ♔e8 4 ♗d7, and on any move of the king follows 5 ♗xe7X.

In Anderssen's attack the primary role was assigned to the two bishops and a pawn, supporting the offensive. In contemporary practice similar mating patterns are seen.

Let's get acquainted with some ways to achieve them.

In the game Stakhovich – Hexler (1955) the pre-requisites for a final attack by White are served by the e6 pawn and the cramped position of the enemy king. The manoeuvre carried out by White is very amusing.

1 ♗h6+ ♔g8 2 ♖f1 f6 3 ♗e8!, and Black resigned, since mate with the bishop on f7 is unstoppable (there is also a dual: 2 ♗e8 fxe6 3 ♖f1).

The same foundations served as a reason for the concluding operation in the game Euwe-Blek (1928).

(See next diagram)

1 ♕h5 ♘e5 2 ♕f7+! ♘xf7 3 exf7+ ♔f8 4 ♘f5X.

And in the following position Alekhine (White) introduced a pawn

into an attacking position in his game with Forrester (1923).

1 e6! ♕f6 2 ♗xd7+ ♔d8 3 ♗c6+! ♕xd4 4 e7X.

* * * *

275. Cardiff – Bristol, 1884

277. Ivanov – Kutyev, 1964

Black to move

Bristol, of course, won. Furthermore it was by correspondence.

Black to move

120 years in a flash ...

276. Horwitz – Popert, 1844

278. Survila – Skoblikov, 1978

Black to move

1 ... c6? (correct is 1 ... ♕xh2+!). And now?

Black to move

1 ... ♗e7. A choice of sacrifice. But first ...

279 Burtslaf – Stark, 1958

Black to move

1 ... ♗g8, and ...

280. Nikolaevsky – Malevinsky, 1975

Black to move

1 ... ♘d8, and ...

281. Nezhmetdinov – Kotkov, 1958

Black to move

1 ... ♛d8, and ...

282. Littlewood – Roth, 1966

Black to move

1 ... b5, and ...

283. Kieseritzky – Dumonche, 1844

White to move

A familiar theme.

284. Beland – Meyer, 1959

Black to move

An uninvited guest.

285. Teichmann – NN, 1914

White to move

1 ♘b5. What happens on 1 ... cxb5 ?

288. Salamon – Bilek, 1976

Black to move

Unravelling the tangle.

286. Steinitz – Wilson, 1862

White to move

Whose king is in danger?

289 Chetkovich – Molerovich, 1951

White to move

Near and far.

287. Lukov – Chistiakov, 1950

Black to move

1 ... ♔xf2+ 2 ♔h1 and the end is nigh.

290. Redikan – NN, 1957

White to move

Only one blow. But what a blow!

199

291. Sergeev – Lebedev, 1928

White to move

Go where it is least expected ...

292. Torman – Sire, 1978

White to move

Lose and become famous!

293. Donnesthorpe – Mundell, 1892

White to move

Columbus' egg.

294. Nimzowitsch – Neuman, 1899

White to move

David and Goliath.

295. W.Speckmann, 1956

White mates in 4 moves

Out of sight!

296. E.Pogosyants, 1977

White to move and win

Warming up

297. A.Troitsky, M.Platov, 1925

White to move and win

Trapping is easy, but how to hold?

298. D.Goldberg, 1931

White to move and win

How to trick the knight?

299 L.Kaiev, 1932

White to move and win

White has three extra pawns but
they might perish ingloriously.
So let them die as heroes!

"... What does this absurd contrast between combinational and positional styles mean? Is it possible to distinguish them purely mechanically? In chess, there are only two styles – good, that is leading to victory, and bad, that is leading to defeat. In each position is hidden a possible combination, and each combination is born out of the position."

M.Chigorin

"Clearly, in chess it is possible to play in every style – and any style is good if it leads to victory. But the more versatile the chess player, the more chances he has of victory, the deeper and better he can play at the board, since during a game he can meet the most diverse positions."

M.Botvinnik

10. Two Knights

Knights, knights! The sound of the chase,
A little bell on the bridle.
Who said the knights must race
In a simple letter 'L'?
I don't walk, I prance
Among all the chess men
And only for the master
Do I slow now and then.

Evgeny Ilin. *A Piece for a Piece.*

An eastern bazaar in the Middle Ages. A riot of colours, the din of the multitude in the crowd. An empire of trade and deceit. Among the fat merchants, the clamoursome shills, the dusty dervishes, the swift-handed conjurers and plain thieves is a man with a chessboard on a dirty dishcloth. And around him is a ring of onlookers, people who like to argue, to play or at a pinch give some advice, at least.

"Well, believers, who wants to get himself a coin from my pouch? A whole dirham for the right answer! I swear to Mohammed, you cannot do this! A whole dirham! It's tempting ... " And then from the crowd a believer volunteers, or to be more precise a gullible challenger. Even in those long-gone days weak chess players often considered themselves great players.

The pieces were quickly placed on the board.

"Tell me, precious, is it or is it not possible to give a check to the black king and mate it in two moves?"

"You've lost, oh wise one!" the 'great player' exclaims. "I see a mate in two!" And with glee he demonstrates his cunning solution: 1 ♖f2+ ♘xf2 2 ♘g3X.

"Ay-yay-yay! Woe is me, the absentminded jackal!" the loser wails. "I forgot to put the white king on the board!"

And he puts it on g4.

"Nothing has changed, honourable one," the 'great player'' smiles smugly. "You get mated in exactly the same way!"

"Hunt for the coin, the problem is not solved, I take your rook with check." The crowd laughs. The 'great player' sheepishly gropes for a coin.

"But you can get your own back," the hustler continues, and moves the white king from g4 to h3.

"Tell me, now can you give a check to the black king and mate it in two moves?"

"What's this, do you take me for an ass?" the 'great player' starts getting angry. "Of course not, the rook is taken with check ... "

"You will have to find another dirham – I take the knight with the rook and on any reply I declare mate. But I will forgive your loss if you tell me if it is or is not possible to give a check to the black king and mate it in two moves."

And he adds a black pawn ...

The 'great player' is uneasy, he doesn't see the point of the modest c4 pawn, and literally spellbound plays 1 ♖xg2, but after 1 ... c3! he can't find the final blow at all.

He pays three dirhams and quickly recedes to the derisive shouts of those around him. And the artful hustler is already setting up a new problem, offering the baited crowd 'easy money'.

All these amusing stories and scenarios are the stuff of history, but the chess content of the ancient problems hasn't been shelved yet and is still useful for training. This is the final setup of one of the most famous ones. This position is 600 years old.

To 'construct' such a mate does not require a whole herd of horses, but his pair need to be managed skilfully.

NN – Blackburne (1902): **1 ... ♘g3+ 2 ♔g1 ♕g2+! 3 ♖xg2 ♘h3X**.

Westerinen – Razuvaev (1969). After 1 g3 ♘xd3 2 ♕xd3 ♕f2+ 3 ♔h1 ♘f1 White resigned. But what had the Muscovite prepared on 1 fxe5? A beautiful mating finish: **1 ... ♘f1+ 2 ♔g1 ♘xh3+ 3 ♔h1 ♕g1+! 4 ♘xg1 ♘f2X**.

Here we see the basic prerequisites to carry out such operations – the cramped position of the enemy king, and the typical tactical device – blockade.

In the game Gennikov – Radchenko (1958) a similar finish came about after sharp introductory play.

With his last move (f2-f3) White attacks the bishop g4 and, in addition, offers an exchange of queens, which favours the defending side. However Black has an interesting tactical possibility.

1 ... ♗h3! (threatening no more no less than mate on g2) **2 gxh3 ♕xh3 3 ♖f2.** On 3 ♕f2 quite simply 3 ... ♗xe5. But now arises a well known configuration.

3 ... ♘g3+ 4 ♔g1 ♕g2+! 5 ♖xg2 ♘h3X.

In the game Hassle – Kumur (1965) White succeeded in carrying out a headlong mating attack even without queens.

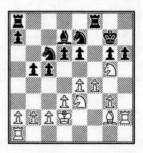

1 **Ξxh6!** **⍟xh6** 2 **Ξh1+** **⍟g7** 3 **Ξh7+** **⍟g8** 4 **⍀g4.** Threatening 5 **⍀h6X.** Upon a move of the rook f8 along the 8th rank by 4 ... **Ξfd8**, Black gets mated in another way: 5 **⍀f6+** **⍟f8** 6 **Ξf7X.** He has to give back material, but the attack is not weakened.

4 ... **Ξxf4** 5 **gxf4** **⍟f8** 6 **⍀f6** **⍀d8** (threatening mate on f7) 7 **⍀xd7+** **⍟e8** 8 **⍀f6+** **⍟f8** 9 **Ξf7+!** **⍀xf7** 10 **⍀xe6X.**

A quite unique mating construction was set up by I.Zaitsev (White) against Storozhenko (1970).

1 **Ξg4+** **⍟d6** 2 **e5+** **⍟c5** 3 **⍑xa3+** **⍀xa3** 4 **⍀e4+** **⍟b5** 5 **⍀ec3+** **⍟a6** 6 **Ξa4+** **⍀a5** 7 **Ξb5+!** **⍀xb5** 8 **⍀b4+** **⍟b6** 9 **⍀a4X!**

We must immortalise this position with a diagram.

The game was played in a simultaneous exhibition. When it appeared in print (it was published in *Moscow Chess*), I.Zaitsev said to the editor: "After the session, I specifically wrote down the name of my opponent.

Otherwise you would not believe that the position is 'legal' ..."

The 'two horse power' mate is readily utilised by chess composers. Among the best contemporary compositions, we note the following two works.

M.Havel, 1955

White mates in 5 moves

1 **Ξhh2.** Now on 1 ... **Ξa1** follows 2 **Ξhg2+!** **⍀xg2** 3 **⍀f3+** **⍟f1** 4 **Ξf2+** **⍀xf2** 5 **⍀g3X.** The second thematic (or, as composers say, echo-chameleon) variation arises after 1 ... **⍟f1** 2 **Ξef2+!** **⍀xf2** 3 **⍀g3+** **⍟g1** 4 **Ξg2+** **⍀xg2** 5 **⍀f3X.** A third mate is delivered if Black plays 1 ... **Ξc2** 2 **Ξxc2** **⍀xc2** 3 **⍀f3+** **⍟f1** 4 **Ξxc2** **⍀f2** 5 **Ξxf2X.**

M.Mikhailov, 1955

White to move and win

1 g7! ♘xg7 2 f6+ ♔f8 3 ♘c5! It seems that the white pawn will go on unhindered to queen (4 ♘cd7+, 5 f7+ and 6 f8=♕+), but Black finds counterplay, reviving the harboured pieces on the 1st rank.

3 ... a2! 4 ♔xa2 ♘c3+ 5 ♔b3 ♗a3! 6 ♔xa3 ♘b5+ 7 ♔b2 ♘d6 (detaining the pawn but now a mating situation arises on the board) **8 ♘cd7+ ♔g8 9 f7+! ♘xf7 10 ♘f6+ ♔f8 11 ♘g6X**

Let's get acquainted with a few variations on the cavalry theme.

In such schemes, the operational task becomes the entry of one of the knights to the shaky square f6 (f3). In the game Has-Taksis (1968), the knight is under fivefold attack when it delivers the double check.

1 ♕h7+! (the king is drawn into a double attack) **1 ... ♔xh7 2 ♘f6+ ♔h8 3 ♘g6X**.

The encounter Wirthensohn – Niklasson (1978) ended with beautiful and rich tactical content.

1 ♗g5! (by means of a bishop sacrifice White introduces the knight f3 to an attacking position) **1 ... hxg5 2 ♘xg5** (threatening 3 ♘xf6+ and 4 ♕h7X; on 2 ... g6 sufficient is 3 ♘xf7) **2 ... ♘e4** (hoping for a respite after 3 ♘xe4) **3 ♘xf7! ♘c5 4 ♘g5!** Black resigned. If 4 ... ♕xg5, then 5 ♘f6+ ♔h8 6 ♕h7X, while after 4 ... ♘xd3 White has the choice between 5 ♘e7+ ♔h8 6 ♘g6X and the even nicer finish – 5 ♘f6+ ♔h8 6 ♘f7X. Also here the double check brought the knight 'among the people'.

A knight jump can be secured by associated threats.

Erdes – Lichtner (1922): **1 ♘f6!** Creating the threat of 2 ♕g6. The white knight is untouchable: 1 ... hxg5 2 ♕h5X; 1 ... gxf6 2 ♕h7X; 1 ... ♕xf6 2 ♕e8+.

1 ... ♘e7 (it seems that Black is defending against the basic threats...) **2 ♕g6!!** (all the same) **2 ... ♕g8 3 ♕h7+! ♕xh7 4 ♘f7X**.

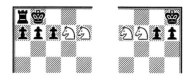

Driving the king into the corner is achieved by means of an elementary mechanism, but this must first be set in motion,

Baumgartner – Toth (1961). **1 ♖xd8** (removing the defence) **1 ... ♖xd8 2 ♘e7+ ♔h8 3 ♘xf7X**.

In the game Eggenberger – Schumacher (1959) a decisive check with the knight on e7 is prevented by ♛b4. Can this obstacle be removed?

1 ♛d2! ♛xd2 2 ♘e7+ ♔h8 3 ♘f7X

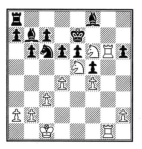

Chistiakov – Dunaevsky (1944): **1 ♖g7+! ♗xg7 2 ♖xg7+ ♔d8** (on other king moves the rook mates on f7) **3 ♘g6!** (the gun is cocked and there is nowhere to hide) **3 ... ♔c8 4 ♖g8+ ♘d8 5 ♘e7+ ♔b8 6 ♘d7X**.

Vasiliev (White) suddenly led his knights into the attack against Burlyaev (1974).

1 ♘xd5! ♛xd3 (there is no choice) **2 ♖xc8! ♘f8 3 ♘e5!!** He can only defend against the cavalry attack 4 ♘e7+ and 5 ♘xf7X at the cost of enormous material loss. Black resigned.

It was P.Morphy who discovered one of the most spectacular mating positions.

In a game against Marache (1857) he delivered a blow which will not be forgotten as long as chess exists.

1 ... ♞g3!! 2 ♕xg6 ♞de2X!.

In modern practice, such episodes can be counted on the fingers of one hand. And regarding final mating patterns, our guiding star can be served by Tal's attack with the white pieces against Portisch (1976).

1 ♘g5! The king is left all alone to face the enemy. If 1 ... ♖f8, then 2 ♕h5 h6 3 ♕g6 hxg5 4 ♕h5+ ♔g8 5 ♘e7X.

1 ... ♗f6 2 ♘h6!

Here L.Portisch could not go on and resigned the game. Dangers approach from all four 'corners of the world': 2 ... gxh6 3 ♕xh7X; 2 ... ♗xg5 3 ♕g8+ ♖xg8 4 ♘f7X; 2 ... ♖e7 3 ♕xe7! ♗xg5 4 hxg5 gxh6, and mate on g7. But where is the fourth mate? The fourth is 'our's' – 2 ... ♖e7 3 ♕xe7! ♗xe7 4 ♘gf7X! 'à la Morphy', only in the corner.

And finally, the extraordinary epaulettes of the 'cavalry general'.

Mislivetz – Petz (1977): **1 ... ♘d2** (threatening mate on g2) **2 ♕h3 ♕h1+**

3 ♔f2 ♘e4+ 4 ♔e1 ♘xc2X! There you are!

An amazing mating pattern can be found in the Arab mansubah.

Found by an unknown chess player about a thousand years ago, it is unusually beautiful and economical. Many chess composers inscribe it in their tasks and studies, drawing the admiration of lovers of chess. Also the famous French poet Alfred de Musset could not remain indifferent to the beauty of chess. Here is a problem of his, dated 1845.

White mates in 3 moves

1 ♖d2! ♘xd2 **2 ♘c3**, and on any move by the opponent's knight White mates by **3 ♘f3X**.

"Alas, this happens only in chess composition, in an artificially composed position – said one Moscow grandmaster – In practice, I have not seen anything like it."

So it also seemed to me, until one day I came across the end of a game Turover – Arzumanian (1957).

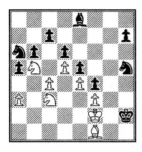

Black has an extra pawn on the kingside and threatens, after ♘h5-g3, to get it moving. Therefore White starts to force the game with the aim of obtaining counter-chances on the other side of the board.

1 c5. Played on the calculation 1 ... bxc5 2 ♘a7 ♘b8 3 ♘cb5 or 1 ... dxc5 2 d6 cxd6 3 ♘xd6 ♘c7 4 ♘c4, in both cases with counterplay for White. After the opponent's reply, White apparently considered the opponent's following response to be impossible because of a combination, which took an unexpected turn.

1 ... ♗xb5 2 cxd6 (continuing his line; the lesser of two evils was 2 ♘xb5) **2 ... ♗xf1! 3 d7.** This is White's idea: the pawn cannot be stopped from queening. However, the exceptional nature of the position allows Black to create a mating attack.

3 ... ♘c5!

White resigned. After 4 ♔xf1 ♘xd7 Black remains a piece ahead and 4 d8=♕ ♘d3 5 ♔xf1 leads to a knight

mate rarely seen in practical play – 5 ... ♘g3X!

An elegant combination with almost the same finish was played by Togonidze in a game with Bilek (1960), the only difference being that compared to the previous example, the role of the white king had been assumed by a pawn.

1 ♖h8+! ♗xh8 2 ♘e6+ ♔g8 3 ♘h6X

It is well known that on correct defence two knights cannot mate a lone king. However, theoretically, there are these finishes:

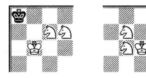

But they would arise only in the case of gross errors by the defending side.

Here 1 ♘c6, intending 2 ♘c7X, cannot be played since Black is stalemated already on the first move.

Also no good is the attempt to draw close to the enemy king from the other side: 1 ♘d6 ♚b8 2 ♘d5 ♚a8 3 ♚c7 ♚a7 4 ♘b5+, because Black plays not 4 ... ♚a8?? 5 ♘b6X, but 4 ... ♚a6, escaping from the mating net.

In this position White wins thanks to the black pawn – which prevents the stalemate.

White manages to mate his opponent before his new queen enters the fray: **1 ♘b4 d3 2 ♘ec6 d2 3 ♘d5 d1=♕ 4 ♘c7X**.

In tournament practice such finishes are rare. Here is an interesting example.

After **1 ... ♘xa5? 2 ♚b6!** Black, in the game Bayer – Barabas (1961), was already in no position to safely defend himself against 3 ♘d7+ and ♘d6-e8-c7X. No help is 2 ... ♘c4+ 3 bxc4 ♗a4 in view of 4 ♘fe4 and 5 ♘c5.

Black's chances of saving himself in the game Bilek – Ciocaltea (1972) are linked to the hope of giving up his knight for the h5 pawn, although even in this case he should lose, as shown in a well-known analysis by A.Troitsky.

However White denies the opponent even the faintest hopes, not allowing the knight to draw close to the main theatre of military operations, and slowly tightening the noose.

1 ♘f5+ ♚h7 2 ♚d5 ♘b4+ 3 ♚e6 ♚g8 4 ♘e5 ♚h8 5 ♚f7 ♘d5 6 ♘e7. Black resigned: the exchange of knights is tantamount to defeat.

300. NN – Kashdan, 1948

Black to move

It's not worth going after the queen ...

301. Maevskaya – Kirienko, 1974

White to move

We started with something pleasing and finish the same way.

302. Labutin – Panov, 1969

White to move

Everybody is looking to the right ...

303. Gerulak – Kakhan, 1909

White to move

Shades of the great Morphy ...

304. Capablanca – NN, 1935

White to move

One of the famous Cuban's 'little combinations'.

305. Averkin – Berdichevsky, 1963

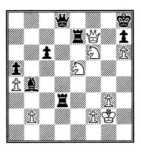

Black to move

And he played 1 ... ♗d6?

306. Somov – Razumov, 1971

White to move

Watch out: the rook on e1 is under attack.

307. Wersteg – Fritchi, 1976

Black to move

Free range for the herd.

308. A.Grunenwald, 1960

White mates in 3 moves

What is the question – this is the answer ...

309 E.Pogosyants, 1973

White mates in 4 moves

Focus with a change of clothes.

310. I.Kupper, 1957

White mates in 8 moves

The knight on g4 should go to e6 when the opponent's bishop would be unable to control the critical squares ...

311. A.Gurvich, 1927

White to move and win

Don't forget that Black is threatening to queen! But the cavalry are not asleep.

312. T.Gorgiev, 1928

White to move and win

If Black manages to give up his knight for the pawn, then it will be a draw. At first he succeeds, but ...

* * * *

"When you see a good move, wait and don't make it; you might find a better move."

Em.Lasker

"If you think your move is good – make it! Without hesitation, you must do what seems good and correct."

J.Capablanca

"What move should you be looking for...The best one (like Rubinstein), the strongest (like Lasker), or the most energetic (like Alekhine)?
Our advice, based on practical experience, is always to go for the most illogical move!"

S.Tartakower

"The desire to find out how to take advantage of a hasty move by the opponent, which at first sight seems unnatural, mistaken, can lure you away on a false trail to an attack. Only with a steady development of forces and extremely circumspect play can you little by little acquire certain advantages in a position and then already an opportunity will arise to deliver a decisive blow."

M.Chigorin

"It is not enough to know that combinations consist of a series of forcing moves – it is necessary to be able to point out the basic reason why we conclude that in this or that position there is the possibility of a combination."

Em.Lasker

11. Bishop and Knight

Mayakovsky's humorous 'Poems on the difference of tastes' goes like this:

> The horse said,
> looking at the camel:
> "What a giant
> mongrel-horse."
> The camel exclaimed
> "Are you really a horse?
> You look like simply
> an underdeveloped camel."
> And only the
> greybeard God knew,
> that these were
> different species of animals.

If only chess pieces had the gift of speech, just such a dialogue might occur between the bishop and knight. Meanwhile chess players would argue. Some would sympathise with the long-range bishop, others – the quirky knight. But experienced players would know 'that these were different species of animals' and try to utilise their individual qualities for a common objective. And the objective in a game of chess, as you know, is to checkmate the opponent's king. In this sense, the 'different species' symbiosis is very successful.

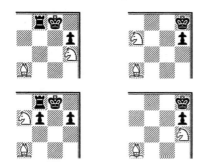

The basic pre-requisite for an operation of this sort against the short castled position is control of the long diagonal.

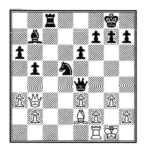

Glass – Roessel (1958): **1 ... ♕g2+ 2 ♔xg2 ♘f4+ 3 ♔g1 ♘h3X** (also possible is 3 ... ♘xe2X).

Anticipating that victory was close, Safronov (Black) against Satikova (1953) boldly played **1 ... ♘g4?** and was probably shocked by the fatal denouement: **2 ♕xg7! ♔xg7 3 ♘f5** Black resigned (3 ... ♔g8 4 ♘xe7X).

In both cases the knight enters its ensuing position with the help of a double check and delivers the last blow from one of two free squares.

Any obstacle standing in the way of a bishop may not only be removed by destroying it with a sacrifice, but also by deflection.

Honfi – Lokvenc (1962). To defend against the threat of ♖f3-h3, Black played **1 ... ♗g7** on which followed a stunning blow – **2 ♘d5!** Now, leading to mate are both 2 ... ♗xh6 3 ♘e7X, and 2 ... ♘xd5 3 ♕xg7X. On 2 ... ♗xb2 the queen is lost – 3 ♘e7+, while after 2 ... f6 3 ♘e7+ ♔f7 4 ♕xh7 White obtains an irresistible attack. Therefore Black resigned.

Usually the way to the king is blocked by the g7 (g2) pawn. But this too is not made of steel.

Lepeshkin – Kosterin (1963) **1 ... ♖xg2+! 2 ♔xg2 ♖g8+ 3 ♔h1 ♕g5!** White resigned (4 ♘xg5 ♘g3+ 5 ♔g1 ♘xe2X or 4 ♖g1 ♕xg1+ 5 ♘xg1 ♘xf2X).

Gusti – Nutrizio (1958): **1 ... ♕h3!** This move contains two threats: the direct – 2 ... ♕xh6 and the indirect – 2 ... ♘g3+ and 3 ... ♕xg2X.

2 gxh3 (the diagonal is opened, and the mechanism of double check swings into action) **2 ... ♘f2+ 3 ♔g1 ♘xh3X.**

Torres – Alekhine (1922): **1 ... d4!** (Black opens the main highway for the bishop b7) **2 cxd4 cxd4 3 ♗xd4 ♗xd4 4 ♖xd4 ♖xd4 5 ♘xd4 ♕xh3! 6 gxh3 ♘f2+ 7 ♔g1 ♘xh3X.**

With a knight on f5 (f4) the g7 (g2) square is subjected to an even heavier bombardment, and here the queen sacrifice on h6 (h3) remains the focal point of tactical operations.

Verein – Salminger (1902): Here the black queen has already thrown herself on the sacrificial altar, all that is needed is to add fuel to the fire: **1 ... ♘xe4!** White resigned: 2 ♗xe4 ♗xe4 leads to the loss of a piece, while in the event of 2 gxh3 on the board arises a stereotype mating situation, looked at in the previous example.

The mechanism of the tactical operations in the last two examples is typical: the queen deflects the g-pawn, while the knight goes into an attacking position, opening the diagonal of the bishop. The relative positions of the attacking pieces are also typical and can serve as a benchmark for more complex combinations.

Lvov – Radchenko (1955). It seems simple: take the g2 pawn and thereby open an approach to the enemy king. But White has an extra piece, and after 1 ... ♗xg2!? 2 d3 he retains chances of defence.

The outcome of the battle is decided by the same sacrifice – **1 ... ♕h3!** The threat of mate forces White to capture the bold queen – **2 gxh3**, but then a familiar picture emerges – **2 ... ♘xh3X.**

There are other possible methods of deflecting enemy pawns, standing in the way of attacking pieces.

216

Troianescu – Dumitrescu (1970): **1 ♗a6!** Black resigned. Why? Because White, with tempo, frees the way for the queen to the king's flank and after 1 ... ♕xa6 2 ♕g4, the g7 pawn would have to make a fateful step forward, handing over the field of battle to the heated knight (2 ... g6 3 ♘h6X).

Lunenkova – NN (1976): **1 ♕g5+!** Black resigned.

Teplov – Balgin (1959). With his last move ♖a1-d1 White attacks the enemy queen. He hardly counted on winning it since Black has available a counterattack – 1 ... ♗f8. But now there

is a roar of thunder from the other side of the river: **1 ... ♘h3+ 2 ♔h1 ♕xf3!**, and White resigned.

If necessary, a wide variety of tactical methods can be utilised to quickly transfer a bishop for a strike on an attacking diagonal. Here are three examples of the demolition of a defence.

Bachwinkel – Djordjevic (1975): **1 ♕xd4+!** Black resigned.

Aleksandrov – Pokrovsky (1939): **1 ... ♕xe4+! 2 dxe4 ♗f3+ 3 ♔g1 ♘h3X.**

Stein – Portisch (1962): **1 ♘xg7!** ♗xc4 (1 ... ♔xg7 2 ♗f6+ ♔g6 3 ♕e1)

217

2 ♗f6! The threat is 3 ♘f5+ ♔g8 4 ♘h6X. There is no escape, since on 2 ... ♖fd8 he is immediately put out of his agony by 3 ♘e6+ ♔g8 4 ♕g4X.

2 ... ♗e7 3 ♕f3. Black resigned.

Time is one of the decisive factors in the chess struggle, especially when attacking the king.

Kinnmark – Strom (1927): **1 ♗f6!** Since neither 1 ... gxf6 2 ♕h6, nor 1 ... ♕xf6 2 ♘h6+ suits Black, he replied **1 ... ♕c5+ 2 ♔h1 ♕xc4.** But then there followed the standard but always effective operation **3 ♕h6!**, and Black resigned.

Koretsky – Engert (1942). **1 ♗f6 ♗e5** (if the queen moves then 1 ... ♕c5 2 ♕h6 is decisive) **2 ♘f5!** Black resigned.

Let's look at positions in which the bishop on a short diagonal stalemates the enemy king, blocked by its own pieces. In such cases any check by the knight will be killing.

When, for one reason or another, the king does not manage to get castled and retires with 'his own moves' to the edge of the board, he might suddenly be astonished to discover that his place of residence is occupied by a rook, and that this environment will cast a long-lasting shadow over his life.

In this position from the game Green – Lynn (1919) the rook could deliver a decisive blow on g5 if it were not for the knight e4, controlling the critical square. By creating a threat to deflect the knight, White changes the direction of the main blow.

1 ♘d2 d6 2 ♘xe4! dxe5 3 ♘xf6X

Kazic against Vukovic (1940) did not spare himself even greater expense.

The knight e4 is taking explicit aim at the black kingside. He is firing at the f6 square but it is still holding on.

Volunteers are needed.

1 ♘xe5! ♗xd1 2 ♘d7! ♗e7 (removing himself from the front line crack troops) **3 ♘exf6+ ♗xf6 4 ♖e8+** (a raid on the command post) **4 ... ♕xe8 5 ♘xf6X**.

In the game Golenev – Lokhanin (1962) White, by sacrificing the exchange, has obtained an attacking position, where the principal role is assumed by the brave knight.

1 ♗h6 (not only defending the stray knight, but also threatening to discover check by moving the knight to h5) **1 ... ♔g8 2 ♘e8!** The knight suddenly becomes restless and embarks on a dangerous raid.

2 ... ♕d4+ 3 ♕xd4 ♘xd4 4 ♘c7 ♖b8. The exchange of queens creates the impression that White's attack has petered out. But he still has his reserves.

5 ♖d1 ♘c6?. In reply to 5 ... ♘e6 Black feared the move 6 ♘d5, but 5 ... b5! was worth considering.

6 ♖xd6! For the concluding manoeuvre it is necessary for White to deflect the e7 pawn from its defence of the f6 square.

6 ... exd6 7 ♘e8! A 'quiet' move with major consequences. Mate with the knight on f6 cannot be averted. Black resigned.

A typical method of rapid redeployment of forces from deep defensive lines was illustrated by the game R.Pletner – V.Pletner (1958), in which the father, playing Black, gave his son a useful lesson in tactics.

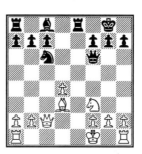

1 ... ♕xf3! 2 gxf3 ♗h3+ 3 ♔g1 ♘xd4. A typical situation has arisen. There is the threat of 4 ... ♘xf3X, attacking the queen. Upon 4 ♗xh7+ ♔h8 5 ♕d3 ♘e2+ 6 ♕xe2 ♖xe2 White's position is completely hopeless.

4 ♕d1 (and this we have already 'studied'...) **4 ... ♖e1+! 5 ♕xe1 ♘xf3X.**

In the following example, access for the bishop to h6 was provided by a rook sacrifice.

Trayanov – Pinkas (1922): **1 ♖xg7! ♕d6.** There is also no salvation in 1 ... ♖b6 2 ♘xb6 ♔xg7 3 ♗h6+ ♔g8 4 ♘d7! (with the threat of 5 ♘f6+ ♕xf6 6 ♕e8X). The main idea of the combination is 1 ... ♔xg7 2 ♗h6+ ♔g8 3 ♕e8+! ♕xe8 4 ♘f6X. But all the same there is no escaping his fate.

2 ♗h6! Black resigned (2 ... ♕xc6 3 ♖g8+! ♔xg8 4 ♘e7X).

Not only the rook, but also the bishop can play the role of uninvited guest.

Bonch-Osmolovsky – Ragozin (1951): **1 ♗h6 ♗h8?? 2 ♘d5!** Black resigned.

It is easy to see that the position in the diagram was 'produced' from the Sicilian Defence. The jump of the knight to d5 and the associated double attack (on the queen a5 and e7 square) has destroyed countless Sicilians.

Every cramped position contains the germ of defeat – said the followers of Steinitz. It would be a mistake to elevate this to a rule, but there is a undoubtedly a grain of truth here.

Semenov – Loginov (1952): **1 ♕f6+!** (the queen, with tempo, frees a square for the knight) **1 ... ♗xf6 2 ♘f7X.**

With an attack on the long castled position a 'special assignment' is carried out by the bishop, located on the h2-b8 (b1-h7) diagonal. We have already drawn attention to its firepower in the 'Two Bishops' chapter. Moreover, if the castled position is weakened by

an advance of the c-pawn, then the knight may strike the enemy king with an unexpected shot from 'behind a corner' – on the a7 (a2) and b6 (b3) squares.

The danger of such a strike occurs when a knight has advanced to the b5 (b4), d5 (d4) and c6 (c3) squares.

Mishneev – Motylev (1971): **1 ... ♕a4!** (the knight is diverted from defence of the critical a2 square, while at the same time mate is threatened on c2) **2 ♗d3 ♗xd3.** White resigned.

Sharokovsky – Mikhnev (1974): **1 ♘xc6!.** Black resigned. The loss of the queen or mate on a7 cannot be averted.

Dikstra – Holaszek (1961): **1 ... ♘xc4 2 ♗xc4 ♕xc4+ 3 ♘c3 ♕xa2!** White resigned.

These methods represent a 'technical passport' to many mating combinations with the participation of knight and bishop.

In a famous game, Consultants – Blackburne (1901) the energetic Englishman took full advantage of a 'gentleman's agreement' to employ tactical means.

1 ... ♕f6 2 c3 ♘b4! 3 ♗c4 (defending against the check on d3) **3 ... ♕a6!** (deflecting the bishop c4) **4 g4 ♕xa2!** (or 4 ... ♕a4) **5 ♗e3** (an attempt to escape) **5 ... ♗xc3.** White resigned.

Planinc (Black) finished the attack beautifully against Vaganian (1974/75).

First he brings his bishop to an attacking position, in the process sacrificing a rook – **1 ... ♗f5! 2 ♕xa8**, then he creates a mating threat – **2 ... ♕d6+ 3 ♔c1 ♘a1!**, and when White defends the b3 square – **4 ♕xb7?**, the enemy queen is deflected with one more sacrifice – **4 ... ♕c7+!** White resigned.

A similar mate was the final objective in the operation carried out by Spassky (White) in his game with Larsen (1978).

1 ♖d6! ♗xd6 2 ♖xd6 ♕c5 3 ♖d5. Black resigned. There might follow 3 ... ♕b6 4 ♕xc4+ ♕c6 5 ♘b5.

And here is a peculiar twist to the story line.

Kunde – Kapfhenkel (1957). White is a rook ahead, and he gladly offers an exchange of queens. However Black carries on 'without authority'.

1 ... ♖c8! 2 ♕xd6. 'If I die – then let it be to the music!' After 2 ♕xc8+ ♗xc8 Black also captures the knight on a8, obtaining a decisive material advantage.

2 ... ⌐xc2+ 3 ♔b1 ⌐c1+ 4 ♔xc1 (the alternative is **4 ♔a2 ♗b1+ 5 ♔a1 ♘c2X**) **4 ... ♘b3X.**

There is no rest for a chess king in the centre. The 'bishop-knight' will catch up with it everywhere.

Mate, as we see, is constructed along the same lines.

Leussen – Duras (1905): **1 ♘7e6+ ♔e8 2 ♕f8+! ♘xf8 3 ♘g7X.**

The mechanism of double check and a queen sacrifice, typical for the 'smothered mate' operation, also frequently accompanies the finales of our theme.

Borik – Novak (1969): **1 ♘d6+ ♔d8 2 ♕e8+ ♘xe8 3 ♘f7X.**

It is enough to catch a glimpse of the position in the game NN – Jankovich (1952), to condemn White's weak play in the opening.

Immediate punishment follows: **1 ... ♘xh2 2 fxe5 ♕xf1+! 3 ♗xf1 ♘f3X.**

Surprises of this kind occur in openings that are played according to the latest word of science and technology.

This position is reached in the Polugaevsky variation of the Sicilian Defence after 1 e4 c5 2 ♘f3 d6 3 d4 cxd4 4 ♘xd4 ♘f6 5 ♘c3 a6 6 ♗g5 e6 7 f4 b5 8 e5 dxe5 9 fxe5 ♕c7 10 ♕e2 ♘fd7 11 0-0-0 ♗b7 12 ♕g4 ♕xe5 13 ♗xb5 axb5 14 ♘cxb5.

The Encyclopaedia of Chess Openings and indeed L.Polugaevsky himself in his book *Birth of a Variation* looked only at 14 ♖he1 h5 with a double-edged, but approximately equal game.

The idea associated with the move **14 ♘cxb5**, was found by grandmaster I. Boleslavsky and he introduced it to his Belarus children in preparation for the All-Union school sports day in 1976.

When the position in the diagram arose in the game Bereznuk (Belorussia) – Izhnin (Ukraine), Black, without hesitation, played according to theory – **14 ... h5** And here is what happened next: **15 ♘c7+! ♕xc7 16 ♘xe6!** (threatening mate on c7) **16 ... ♕e5 17 ♘c7+!!** (extremely impressive: the second knight is sacrificed on the same square!) **17 ... ♕xc7 18 ♕e2+ ♘e5 19 ♕xe5+ ♗e7 20 ♕xc7 ♗xg5+ 21 ♔b1 0-0 22 ♕xb7**, and White won.

It's funny that a year later Black fell into the same net in the game Hoffman – Grunberg. No wonder S.Tartakower called theory a 'short-sighted lady'!

Let's show another surprising mating construction, based on a pin.

Benkovich – Kachaev (1969): **1 ♘xe6! ♕xe5**. He cannot take the knight because of 1 ... fxe6 2 ♕h5+ g6 3 ♗xg6 (or even 3 ♕xg6+) 3 ... hxg6 4 ♗xg6X. Black's move also leads to an immediate climax: **2 ♘c7X!**.

Have you noticed that all the preceding examples featured only queen's bishops? They were herded into a blind alley of black and white kings, which allowed the knights to frolic around. And it is no accident.

You can, of course, produce the same mating situations with the participation of king's bishops, e.g. by moving any of the positions one file to the left or right. But under natural conditions, each pair of opposite-coloured bishops goes to the 'water-hole' and 'hunts' along its habitual paths. The king's bishop has its own well-trodden diagonals. Nor will it turn off these paths when encountering the enemy king and delivering a very heavy offensive against him.

White's position in the game Albin – Shipley (1894) is overwhelming. But it is always nice to find the shortest way to victory.

1 ♘d5! fxg6 (On 1 ... ♔h8 would have followed 2 ♘e5 ♕e8 3 ♘e7) **2 ♘e7+ ♔h8 3 ♘xg6X**.

Spassky (White) had the same finish in mind when embarking on his brilliant combination against Bronstein (1960).

1 ♘xf7! exf1=♕+ 2 ♖xf1 ♔xf7. White is already a rook and minor piece down, and where is the compensation? Here it is: **3 ♘e5+ ♔g8 4 ♕h7+! ♘xh7 5 ♗b3+! ♔h8 6 ♘g6X!**

Alas, this did not happen in the game. Bronstein saw White's intention and did not accept the second sacrifice. After 2 ♖xf1 he tried to pay off with the bishop – 2 ... ♗f5, which, however, did not save him from defeat: 3 ♕xf5 ♕d7 4 ♕f4 ♗f6 5 ♘3e5 ♕e7 6 ♗b3 ♗xe5 7 ♘xe5+ ♔h7 8 ♕e4+. Black resigned.

Sometimes a knight holds his ground on a mating square thanks to a pin. A rook or queen can serve as a 'stopper'.

In the game Wade – Boxall (1953) the white rook pins the h7 pawn. If the f7 pawn were eliminated, then the knight could go to the g6 square with very serious intentions.

The objective is achieved by a simple capture – **1 ♗xf7!**, and Black resigned, since there follows the inevitable 2 ♘g6X with mate or win of the queen.

Subaric – Trifunovic (1947). If it were not for the knight d4, Black would deliver mate with the knight on f3. This circumstance prompts another idea: **1 ... ♕xd4! 2 ♗xd4 ♘f3+ 3 ♔f1 ♗b5+ 4 ♕c4 ♗xc4X**.

The role of the queen, cutting off the f1 square from the white king, is taken by the bishop. The fact that these pieces can interchange on the diagonal allows one of them to be sacrificed.

Smit – Dementiev (1970). After **1 ♘d5 ♕a5+?** (1 ... ♕b8!) **2 b4** Black noticed too late that 2 ... ♕d8 leads to a surprising mate – 3 ♘e6! fxe6 4 ♗h5+. Also there is no escape from a lethal outcome by **2 ... ♕a4 3 ♘c7+ ♔d8 4 ♘de6+! fxe6 5 ♘xe6+ ♔e8 6 ♗h5+ ♖xh5 7 ♕xh5+ g6 8 ♕xg6X**.

In this mating picture the bishop was replaced by the queen, but she has already introduced herself to us in various roles. A similar finish comes against a king placed on the edge file, when the attack is increased. Here a 'special sign' is given by the blocked squares g8 (g1) and g7 (g2).

Boleslavsky – Mosionzhik (1967): **1 ♘gxf5! exf5 2 e6 ♕f6 3 ♕xf5+!** Black resigned (3 ... ♕xf5 4 ♗xf5+ ♔h8 5 ♘g6+ ♔h7 6 ♘e5+ ♔h8 7 ♘f7X. Note the manoeuvre of the knight: it transfers to the mating square with the help of a discovered check.

A means of blockading the king can be traced to the game Sapunov – Bobotsov (1949).

1 ... ♖e8! In this way Black neutralises the opponent's passed

pawn. Now no good is 2 ♕xe8 because of 2 ... ♕d6+ 3 ♔h1 ♘g3+ 4 ♔h2 ♘f1+ and 5 ♔h1 ♕h2X, also bad is 2 ♕xd5 ♗f4+! On 2 ♖f7 follows 2 ... ♖xe7 3 ♕xe7 ♗f4+!.

After **2 ♖xd5** the game ended with a thematic mate: **2 ... ♗f4+ 3 ♔h1 ♘f2+ 4 ♔g1 ♘xh3+ 5 ♔h1 ♕g1+ 6 ♖xg1 ♘f2X**.

Perhaps the most beautiful mating finish came in a game played (by correspondence!) between Tsivits and Gergeya (1970-1972).

1 ... e3! Black wants to play 2 ... exf2. If 2 f3, then 2 ... ♘f2 (with the threat of 3 ... ♘h3 – 4 ... ♕g1X), and 3 ♕d7 does not save him because of 3 ... ♖e6. He has to take the pawn.

2 fxe3 ♕g3! 3 ♔g1 ♕xe3+ 4 ♔h1 ♘f2+ 5 ♔g1 ♘h3+ 6 ♔h1 (now follows a delightful finale) **6 ... ♕g1+!! 7 ♖xg1 ♘f2+ 8 ♔h2 ♗e5X!**

A real anthem to chess combinations!

A bishop can also operate on a very short diagonal, cutting off the king from just one square. In certain situations this will be sufficient.

Wikstrom – Wood (1947). **1 ♕xf7+!** (the f7 pawn, preventing the jump of the knight to g6, is replaced with a piece) **1 ... ♘xf7 2 ♘g6X**.

How such situations arise is shown by the game Soinekken – Shomberg (1957).

1 ♗h7+ ♔f8 2 f4 ♘xe3 Leading to defeat, but also after 2 ... ♘xe5 3 fxe5 Black has a difficult position.

3 ♕e2! ♘xd1?. No help is 3 ... ♘f5 4 ♕h5 g6 (4 ... ♘d6 5 ♕xf7+! ♘xf7 6 ♘g6X) 5 ♗xg6 fxg6 6 ♕xg6.

4 ♕h5 ♗e6 5 ♕xf7+! ♗xf7 6 ♘d7X

As distinct from the previous example, here he had to deflect the

bishop from its control over the d7 square.

In the game Perenyi – Eperjesi (1974) Black, although truly in a difficult position, blithely played **1 ... bxc5?**. It did not take long for the punishment: **2 ♘c6 ♕c7 3 ♕xe6+!** and Black resigned (3 ... fxe6 4 ♗g6X).

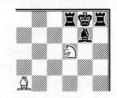

The danger of a mating finish according to the first pattern could arise even at the very start of the game.

Buckley – NN (1840): **1 e4 c5 2 ♘f3 d6 3 ♘c3 e5 4 ♗c4 ♘c6 5 d3 ♘ge7 6 ♗g5 ♗g4 7 ♘d5 ♘d4?** When two people do the same thing ...

8 ♘xe5! ♗xd1 (the lesser evil was 8 ... dxe5 9 ♕xg4) **9 ♘f6+ gxf6 10 ♗xf7X**.

Aronin – Kantorovich (1960): **1 e4 c5 2 ♘f3 g6 3 c3 b6 4 d4 ♗b7 5 ♗c4 d5? 6 exd5 ♗xd5? 7 ♕a4+ ♗c6**.

8 ♘e5! Black resigned.

By a peculiar coincidence, similar action is also taken against a king in its residence on the flank.

Look at the poor knight on h1 in the game Beinke – Danburg (1956).

Such a 'stable' is clearly not by choice but then, encouraged by the enemy, came **1 ... hxg3 2 ♘xg3 ♖h1+! 3 ♘xh1** (3 ♔xh1 ♕h7+) **3 ... ♗h2X**.

'Discovered mate' requires no less dense packing of the king.

Romanishin – Poutiainen (1977): **1 ♕g6!** Black resigned (1 ... fxg6 2 ♘f6X).

A bishop and knight helped by a king will always win against an opponent's lone king. Capitulation is usually forced in the corner of the board.

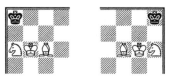

It is easy to see that mate is achieved only in a corner of the same colour as a bishop: with a dark-squared bishop – on the a1 or h8 squares, and the light-squared one – on a8 and b1. But to reach the final position, it is necessary to push the opponent's king into the fatal corner, and this task is not as simple as it may seem at first glance.

A well-known case was when the Kiev master E. Polyak failed to solve it within the given rule of 50 moves, and the game ended in a draw. "Why didn't you drive the enemy king into the right corner?" asked his comrades.

"I was driving, but it wouldn't go," – said the bewildered master.

And indeed, there are certain difficulties in driving back the king, because it constantly strives to break free. The fact is that, unlike the rook or two bishops, which spread a thick veil over the enemy king, the bishop and knight are capable of cutting off the king only when there is ideal coordination, and even then it's just on a limited section of the board.

To deliver the mate White must travel a long and difficult path, which is divided into three stages:

1) driving back the black king from the centre to the edge of the board;

2) driving him into one of the black corners (a1 or h8);

3) direct mate.

Already during the implementation of the immediate objective, assistance should be sought from one's king.

1 ♔b2 ♚c4 2 ♔c2 ♚d4 3 ♗f6+ ♚e4 4 ♔c3 ♚f5 5 ♗d4 ♚e4 6 ♘d2+ ♚d5 7 ♔d3. Now the black king must leave the central squares, yielding the 5th rank. **7 ... ♚d6 8 ♔e4 ♚e6 9 ♘c4.** A zugzwang position: the white pieces have put together an insurmountable barrier and the black king is again forced to retreat. It is clear that he is heading for the safety of the white corner.

9 ... ♚e7 10 ♚f5 ♚d7 11 ♚e5 ♚c6 12 ♘d6. Also here the white pieces purposefully limit the freedom of movement of the black king, forcing it step by step to retreat to the edge of the board.

12 ... ♚d7 13 ♚d5 ♚c7 14 ♗f6 ♚d7 15 ♘b5. One of those positions with a most harmonious coordination of pieces, creating a 'dynamic barrier' in front of the enemy king. **15 ... ♚c8 16 ♚c6 ♚b8 17 ♘c7 ♚a7 18 ♗d4+ ♚b8 19 ♗b6 ♚c8.**

White gets to work on the second task: to prevent the black king from escaping into the open, he drives it into the corner at h8.

20 ♗a7 ♚d8 21 ♘d5 ♚e8 (21 ... ♚c8 22 ♘e7+ ♚d8 23 ♚d6) **22 ♚d6 ♚f7 23 ♘e7! ♚f6 24 ♗e3!** White's last two moves are perhaps the most difficult. The black king's hopes of freedom are shown to be illusory.

24 ... ♚f7 25 ♗d4 ♚e8 26 ♚e6 ♚d8 27 ♗b6+ ♚e8. To conclude the driving away of the king, White repeats a manoeuvre already familiar to us.

28 ♘f5 ♚f8 29 ♗d4 ♚e8 30 ♗f6 ♚f8 31 ♗e7+ ♚g8 32 ♚f6 ♚h7 33 ♚f7 ♚h8

The objective is achieved, the end is nigh. Keep in mind the mating mechanism: **34 ♔g6 ♚g8 35 ♘h6+ ♚h8 36 ♗f6X**.

Here are two more mating patterns, to some extent copies of the previous finish.

In a blitz game Vasyukov – Frankel (1973) an amusing position was reached – which required only half a board.

The tragi-comic position of the black king suggests the solution: **1 ♔e5 d4 2 ♔d6! d3 3 ♔e7 d2 4 ♔f8 d1=♕ 5 ♗g7X**. Funny how none of the black pieces can prevent the manoeuvre of the white king.

Furthermore this idea was seen in a study by I.Kotz and K.Kockelkorn (1875).

White mates in 5 moves

It seems that White can achieve his objective very quickly: 1 ♗b2, 2 ♗a3, 3 ♗f8, 4 ♗g7X, since the zigzag of the bishop cannot be prevented. However in this case there is an indirect defence: 1 ♗b2 ♗h1! 2 ♗a3 g2 3 ♗f8 – stalemate. If, however, 3 ♔f2, then mate is delivered only on the 6th move.

The solution: **1 ♗e5! ♗h1 2 ♗xg3** and only now **2 ... ♗g2 3 ♗d6 ♗h3 4 ♗f8** and **5 ♗g7X**.

Let's now look at a few mating patterns in which a pawn lends a hand to the knight and bishop. Pawns often serve as guards at the royal chamber.

Looking at the situation from the game Jouy – La Bourdonnais (1824), the first impression is that Black's attack has landed in a blind alley. But the famous French player had prepared a decisive tactical operation.

1 ... ♘xd4! 2 ♕xe4+. The threat was 2 ... ♘f3X. On 2 ♗xe4 would have followed 2 ... gxh2+ 3 ♔xh2 ♗e5+. If 2 cxd4, then first 2 ... ♗xd4+ 3 ♗e3 gxh2+, and then as in the previous variation. Now, however, everything is perfectly simple.

2 ... ♕xe4 3 ♗xe4 ♘e2X.
The power of the double check was realised in the following game between two unknown amateurs (1965).

1 f6 (moving the pawn up to the main line of resistance and creating the threat of mate on g7) **1 ... ♖g8 2 ♕h7+! ♔xh7 3 ♘g5+ ♔h8 4 ♘f7X.**

In the game Virtanen – Berkvist (1974) mate was achieved after a rook sacrifice and an exchange of queens.

1 ♖g8+! ♕xg8 2 ♕g7+ ♕xg7+ 3 fxg7+ ♔g8 4 ♘e7X.

Rogul – Zemkov (1977): **1 g6 ♖h1 2 g7+ ♔g8 3 ♘d6!** (threatening **4 ♗c4X**) **3 ... ♖xh6 4 ♘e8! ♖h2+ 5 ♔g3.** Black resigned.

Sometimes the final blow is delivered by a pawn, and the pieces support it, at the same time taking away free squares from the enemy king. Also in these cases the idea of a tactical operation arises thanks to the far advanced pawn, which finds itself at the spearhead of the attack.

Molotkovsky – Deacon (1913): **1 ♕h5+ ♔f8 2 ♗a3+ ♔g8 3 ♕f7+! ♘xf7 4 exf7X.**

Rosh – Krumbach (1918): **1 fxg6! ♗xg4 2 ♘f6+ ♔h8 3 g7X.**

230

In the game Stark – Berthold (1962) the tactical blow was preceded by a subtle manoeuvre.

1 ♕f2 (threatening mate on f7) **1 ... ♗g6**, but now White has already regrouped for a decisive thrust: **2 ♕f7+ ♗xf7 3 exf7X**.

* * * *

313. Gundin – Gurinau, 1915

White to move

This and the next four tactical positions are designed for you to solve instantly.

314. Feld – Tenner, 1933

Black to move

315. I.Rabinovich – Goglidze, 1939

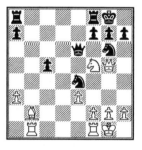

White to move

316. Gutman – Zhdanov, 1948

Black to move

231

317. Maeder – Zunker, 1973

White to move

1 ♗h6 ♗h8? And one more move ...

318. Roizman – Khalilbeili, 1962

White to move

'White rhapsody.'

319 Gitman – Andrlik, 1960

White to move

The last inch.

320. Foldi – Florian, 1958

White to move

Is 1 ♕xb7 good?

321. Shutov – Korostilev, 1968

White to move

A house of cards.

322. Marriott – Arnold, 1938

White to move

Is the knight on d6 in a trap?

323. Rogoff – Bertok, 1971

White to move

This happened in blitz.

324. Steinberg – Gulnin, 1968

White to move

On a precarious throne.

325. Bogda – Ferreira, 1976

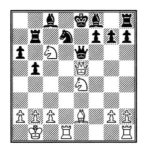

White to move

From Leningrad across to ... Odessa.

326. Mudrov – Henkin, 1958

Black to move

Taking a detour.

327 Ozvath – Ertel, 1970

White to move

1 ♘g4 ♗xg2. Take the exchange (2 ♗h6+) or ...

328. NN – Bird, 1978

Black to move

The pinned castled position.

329 Uhlmann – Liebert, 1976

Black to move

Such a long-range bishop ...

330. Zhuravlev – Glotov, 1962

White to move

Centre and flanks.

331. Elsykov – Ermakov, 1969

Black to move

A bishop in the ambush.

332. Kapsenberg – Norman, 1946

White to move

Infantry dying in battle.

333. Pagenkopf – Gusky, 1958

White to move

Close the gun-port!

334. Ahues – NN, 1934

White to move

The queen is a bad blockader.

234

335. Alekhine – Fletcher, 1928

White to move

The mill.

336. Kopilov – Karlsson, 1961

Black to move

Sheer unpleasantness.

337. J.Roth, 1974

White mates in 3 moves

Forced modesty – also beautifies.

338. W.Speckmann, 1956

White mates in 4 moves

Confused infantry.

339 T.Erlen, 1845

White mates in 4 moves

Masquerade.

340. Z.Birnov, 1952

White to move and win

The black knight is hunted ... but it is the king who dies.

341. *T.Gorgiev, 1938* 342. *G.Nadareishvili, 1947*

White to move and win *White to move and win*

Suddenly a pair of rooks are exchanged and the remaining rook battles against the opponent's minor pieces.

Neither respite nor rest for the exhausted rook.

* * * *

"To be able to withstand a determined attack and repulse an offensive is a great art. When retreating, one should not regard the game as lost because it might be the case that your game will turn from defence into attack."

A.Petrov

"Correct defence is that which has the intention of transferring to attack ... The defender should constantly think about this fact so that he will not miss the moment to go over to the offensive."

S.Urusov

"There never was a master who combined the art of attack and defence to such an extent as Chigorin."

H.Pillsbury

"You should protect your king with the least possible number of pieces. You can only exploit a superiority in pieces when attacking the opponent's king."

J.R.Capablanca

"To defend on technical-strategical, indeed also psychological grounds, is considerably more difficult than conducting an attack."

R.Spielmann

"In general, there are probably no or almost no completely original, new combinations. But in every tournament it is possible to find a fresh arrangement of the original colours of a combination that is already known."

M.Tal

12. Queen and Bishop

Once upon a time, in the days of chatrang, the queen and bishop were the poor relations of the noble chess family. Both barely hobbled along their diagonals, the queen – to one square, the bishop – over a square. For several centuries they languished in darkness and obscurity, while 'land reform' did not allot them a greater expanse of terrain on the chess board. The queen, it is true, later obtained a far greater area than the bishop. But inequality of property rights to some extent was smoothed over by common 'diagonal interests'.

The queen is a universal piece. In all military campaigns she can take the place of a rook or either bishop – with success. And this means that all mating constructions, in which there is at least one of the linear pieces, allow the participation of the queen as an equivalent substitute. Therefore the circle of mating finishes significantly expands and the probability of a successful attack increases, since the queen is capable on its own of taking away the maximum number of squares from the enemy king. The interaction of the queen with other pieces has its own specifics, since it is basically its individual properties that determine the particular methods and techniques of conducting an attack.

The queen and the bishop quickly find a common language when it comes to attacks on the enemy castled position. The topic of their conversation is often the h7 (h2) square, a long way from the main defensive forces and easy prey for the joint attack of long-range pieces.

The queen can deliver a final blow in all directions accessible to it – along the h-file, along the penultimate rank and along the b1-h7 (h2-b8 diagonal). Upon a diagonal attack the queen flies to its target like an arrow shot from a bow. The impression is such as if the bishop is jostling the queen, telling her to speed up. Meanwhile the remaining pieces helpfully clear a path or lure the enemy into the attack in order that 'his excellency', God forbid, will not miss the mark.

Mitchell – Madsen (1967). The noose is pulled tight. But an immediate strike turns out to be a blank shot, since the white king will escape through the

'underground passage'. So the rook diverts the enemy king to charm its own queen: **1 ... ♖h1+!** White resigned.

Gnauk – Böhm (1977): **1 ♗xf6 gxf6** (one guard is eliminated but another takes his place – the rook e7 ...) **2 ♘xd5! exd5 3 ♖xe7** (... but not for long). Black resigned.

Maderna – Villegas (1943). Here the first minister protects the approaches to the king himself. This does not save the army. **1 ♗g7+.** Black resigned.

Shereshevsky – Kupreychik (1976). **1 ... ♘d3** (Opening a double attack, he threatens mate on h2, the bishop on b2 is 'hanging') **2 ♗xh7+? ♔h8** (2 ... ♔xh7? 3 ♕xd3+) **3 ♕h5**. It seems that White is the first to open fire, but a dashing cavalry charge changes the picture of the battle.

3 ... ♘f4 4 ♕h4 ♘h3+! An unexpected interference. White resigned.

When the queen is on a sharp attacking diagonal, the main tactical device becomes the destruction of the enemy castled position.

Troger – Weise (1964). All Black's pieces are on the attack, the offensive has reached a critical point: **1 ... ♖xg3 2 fxg3 ♖xg2+ 3 ♔xg2 ♕xg3+ 4 ♔h1 ♕h2X**.

The destruction of the castled position often starts with the elimination or diversion of the base pawn f7 (f2).

Tolush – Niemela (1959): **1 ♘xf7!**, and on the capture of the knight follows a forced mate – **1 ... ♔xf7 2 ♕xg6+ ♔f8 3 ♕xh6+ ♔g8 4 ♗h7+ ♔f7 5 ♕g6+ ♔f8 6 ♕g8X**.

Perhaps the most logical exploitation of this method was shown by Capablanca (White) against Jaffe (1910).

1 ♖xe6! ♘f6. Of course, the rook cannot be taken: 1 ... fxe6 2 ♕xg6+ ♔h8 3 ♕h7X.

2 ♘e5! c5. After 2 ... ♗xe5 3 ♖xe5 White has an extra pawn and a winning position. As before, 2 ... fxe6 is bad because of 3 ♕xg6! ♔h8 4 ♕xh6+ ♔g8 5 ♕g6+ ♔h8 6 ♗g5 ♕e7 7 ♘g4. **3 ♗xh6+! ♔xh6 4 ♘xf7+!**.

Capablanca has carried out his plan: the king's pawn barrier has been destroyed. Black resigned.

A diagonal attack requires that the bishop is behind the queen. The initiative to reorganise the pieces, according to the master plan, might be in the hands of any of the actors.

Heinicke – Pfeiffer (1957): **1 ... b5! 2 axb5 ♗a7!** White resigned. There is no defence against the manoeuvre ♗a7-b8 with an imminent landing of aircraft on h2.

Johner – Bialas (1962): **1 ♕c1! ♗g4 2 ♕c2.** White is all ready to pull the trigger.

2 ... ♗h8 3 ♖f4! ♗h5 4 ♖h4 ♕f7. Black will not manage to neutralise the diagonal with the move 4 ... ♗g6 because of 5 ♖g4.

5 e5! dxe5 6 ♖xh5 ♕xh5 7 ♕h7+ ♔f8 8 ♗g6 ♕xg6 9 ♕xg6 ♖e8 10 ♗xe5 Black resigned (10 ... ♖xe5 11 ♖xe5 fxe5 12 ♕d6+ or 10 ... fxe5 11 ♖f1+).

Regrouping of the pieces noticeably increases their firepower if the diagonal leading to the king has been weakened by pawn moves. This method works perfectly when there is an attack on the long castled position.

Ed.Lasker – Yates (1924). It is striking that the queen and bishop on the b1-h7 diagonal are not in the order that Black would want. But is it possible to swap them around? The gallant bishop has no objection ...

1 ... ♕f7! 2 ♗h6 ♗g6 3 ♗xg7 ♕f5!, and upon the forced **4 ♕d3** Black

obtains the advantage after 4 ... ♕xd3 5 ♖xd3 ♗xd3 6 ♗xf8 ♖xf8 (In the game 4 ... ♔xg7!? was played).

The same manoeuvre in the game Rabinovich – Romanovsky (1925) brought Black immediate victory.

1 ... ♗g6 2 ♕a4 b5! (not at once 2 ... ♕f5, on which White defends 'à la Lasker' – with the move 3 ♕e4 **3 ♕xa3**, and only now **3 ... ♕f5!** White resigned. If 4 ♕b3, then 4 ... ♖ac8.

Karpov – Hort (1978): **1 ♕e5!** (preventing the move ♗f8-d6 and taking advantage of the open door to the king's refuge on the queen's flank) **1 ... ♖g8 2 0-0-0 g6 3 ♖e1 ♗g7 4 ♕b8+ ♔e7 5 ♖xe6+!** Black resigned (5 ... ♕xe6 6 ♕c7+ ♕d7 7 ♗d6X).

If, for one reason or another, he cannot regroup his forces, the bishop will try to build a 'pontoon bridge' for the queen.

Augustin – Lanz (1975): **1 ♗e8! ♕f5 2 ♖e6!** Black resigned.

Upon a frontal assault along the h-file, the queen can be thrown into the epicentre of the attack, according to the system already familiar to us of 'zero-transportation'.

Sarkisova – Nizhgorodova (1976): **1 ... ♘xh2! 2 ♔xh2 ♕h4+ 3 ♔g1 ♖xf2! 4 ♘f5** (4 ♖xf2 ♗xg3) **4 ... ♗xf5 5 ♕xf5 ♖xg2+! 6 ♔xg2 ♕g3+**. White resigned.

And here are two examples of a bayonet attack.

Manov – Hairabedian (1962): **1 ... ♗e2!** (clearing the file) **2 ♘xe2 ♖h8+ 3 ♔g1 ♖h1+ 4 ♔xh1 ♖h8+ 5 ♔g1 ♖h1+ 6 ♔xh1 ♕h8+**, and mate on the next move.

Sometimes a preparatory bombardment precedes the breakthrough.

Cochrane – Staunton (1842): **1 ... ♘xh3+ 2 gxh3 ♖g4+!** (2 ... ♕xh3 3 ♘f4) **3 hxg4 ♕h2X**.

Herman – Charousek (1896): **1 ... f3! 2 gxf3 ♗xh3 3 ♖g1 ♕h5 4 ♖g5 ♕h4 5 ♔g1**. It's easy to see that all White's replies were forced. The second wave of attack starts with a series of stunning blows, the aim of which is to prevent the enemy king from seeking refuge.

5 ... ♗h2+! 6 ♔h1. Bad is 6 ♔xh2 ♗f1+, and White loses the queen.

6 ... ♗f1! 7 ♕d1. He cannot capture on f1 because of 7 ... ♗g3+ with mate on h2. Now, however, in the event of 7 ... ♗g3+ 8 ♔g1 White, by attacking the bishop on f1, gains a tempo for the defence.

7 ... ♗e2! Forcing closure of the last loophole for the king. White resigned. On any capture of the selfless bishop follows 8 ... ♗g3+ with mate in two moves.

Pak – Pyatov (1970): **1 f5! exf5.** The threat was 2 f6. If 1 ... ♖g8, then 2 fxg6 fxg6 3 ♖f7.

2 ♖xf5! This move is decisive, since it is bad to take the rook because of 3 ♗xf5, and the h7 square is defenceless. Meanwhile ♖f5-h5 is threatened.

2 ... ♗c5 3 ♔h1! The simplest. Black resigned (3 ... ♗xe3 4 ♕xf8X).

The combined effort of queen and bishop sets in motion a particular mating mechanism.

Kotenko – Balendo (1977): **1 ... ♖xe3!** (in order that the wheel is in full spin, it is necessary to deprive the f2 square of defence) **2 ♖xe3** (2 fxe3 ♕h2+ 3 ♔f1 ♗g3 leads to another mating pattern) **2 ... ♗h2+ 3 ♔h1 ♗g3+ 4 ♔g1 ♕h2+ 5 ♔f1 ♕xf2X.**

This mechanism is universal, it meets 'international standards' and unfailingly

operates in the most varied terrain of the chess landscape.

Sokolsky – Kofman (1948). Another moment and 1 ... 0-0-0. Stop, a moment!

1 ♘f7! ♔xf7 (1 ... ♖g8 2 ♕xh7) **2 ♖f1+ ♔c8 3 ♖xf8+.** Black resigned. After 3 ... ♔xf8 the machine starts to work in automatic mode: 4 ♕xe7+ ♔g8 5 ♕e6+ ♔f8 6 ♗e7+ ♔e8 and now on request 7 ♗f6+ ♔f8 8 ♕e7+ ♔g8 9 ♕xg7X or 7 ♗xd6+ ♔d8 8 ♕e7+ ♔c8 9 ♕xc7X.

The opponent tries to cover his Achilles' heel by all available means. One of his defensive resources is the advance of an anti-bishop hedgehog on f5. But for every armour there is an armour-piercing shell.

Safonov – Kutepov (1954). On 1 ♕h5 Black replies 1 ... f5, closing the diagonal, and in the event of 2 exf6 ♘xf6 he brings up the reserves to a dangerous zone of the battle. White carries out a typical operation to blockade the enemy forces.

1 ♘f6+! gxf6. What to do next? If 2 ♕h5?, then 2 ... f5 and the bishop's path to the king is shielded.

2 ♕g4+! ♔h8 3 ♕h4!. The queen must attack h7 namely from this square, where it simultaneously pins the f6 pawn without allowing it to make a saving step forward. Black resigned.

This device happens quite often. Here is one opening trap with a similar ending.

Queen's Pawn Opening
Engels – Badenstein, 1937

1 c4 ♘f6 2 ♘f3 e6 3 ♘c3 d5 4 e3 ♗e7 5 b3 0-0 6 ♗b2 b6 7 d4 ♗b7 8 ♗d3 dxc4 9 bxc4 c5 10 0-0 cxd4 11 exd4 ♘c6 12 ♕e2

12 ... ♘xd4? Black gobbles a poisoned pawn. 12 ... ♖e8 is correct.

13 ♘xd4 ♕xd4 14 ♘d5! ♕c5 15 ♗xf6! gxf6 If 15 ... ♗xf6, then 16 ♕e4, attacking h7 and threatening 17 ♘xf6+ winning the bishop b7.

16 ♘xe7+ ♕xe7 17 ♕g4+! ♔h8 18 ♕h4! The f6 pawn is nailed to the spot. Black resigned.

Dealing with pawns often becomes the main tactical content of the struggle. Let's get acquainted with the two typical methods of blocking.

Dorfman – Romanishin (1977). For better or worse, but on 1 ... ♗e5? White replies 2 f4, avoiding immediate danger. With a sacrifice of a piece Romanishin eliminates one of the pawns, forcing the opponent to block the other: **1 ... ♗xf3+!** White resigned. After 2 ♗xf3 ♗e5 the king freezes like a rabbit under the gaze of a boa constrictor.

Fischer – Benko (1966): **1 ♗xd4.** The introduction to a combination. White frees the way of the e4 pawn, so that if need be he can open the diagonal for the bishop d3.

1 ... exd4. Now 2 e5 suggests itself, but this continuation is premature, after 2 ... f5 Black maintains equality.

2 ♖f6! An excellent move, blocking the f7 pawn. On 2 ... ♗xf6 or 2 ... dxc3 would of course follow 3 e5.

2 ... ♔g8 3 e5 h6 4 ♘e2!. Black resigned: if 4 ... ♘b5, then 5 ♕f5, and no good is 4 ... ♗xf6 5 ♕xh6.

The queen can attack the h7 (h2) square via the 7th (2nd) rank. But this requires good calculation.

Quinteros – Henley (1976): **1 ℤxg6+! fxg6 2 ℤxg6+ ♔xg6 3 ♗e4+ ♔g7 4 ♕c7+.** Black resigned.

Pogacs – Gever (1978): **1 ... ℤf3! 2 ♘b7** (after 2 ♔g1 ♕a7+ 3 ♔h1 ℤxf1+ 4 ♕xf1 ♕d7 5 ♕f6 ♗c7 and the knight d8 is caught in a trap) **2 ... ℤxh3+ 3 ♔g1 ♕a7+ 4 ℤf2 ♗g3.** White resigned.

In the game Zita – Grynfeld (1950) Black has just played e6-e5, reckoning on pushing back the rook d4 and strengthening the position of the king with a retreat of the knight to g8.

White produces a combination with a masked final manoeuvre: **1 gxf6! exd4 2 fxg7+ ♔xg7 3 ♕g4+ ♔h8** (3 ... ♔f7 4 ♕f5+) **4 ♕xd4+ ♔g8 5 ♕a7!** (not 5 ℤg3+? ♕xg3+ 6 fxg3 ℤe1+ with perpetual check). Now, however, Black resigned, since not one square on the 7th rank is accessible to his pieces and he cannot defend the h7 square.

The double attack is a powerful tactical weapon, capable of firing a round of ammunition. Joining forces with the bishop to create a threat of mate on h7, the queen is able to simultaneously attack a considerable number of squares. If in its sphere of activity come undefended pieces or pawns, then they will perish, since first of all the defending side must secure its king.

The threat of a double attack usually occurs when there is an offensive along a diagonal. Practice shows that the queen most often delivers a blow from the e4 (e5) square. In this case a side objective should be sought on the d5-a8 (a1-d4) section of the diagonal or on the 4th (5th) rank.

Attack and defence are the basic means of struggle in chess. Double attack is one aspect of attack and often occurs already in the opening.

Thus, in the French Defence after the moves **1 e4 e6 2 d4 d5 3 ♘c3 ♘f6 4 ♗g5 dxe4 5 ♘xe4 ♘bd7 6 ♘f3 ♗e7 7 ♘xf6+ ♘xf6 8 ♗d3 0-0 9 ♕e2 b6?** arises a well-known theoretical position.

The correct continuation here is ... c5. However the desire to introduce the bishop c8 to the game as quickly as possible induces the careless chess player to make the erroneous move **9 ... b6?**. It is refuted by a typical tactical device: **10 ♗xf6 ♗xf6 11 ♕e4**. Now Black has the rook a8 and h7 square under threat. This is a classic example of a double attack.

Within reach of the queen are also other unprotected or inadequately protected figures. In the game Erglis – Krumkali (1950) this piece was the knight c6.

Under pressure from his opponent, Geller (White) against Tseshkovsky (1974) thought up an exchanging operation: **1 ♖xf5 ♖xf5 2 ♖xf5**, reckoning on 2 ... ♖xg2 3 ♔xg2 ♕xf5 4 ♕e2 with approximate equality. Tseshkovsky, however, 'raised an objection' – **2 ... d4!** 3 ♗a5 (3 ♗d2 ♖xd2 or 3 ♗xd4 ♖e1+) **3 ... ♖e5**. White resigned, since after 4 ♖xe5 (4 g4 ♖xf5 does not change matters) 4 ... ♕xe5 surprisingly the h2 square and the bishop a5 come under threat.

1 d5! exd5 Black has no choice: 1 ... ♘xd5 2 ♘xd5 exd5 3 ♗xe7 loses a piece.

2 ♗xf6 ♗xf6 3 ♘xd5 ♕d6 4 ♘xf6+ ♕xf6. The exchange of pieces, defending the h7 square, also cleared a section of the diagonal on which the knight is barely maintained. And it is the knight that becomes White's prey.

5 ♕e4. Black resigned.

Playing against Tolush in 1959, a certain NN decided to win a pawn in a cunning way – **1 ... ♘xd5**. He does win a pawn, but after **2 ♕xd5 ♗xh4 3 ♕e4** loses a bishop.

With the same ambiguous intentions the queen may also attend to other squares. Accordingly, it shuffles around also with supplementary objectives.

In the following example Black's 1st move already turned out to be a complete surprise for the opponent.

Musil – Karpov (1975): **1 ... ♘f4!
2 ♖d2** After 2 gxf4 ♕xf4 in his sights
are two targets – h2 and c1.

2 ... ♘c3 3 gxf4 (to tolerate such
knights is beyond human endurance)
**3 ... ♕xf4 4 ♖xc3 ♕xh2+ 5 ♔f1 ♕h1+
6 ♗g1 ♗h2**. White resigned.

In some situations, the attack on the
h7 (h2) pawn distracts the opponent
from other defensive duties, and then
his pieces and pawns are left
undefended against blows by the
queen.

Henkin – Lebedev (1961): **1 ♘xd4
exd4 2 ♕a5!** S.Tarrasch said: "If one
piece stands badly – the whole game is
bad". Black loses because of the poor
position of the knight on a6, which has
to lose time saving itself.

2 ... ♘c7 3 ♕f5. A long queen
manoeuvre has led to a position in
which Black can only avoid mate by
the move **3 ... g6**. But then the bishop
f6 is left unprotected. Therefore Black
resigned.

A rarely seen double attack by the
bishop.

In the game Filipovic – Silva (1962)
Black played **1 ... ♘xe4**, hoping to
maintain equality after 2 ♕f5? d5.
White, however, had prepared a
beautiful blow: **2 ♖c7! ♕xc7 3 ♗xe4**,
and Black resigned, since he is left a
piece down.

Another kind of double attack is
illustrated by the conclusion of the
game Vasyukov – Holmov (1964).

1 ♘xc5 ♕xc5 2 ♗xg7! ♗xg7 3 ♕h5.
He not only threatens mate on h7, but
also 4 ♗xh7+. Black resigned.

Finally, a curiosity which cost the
loser dearly.

In this position the Romanian master Marco, playing Black against Popiel, resigned, assuming that he would lose the pinned bishop on d4.

Meanwhile he could have won if he had noticed the surprising shot **1 ... ♗g1!** with a simultaneous attack on the h2 square and the queen d3.

But here Trifunovic (White) against Aaron (1962) did not miss such a chance.

In reply to **1 ... ♖b6?** he played **2 ♗g8!** and forced the opponent's immediate resignation.

The hottest point in the starting position of the chess armies is the f7 (f2) square. While the king remains uncastled, he has to personally oversee his own safety. This menial task is not for a piece in whose veins flows blue blood. Meanwhile, it is sufficient to introduce the bishop to c4 (c5), and real danger is not far off.

For 'educational' purposes we mention the world famous 'Scholar's mate' – **1 e4 e5 2 ♗c4 ♘c6 3 ♕h5 ♘f6 4 ♕xf7X** – and proceed to a more instructive example.

In the Philidor Defence after the moves **1 e4 e5 2 ♘f3 d6 3 d4 ♘d7 4 ♗c4** there arises a position in which inexperienced chess players, fearing the thrust ♘f3-g5, anticipate it by **4 ... ♗e7?**.

This move loses at least a pawn – 5 dxe5 ♘xe5 6 ♘xe5 dxe5 7 ♕h5, simultaneously attacking f7 and e5, while after 5 ... dxe5 – a whole piece because of the simple 6 ♕d5!, and the f7 square is defenceless (6 ... ♘h6 7 ♗xh6).

The correct continuation (in place of 4 ... ♗e7?) is 4 ... c6 (5 ♘g5 ♘h6) 5 0-0, and only now 5 ... ♗e7, since the d5 square is inaccessible to the queen.

The danger of a double attack, one of the objects of which is the f7 (f2) square, arises already in the opening. Even in those cases where the king has managed to castle, he cannot feel safe, particularly if the king's rook has already left the f8 square.

By way of illustration we offer a few disasters that occurred in different openings.

Spanish Game
Mohrlok – Kramer, 1962

**1 e4 e5 2 ♘f3 ♘c6 3 ♗b5 a6 4 ♗a4
d6 5 d4 b5 6 ♗b3 ♘xd4 7 ♘xd4 exd4
8 c3.** A correct sacrifice of a pawn.
After 8 ... dxc3 9 ♘xc3 White has an
advantage in development and a good
game. On the other hand, 8 ♕xd4? is a
mistake because of 8 ... c5. Now it
seems that White can deliver a double
attack – 9 ♕d5, but on this follows
9 ... ♗e6 10 ♕c6+ ♗d7 11 ♕d5 c4, and
Black wins a piece.

8 ... d3 (losing time, better is
8 ... ♗b7 9 cxd4 ♘f6) **9 a4 ♗d7**
(inaccurate, 9 ... ♖b8 is correct)
10 axb5 axb5? But this is already
the decisive mistake. Necessary was
10 ... ♗xb5, though after 11 ♘a3 ♗d7
12 ♕xd3 White has an appreciable
advantage.

11 ♕h5! The roar of thunder! The f7
square can be defended only by the
move 11 ... g6, but then follows
12 ♕d5! with a simultaneous attack on
the same ill-fated square and the rook
a8.

11 ... d2+. The so-called 'check
before dying', albeit in the faint hope of
12 ♘xd2? ♘h6.

12 ♗xd2. Black resigned.

In one of the variations of the
Spanish game after the moves **1 e4 e5**

**2 ♘f3 ♘c6 3 ♗b5 a6 4 ♗a4 ♘f6
5 ♕e2 b5 6 ♗b3 ♗e7 7 c3 d6 8 a4**
arises a well-known theoretical position.

Here 8 ... ♖b8 or 8 ... ♘a5 is played,
only not **8 ... b4?** because of **9 ♕c4!**
with a double attack on f7 and c6.

As you can see, the rotation of the
queen on the board may bring untold
disasters.

Caro-Kann Defence
Borges – Rocha, 1933

**1 d4 d5 2 ♘c3 c6 3 e4 dxe4 4 ♘xe4
♗f5 5 ♘g3 ♗g6 6 h4 h6 7 ♘f3 ♘d7
8 ♗c4 e6 9 ♕e2 ♗d6 10 0-0 ♘gf6
11 ♘e5 ♗h7?** Obligatory was 11 ... ♗xe5
12 dxe5 ♘d5.

12 ♘xf7! Black resigned: 12 ... ♔xf7
13 ♕xe6+ leads to mate.

We are familiar with the knight
sacrifice on f7, smoking the king out of
its refuge and opening the a2-g8

diagonal for a coordinated attack by the queen and bishop. This sacrifice is met very frequently in tournament practice.

French Defence
Van Steenis – Gommes, 1939

1 e4 e6 2 d4 d5 3 ♘d2 dxe4 4 ♘xe4 ♘d7 5 ♘f3 ♘gf6 6 ♗d3 b6 7 0-0 ♗b7 8 ♕e2 ♗e7 9 ♖e1 0-0 10 ♘eg5 ♖e8?

Unlike the previous game Black has already managed to castle, but the scheme of attack remains unchanged.
11 ♘xf7! ♗xf3 12 gxf3. Black resigned: after 12 ... ♔xf7 13 ♕xe6+ ♔f8 14 ♗c4 mate in unstoppable.

But operations do not always proceed so smoothly.

In the game Cheremisin – Myasnikov (1960) after the obvious sacrifice **1 ♘xf7 ♔xf7** White played **2 d6+!**.

But why not at once 2 ♕e6+ ♔f8 3 d6 ? In this case White must reckon on the possible defence: 3 ... ♗d5 4 ♖xd5 exd6, and it is necessary to sacrifice further a bishop (5 ♗xd6+), which leads to not quite clear consequences. But after 2 d6+! there is already no sense in 2 ... ♗d5 3 ♖xd5. Also no good is 2 ... e6 3 ♗xe6+ ♔f8 4 dxc7 ♕c8 5 ♗d6+, and likewise 2 ... ♔f8 3 dxc7 ♕c8 4 ♕e6.

Black replied **2 ... ♘d5**, but after **3 ♕e6+ ♔f8 4 ♖xd5 exd6 5 ♖f5+!** resigned.

An invitation to a 'tango of death' might also follow from the rook.

Hartston – Penrose (1963): Here White failed to play **1 ♖xf7! ♔xf7 2 ♗c4+ ♔f8 3 ♖f1+ ♗f6 4 ♖xf6+! gxf6 5 ♕g8+ ♔e7 6 ♕e6+ ♔f8 7 ♕xf6+** winning.

In the schemes of attack we have looked at, of paramount significance is the timely transfer of the bishop to an attacking diagonal.

Drimer – Gunsberger (1959): **1 b4!** (removing the attack on the d5 square, to which the white bishop will soon be striving) **1 ... ♖c4 2 ♖xh7+! ♔xh7 3 ♕h5+ ♔g8 4 ♘e7+!** (freeing the d5 square for the bishop) **4 ... ♕xe7 5 ♗d5+ ♔f8 6 ♕h8X.**

In the game A.Petrosian – Moldagaliev (1969) White cannot delay, since his king is not sufficiently secure (the threat is 1 ... ♕e1+ 2 ♔g2 ♖d2+). But an immediate 1 ♗e6+ ♔f8 2 ♕g6 is no good, since it gives the opponent necessary time for an counterattack. A forcing operation now decides: **1 ♖h8+! ♔xh8** (1 ... ♔f7 2 ♕g6+). **2 ♕h5+.** Black resigned: after 2 ... ♔g8 the bishop transfers to the a2-g8 diagonal with check, 3 ♗e6+, and the queen mates on the f7 square.

In the game Euwe – Reti (1920) the entry of the bishops to the front line was prepared by the sacrifice of two rooks.

1 ... ♗d6! 2 ♕xh8 ♕xg5. The threat

is 3 ... ♗h3, while on 3 ♕xh7 follows 3 ... ♗f5 trapping the queen.

3 f4. Exploiting the fact that not possible are either 3 ... ♕xf4 4 ♖f1, or 3 ... exf3 4 ♕e8+, White tries to drive away the black queen from its dangerous position, but upon this he weakens the g1-a7 diagonal.

3 ... ♕h4 4 ♖xe4 ♗h3! 5 ♕xa8 ♗c5+ 6 ♔h1 ♗xg2+! 7 ♔xg2 ♕g4+. White resigned (8 ♔f1 ♕f3+ 9 ♔e1 ♕f2X).

Operating on the a2-g8 (g1-a7) diagonal, the bishop drives the king into the corner. In these cases the queen might deliver a blow via the last rank or the h-file.

In the game Dyakov – Ayansky (1962) we should note the 'geometrical motif', characteristic for carrying out the white queen's trade.

1 ♕c3+ ♔g7 2 ♕c8+ ♔g8 3 ♕xg8X (Dyakov did not hear the 'melody' and sent the queen in completely the opposite direction – 1 ♕d5!? ♔g7 with a draw).

The direction of the blow may vary defending on the state of play, as happened in the game Felner – Bancroft (1960).

1 ♗g5!, and Black resigned, since on **1 ... hxg5** (1 ... ♕xg5 2 ♕g8X) follows **2 ♕h5X**.

White's tactical operations are based on the idea of deflecting the h-pawn, which often features in combinations against the short castled position.

Lukovnikov – Sergeev (1974): **1 ♗g5! hxg5 2 ♘xe5!**, with tempo (the threat is 3 ♘g6+) freeing the way for the queen to h5. Black resigned.

Pereisa – Motta (1937): **1 ... ♕g3! 2 hxg4 ♕h4X**.

The short queen manoeuvre, to which can be assigned the conditional sign <–>, forces the opponent to accept the knight sacrifice and expose the h-file. This manoeuvre is typical and crowns many tactical operations in such like positions.

Lematchko – Merdinian (1976): **1 ♕h5 h6 2 ♖xe6! ♗xe6** (2 ... ♕xc4 3 ♖xh6) **3 ♗xe6+ ♔h8** and now according to the stereotype – **4 ♕g6**. Black resigned.

With the same thematic idea the knight can be sacrificed on the g6 (g3) square.

Spasov – Popov (1977): **1 ♘g6+! hxg6 2 ♕g4 ♘f8 3 ♗f7!** Only this move guarantees victory. If at once 3 ♕h4+ ♘h7 4 ♗f7, then 4 ... f5 5 ♕h3 ♗g5 6 ♗xg6 ♗h6. Also no good is 3 ♕h3+ ♘h7 4 ♗f7 ♗c8.

3 ... ♘h7 4 ♗xg6. Black resigned (4 ... ♔g8 5 ♕e6+ ♔h8 6 ♕h3).

A rook sacrifice, opening the edge file to please the queen is also a good way to promote an attack.

Marovic – Ciric (1962). After the careless **1 ♕xb7?** the offensive quickly unfolds: **1 ... ♕e4+ 2 ♔a1** (2 ♖c2 ♗f5) **2 ... ♖xa2+! 3 ♔xa2 ♕a4+ 4 ♔b1 ♗f5+**, and White resigned (5 ♖c2 ♕xc2+ 6 ♔a2 ♕a4X).

When the royal infantry has been completely annihilated the enemy's command post is surrounded, in accordance with all the rules of the art of warfare.

Here, depending on the situation, capitulation is forced by one of the attacking pieces. A tactical clearance operation begins with the destruction of the castled position, while the main direction of attack remains the a2-g8 (g1-a7) diagonal.

Klinger – Kenerlich (1963): With the surprising move **1 ♖c6!** White covers over the 6th rank and shuts off the black queen from defence of the king's flank. After the forced **1 ... bxc6** White exploits the pinned f7 pawn – **2 ♕xg6+**, destroying the cover of the enemy king.

There followed **2 ... ♔h8 3 ♕h5+ ♔g7 4 ♕xg5+ ♔h8 5 ♕h6+ ♔g8 6 ♗e4 f5 7 ♗c2!**, and Black resigned, since the bishop transfers to the a2-g8 diagonal with check.

Donchev – Cramling (1975): **1 ♖xh5! gxh5 2 g6 hxg6 3 ♕xg6+ ♔h8 4 ♗xf7** Black resigned.

An illustration of the tactical pre-requisites required for redeploying pieces to attacking positions is shown by the game Grunfeld – Torre (1925), where White's last move f2-f3 carelessly weakened the diagonal leading to the king.

1 ... ♘xe5! 2 dxe5 (2 fxe4 ♘g4 3 e5 ♕h6 leads to material loss in view of the threat 4 ... ♕xh2X or 4 ... ♘e3). But now the g1-a7 diagonal is cleared of white pawns and Black delivers the decisive blow: **2 ... ♗c5+ 3 ♔h1 ♘xg3+!** White resigned (4 hxg3 ♕h6+ 5 ♗h3 ♕xh3X).

These finales are a reward for a successful attack, both on the kingside and on the queenside. The privilege of concluding the campaign is available here for the queen or bishop, the only difference being that the queen transfers to its active operations along the rank.

Milev – Minev (1961): **1 ... ♘e2+! 2 ♗xe2 ♗d4+ 3 ♔f1 ♕h1X**.

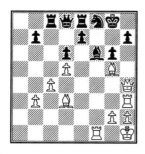

Portisch – Reshevsky (1973): **1 ♗xg6 hxg6 2 ♖xf6!** Black resigned (2 ... exf6 3 ♕h8+ ♔f7 4 ♖h7+ ♘xh7 5 ♕xh7+ ♔f8 6 ♗h6X).

Ljubojevic – Durao (1974): **1 ♗b5!!** 'Simply' defending the 1st rank against a queen check. Now White has three pieces under attack, but not one of them can be taken: 1 ... ♕xe4 2 ♗a6X or 1 ... cxb5 2 ♕a6+ ♔b8 3 ♗xd6X.

Black resigned, in the opinion of several commentators, prematurely, though even after the better 1 ... ♖df8 2 ♗xd6 ♕f1+ 3 ♗xf1 ♖xf1+ 4 ♕g1 ♖xg1+ 5 ♔xg1 White, by taking the pawn on e5, remains with two extra pawns.

The effectiveness of the co-ordination between the queen and bishop reaches its climax when an attack is conducted via a long diagonal. The direction of the blow is through the centre squares; it ties down the defensive capabilities of the enemy and allows the attacking pieces to transfer quickly to any sector of the battle.

If the short castled position is weakened by the advance of the g-pawn, then the long diagonal extends to the edge of the board, as if aspiring for infinity. But the pieces are subject to the laws of 'chess gravity', and the flight of the queen is limited to 'orbiting around the king'.

Thus has ended the existence of many royal dynasties.

Belenky – Pirogov (1957). All three critical points – g2, h1 and h5 – are covered by enemy pieces. But their 'personal interests' come together on the e1 square. There too arrives the 'floating' black rook, disturbing the peace and quiet: **1 ... ♖e1!** White resigned. Already there is no return to Idyll: 2 ♕xe1 ♕h5X; 2 ♖xe1 ♕g2X; 2 ♕g4 ♕h1+ 3 ♖xh1 ♖xh1X.

Fraguela – Larsen (1976): On the long diagonal stands the knight f3. It is defended by two white pieces. But how many times is it attacked? Only by the knight on e5. Yet a moment later it will be attacked by the whole black pack:

1 ... ♘d2! White resigned. (2 ♕xd2 ♘xf3+ 3 ♗xf3 ♕xf3, and mate is unstoppable, or 2 ♗b4 ♘exf3+ 3 ♗xf3 ♘xf3+ 4 ♔h1 ♘d2+ 5 f3 ♘xf1).

Note that in the diagram position 1 ... ♘c3? is no use because of 2 ♕xe5 ♘xe2+ 3 ♔h2, and Black is unable to take the queen on f3 in view of the threat of mate on g7.

Illingworth – Alexander (1931): According to the rules of etiquette an attacked queen must move. But here this is not the case: **1 ♘d5!** Black resigned: he loses a piece since his own queen is taken with check.

A diagonal attack is swift and merciless, so the main tactical task of the offensive is often to point the queen in an attacking direction.

Makov – Vazhenin (1976). The white king is on the edge of a precipice and there is no time for the move ♕h4-f6. And yet the queen manages to get to the launch pad without giving the enemy any respite: **1 ♕d8+! ♚h7** (1 ... ♖xd8 2 ♖xd8+ ♚h7 3 ♖h8X) **2 ♖xh5+! gxh5 3 ♖h6+ ♚xh6 4 ♕f6+.** Black resigned.

Here is another operation along a captured diagonal. **1 ♖xc5! ♖xc5 2 ♕d4 ♕f8.** Now it is not enough to take on c5, since the bishop on d5 would be lost. But White has more serious intentions.

3 ♘f6+! A typical device. As soon as the queen leads the storm troopers, his aides are trying in every way to force a breach in the enemy defence. Upon 3 ... gxf6 4 ♕xf6 mate is inevitable.

3 ... ♚h8 4 ♕e4. Black resigned. When the g7 pawn leaves its post, the white army will rush into the breach.

A weakened diagonal might provoke threats.

Kupreychik – Romanishin (1976): **1 ... ♘h4 2 g3 ♕f7** (attacking the bishop a7) **3 ♖xe8 ♘f3+!** White resigned.

We have already repeatedly seen how the queen, by creating a threat of mate, can in passing strike other objects. Such 'curiosity' can come at a high price to its environment, and therefore the very useful advice of experienced players is: before making a move, make sure that you do not blunder. Alas, this is often overlooked. Even by grandmasters ...

In the XIX Olympiad in Siegen (1970) the game Portisch – Gligoric arrived at the following position:

It is White to move, and if the Hungarian grandmaster had just played 1 a3, then he would have preserved his advantage. Portisch, however, made a gross oversight – **1 h5??** and after **1 ... ♕b4** immediately resigned, since besides the mate on b2 there is the threat of 2 ... ♕xe1.

"A beginner's mistake" – said the tournament bulletin. "An unfair comparison – objected grandmaster M.Taimanov. – show me a beginner who is able to withstand five hours of fierce fighting against a world class player before he makes a mistake!"

But it was not easy to predict the disguised manoeuvre of Konstantinopolsky (White) in his game against Bivshev (1951) even with a 'fresh' mind.

1 ♘xc6 ♗xc6 (first exchanging) **2 b4 ♗d6** (then driving away the bishop to an unstable position) **3 ♕d3** (and finally regrouping his pieces for the decisive blow). Black resigned. On any move by the bishop or defence of it (3 ... ♖fd8) follows 4 ♕c3 with a simultaneous attack on the g7 square and the bishop c6.

Note that instead of 3 ♕d3 insufficient was 3 e5? ♗xg2 4 exd6 in view of 4 ... ♕b7.

Upon a diagonal offensive the danger of a double attack is increased further, because an intermediate blow by the queen passes through the centre and the shock waves reverberate in concentric circles over the whole board.

Panchenko – Koslov (1970): **1 ... ♖xc4!** The queen is heading for d5, so that in the event of 2 ♘xc4 it can deliver a double attack on the g2 and c4 squares. But what good will come of this if White can move the knight to e3, simultaneously defending against

mate? Well, then the bishop g5 will be left without support and in the sights of the ubiquitous queen.

2 ♗xf6 ♕d5 3 f3 ♗xf6 4 ♘xc4 ♕xc4. White resigned.

In the combination played by Larsen (White) against Matanovic (1965) one of the tactical elements was also a double attack.

1 ♘xe6! The basic idea of this sacrifice is revealed later, while on 1 ... fxe6 White had prepared 2 ♕c3! with a simultaneous attack on g7 and c8.

1 ... ♖xc4. Black forestalls the double attack by exchanges, the 'sacrificial symphony' continues.

2 ♘h6+! Black resigned. If he doesn't want to be subjected to a piquant mate: 2 ... ♔h8 3 ♗xg7X, then he should take the knight – 2 ... gxh6. But then 3 ♕xh6 leads to mate, since it is impossible with a single move to render harmless both the knight e6 and the bishop b2.

If a bishop is taking aim at the enemy castled king position on the long diagonal, the queen can support it or deliver the final blow on the g-file. In these cases an acute attack is also directed against the g7 (g2) squares with the immediate task being to blow up the castled position and immediately destroy the pawns on f6 (f3) and g6 (g3).

Tuzovsky – Korolev (1975). To defend against the mate on g2, White played **1 f3**, on which followed the devastating sacrifice – **1 ... ♞xf3! 2 gxf3**, and then the deflection – **2 ... ♜e1+**. White resigned.

Upon 1 ♗f1 Black could continue the attack by 1 ... ♞f3! 2 ♜e2 (2 ♜d3 ♜e1) 2 ... ♛f4 etc.

Keres (Black) against Blumenov (1933) decisively cleared a way to the king.

1 ... ♞xe3! 2 fxe3 ♗xg3+! 3 ♚xg3. Also 3 ♚g1 ♗h2+! does not change matters.

3 ... ♛g5+. Not at once 3 ... ♛e5+!? because of 4 ♚f2 with an escape via the e1 square. Now, however, this attempt is stopped by the check on h4.

4 ♚h2 ♛e5+ 5 ♚g1 ♛g3+, and mate on the next move.

In an attack against the long castled position the 'war path' becomes the b-file. Most often the pawn located there is just destroyed.

Zhuravlev – Koskin (1936). The a1-b8 diagonal is crammed like a bus in the 'rush hour'. But see how deftly the 'passengers without a ticket' scatter.

1 ... ♞xf3! 2 ♞xf3 (one pair is no longer there) **2 ... ♞xe4! 3 ♞xc4** (all clear) **3 ... ♜xb2+ 4 ♚c1** (what to do next? Two knights have been given up!) **4 ... ♜b1+! 5 ♚xb1 ♛b8+**. The 'ticket collector' has arrived. White resigned.

Let's familiarise ourselves with the queen's methods of attack via the h-file. This operation is based on a pin and so cunningly masked that it was once overlooked even by such a 'great combinationalist' as R.Spielmann.

Fazekas – Spielmann (1938): **1 ... ♜e2? 2 ♜c8+ ♚h7 3 ♜h8+!**. Black resigned. The king is lured to h8, and the g7 pawn falls into a pin. After 4 ♛h6+ a meeting with the queen promises no happiness.

A rather more complicated version of this scheme appeared in the game Sherbakov – Barskauskas (1959).

It starts with a deflection – **1 ♘xd5!**, and then after **1 ... exd5** the e-file was opened and everything went like clockwork: **2 ♖e8+ ♔h7 3 ♖xh8+ ♔xh8 4 ♕h6+**, and Black resigned.

It's not always so easy to open the casket, but the familiar configuration helps us to pick up the key even to a lock with a 'secret'.

Alekhine – de Cassio (1944): **1 ♘f6+ gxf6 2 ♗xf6.** Black resigned: after 2 ... ♘d8 3 ♕h6 ♘e6 4 ♗xe6 he is mated.

In this example Black was totally unarmed and could not put up any resistance. In most cases when the queen is flying beyond the clouds it still has to reckon with earthly matters.

Sakharov – Cherepkov (1969): **1 ♗xh7+! ♔xh7 2 ♖xd6 ♗xd6 3 ♖h4+** Black resigned. If 3 ... ♔g8 4 ♖h8+ ♔xh8 5 ♕h6+ ♔g8 6 ♕xg7X. As you can see, the same opera, but with an overture.

When a long diagonal is blocked by an impregnable barrier, the bishop looks for a loophole to get on to the f6 (f3) square. Here, it is also in the area of a long diagonal, but it cannot carry a warhead loaded with the 'queen's explosives': it is too crowded to set up a launching pad for a two-stage missile. The task for the bishop is to hold on to its position until the queen enters into its orbit at the h6 square.

Eslon – Hutchings (1975). Naturally it is White to move. It seems that the queen could simply 'throw herself' at h6, with the aim of grabbing space around the king. However Black delivers a pre-emptive strike – 1 ... ♗xf3+ 2 ♔g3 (2 ♔g1? ♖d1+) 2 ... ♗h5+ 3 f3 (3 ♔h4? ♕d4+ 4 f4 ♕f2+) 3 ... ♖xf3+ 4 ♔g2 ♖xf6 5 exf6 ♕d5+ with a guaranteed draw.

So before starting all-out war White tries to disorganise the retaliatory system;

1 ♖d1 ♖xd1 (1 ... ♗xf3+? 2 ♕xf3 ♖xd1 3 ♕a8+) **2 ♕h6 ♗xf3+ 3 ♔h3** (3 ♔g3? ♖g1+ 4 ♔h3 ♗g2+ 5 ♔h4 ♕d4+ 6 f4 ♕f2+ and Black wins)

3 ... ♗g2+ 4 ♔h4 (4 ♔xg2? ♕d5+ 5 f3 ♕d2+) 4 ... ♕d4+? 5 f4 ♕f2+ 6 ♔g5. Here Black exceeded the time limit, but by now there are no acceptable checks.

Meanwhile there was a way of escape. Instead of 4 ... ♕d4+? he should continue 4 ... ♖d4+! 5 ♔g5 (5 f4? ♖xf4+) 5 ... ♖g4+! 6 ♔xg4 ♕d1+! 7 ♔h4 ♕h5+ 8 ♕xh5 gxh5 9 ♔xh5 with an exchange of queens and even an extra pawn.

This means that Black's rocket launcher was not incapacitated, it was just that his accuracy of fire was off the mark.

Thus, when burning one's bridges, it is necessary to identify the extent of the enemy's counterplay. And this requires accurate calculation.

In the game Pogacs – Ciric (1962) White missed an opportunity. He played 1 ♖e1?, intending to transfer the queen with all amenities (after the manoeuvre ♖e1-e5). Black, however, found a defensive possibility: 1 ... e5! Now no use is 2 dxe5 ♕xd3 3 ♕g5 ♔h7, or an immediate 2 ♕g5 ♖e6 3 dxe5 ♖xf6. After 2 ♗xe5 ♖e6 Black avoided the immediate dangers and the game ended in a draw.

In the diagram position White had a forced way to victory: 1 ♗e4 ♕b3 (the only reply; if 1 ... ♕d7, then, of course, 2 ♕g5 ♔h7 3 ♕xh5+) 2 ♖b1 ♕a2 (the bishop b7, as before, is invulnerable,

but in return the way is opened for the white queen to go to h6) 3 ♕g5! ♗xe4 4 ♕h6 ♕xb1+ 5 ♔f2 ♕c2+ 6 ♔g3, and the king hides from the checks.

The bringing of the bishop to f6 (f3) is achieved by various tactical means.

Durst – Alster (1965): 1 ♘d7!. A highly amusing position! The knight is under fire from three enemy pieces! He can't take it, but neither can he not take it.

1 ... ♕xd7. Black is already beyond good and bad. You see, on 1 ... ♘e8 or 1 ... ♘h5 White would reply with the quite funny – 2 ♘f6+!, which, however, leads to the same situation as in the game.

2 ♗xf6 g6 3 ♕g5. Black resigned.

The motif for White's tactical operation in the game Spielmann – Wahle (1926) is the pin along the diagonal.

1 ♖xe7! ♕xe7 2 ♕f3 ♔g7 3 ♘ge4! dxe4 4 ♘xe4. The black knight is

attacked three times, and the defensive resources are exhausted.

4 ... ♛e6 5 ♗xf6+ ♚g8 (the bishop is established on f6, it's the queen's turn) **6 ♛f4**. Black resigned: The queen is free to go to h6, and the conversation is over.

On the short diagonal the bishop kept the enemy king under house arrest and, as it were, opened the front door on g7 to the queen and the back entrance on f8.

In the spectacle staged by Weinicke and Gross (1961), the white dreamboat queen enters f6 in style.

But she fears retaliation by the black queen, which has the white king in her line of vision. The rook is woven into the plot: **1 ♖d7!**. The plotter will be immediately executed, but a meeting with the king will have to be postponed. Meanwhile, the white queen will solemnly commit her dirty deed. **2 ♛f6**.

In presenting this sentimental story of the language of chess pieces, we note that the occupation by the queen of the f6 (f3) square, in conjunction with a bishop on h6 (h3), becomes a major tactical task in many positions.

In the game Vasyukov – Pfleger (1966) this is prevented by three of the opponent's pieces. But one of these is eliminated, another deflected, and the third forced to exchange: **1 ♖xd5! ♗xd5 2 ♖xd5 ♛xd5 3 ♘f6+ ♗xf6 4 ♛xf6**. Black resigned.

The order that pieces are introduced to the attack can vary depending on the concrete circumstances.

Alekhine – Mikenas (1937): **1 ... ♖c2! 2 ♛xc2** (otherwise he loses the bishop on b2) **2 ... ♛xf3+ 3 ♚g1 ♗h3**.

But all this was not played by Mikenas against the world champion in the international tournament in Kemeri. When Alekhine immediately pointed out the missed opportunity, the young Lithuanian master said in a temper: "It doesn't matter, I will win this game a second time!". And, just imagine, he did win!

At an international tournament in Dortmund (1974) Gaprindashvili defeated master Servati (Black) with a beautiful combination involving the sacrifice of two rooks.

1 ♕d4! ♕xh1+ 2 ♔d2 ♕xa1 3 ♕f6!, and Black resigned, since there is no satisfactory defence against 4 ♗h6.

A few months later, at an international tournament in Halle, a game played by Tal (White) against the German master Paehtz arrived (by transposition of moves) at an exactly identical position. The grandmaster from Riga resorted to 'plagiarism'.

1 ♕d4! ♕xh1+ 2 ♔d2. Here Paehtz unravelled his opponent's plan, but, alas, too late. After **2 ... ♕xh2 3 ♗xf8 ♔xf8 4 ♗f3 d5 5 ♗xd5 ♖b8 6 ♖e1 ♗e6 7 ♖xe6** Black acknowledged defeat.

"I express my sincere gratitude to the world champion – Tal wrote jokingly in the Rigan magazine *Shakhmaty* – for her active participation in my performance in Halle ..."

After the deflection of the g-pawn, the queen, from its original square, delivers a blow on the newly opened file.

Zuckerman – Hartoch (1968): **1 ♖xe7! ♖xe7**. It is clear that the black queen must keep in her sights the g4 square. But now the rook a8 is left undefended.

2 ♕f3! The queen uses this square like a trampoline in order to transfer to g3. Black resigned.

In the resulting position also winning was the move 1 ♗e6, blocking the diagonal of the black queen.

The deflection of the g-pawn from its file is usually achieved by an exchange or a sacrifice on f6 (f3).

Pedersen – Gerger (1976): **1 ♖xf6 gxf6 2 ♗h6**. Black resigned.

Bokuchava – Gurgenidze (1976):
**1 ... ⌶xf3! 2 gxf3 ♗h3 3 ♗e3 ♕f6
4 ♕e4.** Not a single square on the g-file is accessible to the black queen. But this is only for a moment ...

4 ... ⌶b4! White resigned.

The attack might be combined: both against the g7 (g2) squares, and also along the 8th rank (1st) rank. Such an offensive is illustrated by the game Volchok – Nakonechny (1964).

The g2 square is covered by the bishop g3, but it can be deflected by combinational means: **1 ... ⌶xf2!
2 ♗xf2** (2 ⌶xf2 ♕c1+) **2 ... ♗h3 3 g3
♗xf2+.** White resigned: on 4 ♔xf2 comes the decisive 4 ... ⌶f8+, while 4 ⌶xf2 leads to mate in three moves after 4 ... ♕c1+.

In some situations the object of attack becomes the h-pawn. Then the bishop supports the queen from the c1-h6 (h3-c8) or f8-h6 (f1-h3) diagonals.

A mandatory condition of this mating construction is the blockade of the g8 (g1) square. It is achieved in various ways but most of all by direct threats to the royalty.

Kubart – Flasche (1957): **1 ⌶f6! ♗c8**
(1 ... gxf6 2 ♘xf6+ ♗xf6 3 ♕xh6X or 1 ... ♗xf6 2 ♘xf6+ ♔h8 3 ♗xh6 gxh6 4 ♕xh6X) **2 ⌶xh6+!** Black resigned.

Vizantiadis – Spassky (1970):
1 ... ⌶8xf3!, and White resigned, without waiting for the elegant finish – 2 gxf3 ⌶xh2+ 3 ♔xh2 ♕h4+ 4 ♔g2 ♗h3+ 5 ♔h2 ♗f1X.

There was a quite busy crisscross manoeuvre of the white pieces in the game Dolmatov – Rastyanis (1978).

1 ♕d8+ ♕g8 2 ♗f8! Black resigned: after 2 ... ♗e6 there is the threat of 3 ♕f6+, and on 2 ... ♔h7 White simply takes the enemy bishop.

An attack via the 7th (2nd) rank leads to these finishes:

If the radius of action of the attacking pieces is restricted by their own pieces or pawns, they can be sacrificed.

In the game Dobsza – Dinnies (1936) the g7 pawn gets under White's own feet, and provides cover for the black king. If it were not for this pawn, the struggle would be decided immediately.

White carries out a combination which allows him to get rid of the blocking foot soldier and thereby lengthen the diagonal of the bishop on b2: **1 ♖e8+! ♖xe8 2 ♕d5+ ♔h7 3 g8=♕+! ♖xg8 4 ♕f7+**. Black resigned.

And here is one of those rare occasions when the queen enters the service of a bishop.

Corbett – Tyler (1963). **1 ♕f7! ♖xe1+** (1 ... ♖g8 2 ♖e8!) **2 ♔g2**, and Black, despite his enormous material advantage, cannot prevent the threat of 3 ♗g7X (2 ... ♕g8 3 ♕xf6+).

Upon an attack on an uncastled king the mating picture is drawn with the same colours, but in this case the factor of time assumes particular significance. Here it is important not to lose a moment on the finishing touches.

Wilhelm – Fetscher (1975): **1 ... ♕f3 2 ♗d2 ♗b4! 3 ♕xb4 ♖d3! 4 ♗xf7+ ♔xf7 5 ♕xb7+ ♔g6**. White resigned.

Here is a dashing combination by the young Alekhine (Black) against Rodzinsky (1913).

One of two black attacking pieces must be lost. Alekhine gives up the more valuable one, but for a long time the enemy queen will be out of the game. **1 ... ♔d7! 2 ♕xa8 ♕c4 3 f3 ♗xf3! 4 gxf3 ♘d4! 5 d3?**.

Confusion, but by now the game cannot be saved. As pointed out by

Alekhine, also after the best defence – 5 cxd4 ♕xc1+ 6 ♔e2 ♕xh1 7 d5 Black achieves a decisive advantage by continuing 7 ... ♕xh2+ 8 ♔d3 ♕g1! 9 ♕c6+ ♔d8 etc. Now, however, the game ends in three moves.

5 ... ♕xd3 6 cxd4 ♗e7! 7 ♕xh8 ♗h4X.

This enigmatic position arose in the game NN – Steinitz (1873) after the moves **1 d4 f5 2 e4 fxe4 3 ♘c3 ♘f6 4 ♗g5 c6 5 ♗xf6 exf6 6 ♘xe4 ♕b6 7 ♕e2 ♕xb2! 8 ♘d6+ ♔d8 9 ♕e8+ ♔c7 10 ♕xc8+ ♔xd6 11 ♖d1**.

They say that Steinitz once proclaimed in the heat of controversy: "I introduced new principles to chess! What did Morphy do? He castled. He hid his king in a safe corner. But I? I played with my king over the whole board. I forced it to fight! With its help I obtained, as it were, an extra piece!" To which the American master G.Mackenzie, calmly puffing a cigar, noted: "Not a bad idea – both that and the other".

Indeed, looking at the position: the black king is in the thick of things, it is taking a lively part in the struggle. Such bravery must be based on precise calculation. And Steinitz had already prepared a brilliant manoeuvre which dramatically changed the picture of the battle.

11 ... ♘a6! 12 ♕xa8 ♔c7! 13 ♕xa7

(forced, since 13 ... ♗b4+ was threatened) **13 ... ♗b4+ 14 ♔e2 ♕xc2+ 15 ♔f3 ♕f5+ 16 ♔g3** (16 ♔e2 ♖e8X) **16 ... ♗d6+ 17 ♔h4 ♕g5+ 18 ♔h3 ♕h5X**. A sleeping queen in the land of Nod – a familiar tale, but, alas, with an unfortunate epilogue.

In the gallery of mating pictures a special place is reserved for two colourful canvasses, painted from real life. One is portrait, the other landscape.

In the game Loman – Teschner (1950) White had already sacrificed a piece in the very opening.

After 1 ♗c4 the attack might still be menacing (1 ... ♕f7 2 ♗b3). But the play takes a surprising turn: **1 ♘xc7? ♗b4X!**

After a sacrifice the white king also succumbed to a 'double mate' in the game Shaposhnikov – Smolensky (1968).

1 ... ♗c4!, and White resigned, since he did not want to witness the destruction of his own king after 2 ♕xc4 ♗xc3X. Meanwhile, the queen cannot hold the e-file: on 2 ♕e3 follows a new attack 2 ... ♘g4

3 ♕e4 ♗xc3 winning the queen. The vis-à-vis of the queen and the king is one of the signs of an impending storm.

And here is the final exhibit of our opening day.

Regan – Michel (1905): **1 ... ♖xb4 2 cxb4 ♕c1+ 3 ♕d1 ♗xb4+ 4 ♘d2 ♗xd2X.** Black consciously hammers the nail into the wall.

* * * *

343. Lednev – Henkin, 1973

White to move

Cloak and dagger knight.

344. Jamieson – Ortega 1972

White to move

Mining the fortress wall.

345. Negyesyi – Denes, 1948

White to move

Obstruction across the road.

346. Bartrina – Ghitescu, 1974

White to move

One mate, few checks.

347. Wexler – Bazan, 1960

Black to move

A wide assortment.

348. Kirillov – Suetin, 1961

White to move

Mating choices.

349 Peev – Pederson, 1972

Black to move

No frills.

350. Vasyukov – Polugaevsky, 1966

White to move

Forcing a capture.

351. Biering – Hay, 1977

Black to move

Deprived of hope!

354. Kapengut – Vaganian, 1970

Black to move

The highest wave.

352. Arinbern – Gutmunder, 1957

White to move

If 1 ♗b2, then 1 ... ♕d1+ 2 ♖c1 ♕d8. Play more resolutely.

355. Belavenets – Balashova, 1979

White to move

Fearless.

353. Romanovsky – Vilner, 1925

White to move

Hardly moving a muscle ...

356. Debarnot – Rogoff, 1976

Black to move

Doubles play.

357. Grigoriev – Nadiseva, 1973

Black to move

Maid-servant's windfall.

358. Csalai – Barabas, 1959

Black to move

One amidst enemies.

359 Delplanche – Felsing, 1958

White to move

Let the guns do the talking ...

360. Martin – Gimenot, 1957

White to move

1 ♕f7? ♖d3+! and Black opens fire first ...

361. Rukavina – Larsen, 1973

Black to move

As in the days of the Vikings ...

362. Lemerre – Nora, 1959

Black to move

And if 1 ... ♘xd4 ?

363. Smachanska – Murezan, 1976

White to move

Like an avalanche down the mountain.

364. Wibe – Schneider, 1975

White to move

Pin and do not release it!

365. Horowitz – NN, 1944

White to move

1 ... ♕f1+ is threatened ...

366. Cabral – Molinari, 1943

Black to move

Has the attack been beaten off? No carry on!

367. Reshevsky – Tan, 1973

White to move

1 ♖xf6 ♖a1+. What escaped him?

368. Eisinger – Kieninger, 1931

White to move

Wave after wave.

369 Elstner – Holze, 1959

White to move

1 g4 Black replied 1 ... ②d4?, failing to detect the opponent's trap. What?

370. Hennings – Uhlmann, 1963

Black to move

What follows on 1 ... ②xd4 ?

371. Bilek – Farago, 1973

White to move

Almost a draw. But ... be careful!

372. Keres – Szabo, 1955

White to move

No peace under the olives.

373. Hennings – Lein, 1959

Black to move

Draw? asked Black – Draw! – said White. Who had regrets afterwards?

374. Marshall – Petrov, 1930

White to move

1 ♕b4 ♔h8? (correct is 1 ... ♖fe8). And now ...

375. Kinzel – Duckstein, 1958

White to move

While the black queen slumbers ...

378. Samarian – Kolosov, 1973

Black to move

While the king remains uncastled ...

376. Luboshits – Shagalovich, 1956

White to move

The bishop-labourer.

379 Nordstrom – Wennestrom, 1964

Black to move

Watershed.

377. Salwe – Speyer, 1910

Black to move

From place to place.

380. Sorokin – Kapustin, 1959

White to move

No right to make a mistake.

381. Rozov – Kozlov, 1973

Black to move

"A knight on the edge is in disgrace" – said S.Tarrasch.

382. Maedler – Uhlmann, 1963

White to move

And if 1 ♖c7 ?

383. Delannoy – Morphy, 1858

Black to move

1 ... ♖fe8 2 ♗xc7. Was it worth coming to Europe?

384. Gligoric – Tolush, 1957

White to move

Lassoing the king.

385. Grippa – Halle, 1963

White to move

1 ♖af1 ♘xf1 and ...

386. Reggio – Mieses, 1901

Black to move

To the left and to the right and even an epaulette!

387. Buinoch – Matocha, 1968

White to move

Go back!

388. Apishenek – Hartman, 1959

White to move

Black threatens to take the knight on c5. What to do?

389 Chukaev – Malev, 1964

White to move

The grand hunt.

390. Ivanov – Litvinov, 1972

White to move

'The mark of Zorro'.

391. L.Kubbel, 1935

White to move and win

Lassoing the queen.

13. Queen and Knight

Like a bishop, a knight knows from his own experience that the world consists not only of one black or white diagonal. Changing the colour of his square on each move, he can step by step circumvent all 64 geographical points of the chess kingdom. The ability to break through the enemy ranks, negotiating all obstacles, gives the knight definite advantages even over the rook. And if we also take into account the universal qualities of the queen, then it becomes clear that the tandem of 'queen-knight' is superior in its own 'cross-country capacity' than all other chariots.

We know that the relative values of the pieces vary depending on the nature of the position. For example, in open positions the bishop is usually stronger than a knight, and the rook even more so. But the strength of each individual piece also depends on the degree of interaction it has with its partners. In tandem with the queen, the 'energy capacity' of the knight increases dramatically.

How often the mighty queen, leading the battle and surrounded by enemy troops, is short of reliable support! It is then, looking hopefully around the battlefield, she, like a Shakespearean hero, exclaims: "A horse! My kingdom for a horse!"

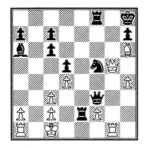

In the game Vorself – Pleim (1959) the opponents are waging a fierce offensive against the kings. But it's Black's move, and he achieved victory by a total sacrifice of pieces, apart from those administering the swift checkmate: **1 ... ♖xc2+! 2 ♔xc2 ♕d3+ 3 ♔c1** (otherwise 3 ... ♖b8+) **3 ... ♕xc3+ 4 ♔d1 ♗e2+! 5 ♔xe2 ♘xd4+ 6 ♔f1 ♖xf2+! 7 ♔xf2 ♕f3+ 8 ♔e1 ♕e2X**.

Let's look at ways to attack the short castled position with the queen and knight. Usually the knight sets the tone and the direction of the attack depends largely on his possibilities. The queen is much more mobile and can more easily adapt to the customs and habits of her fighting comrades.

The knight's favourite pasture is the g5 (g4) square. It is located just two jumps from the royal stables, and one from a tempting target such as h7 (h2).

Black's last move in the game Yates – Marin (1930) was c5-c4. What's this? Inattention? Ignorance? Or ... fatalism? **1 ♗xh7+ ♔xh7 2 ♕h5+ ♔g8 3 ♘g5.** Black resigned.

Pestalozzi – Duhm (1908). Also here Black was remarkably careless in just playing ♘b8-c6? Retribution followed immediately: **1 ♗xh7+ ♔xh7 2 ♕h5+ ♔g8 3 ♘g5 ♖e8** (an attempt to escape) **4 ♕xf7+ ♔h8 5 ♕h5+ ♔g8 6 ♕h7+ ♔f8 7 ♕h8+ ♔e7 8 ♕xg7X**.

Let's familiarise ourselves with other methods of attack against the h7 square.

Of the tactical blows, the demolition of the royal fortress with a bishop sacrifice on h7 undoubtedly takes first place. This ancient combination is often crowned with a mating finish.

Alekseev – Chernenko (1961). The black queen is waiting for cavalry reinforcements. However the immediate knight jump – **1 ... ♞g4?** is premature because of 2 f3, and if 2 ... ♝d3 3 ♛d2 ♝xf1, then 4 fxg4!. First it is necessary to deflect the enemy queen from the 2nd rank: **1 ... ♝d3! 2 ♛xd3**, and only now **2 ... ♞g4**. White resigned.

And so, deflection. We have repeatedly met this technique in previous chapters. It is perhaps the most common tactical element in the chess kingdom.

Flohr – Gilg (1934). It seems that the black king is well protected and in no danger. However, this impression is deceptive. The knight f6 is tied down to protecting two critical points in the position – h7 and d5. After **1 ♞d5!** the servant of two masters cannot cope.

This theme with different nuances roams from game to game at all levels of competition.

Szabo – Kotov (1946). In reply to **1 ... h6?** Black played **2 ♞d5!**, and

after a few moves it was all over (2 ... exd5 3 ♝xf6 ♝f5 4 ♛xf5 g6 5 ♛xg6+ fxg6 6 ♝xd5+ ♜f7 7 ♝xe7, and Black resigned).

Balashov – Romanishin (1976). Black played **1 ... dxc4?**, so that after 2 ♞e5, he has the variation 2 ... ♞xe5 3 ♝xa8 ♝a6 with advantage. But the white knight, though turning its head to the left (as we assume from the diagram), looks askance in the other direction: **2 ♞g5!**, and the thrust ♞c3-d5 can be averted only at the cost of a piece.

In the last examples the threat to deflect the knight f6 is accompanied by the threat to eliminate it. These two methods are closely intertwined in positions requiring a 'surgical operation'.

Gonsior – Novak (1963). The h7 square is defended by two pieces. One is eliminated, the other deflected: **1 ♜xf8+! ♛xf8 2 ♝xe6+!** Black resigned.

The opposite technique – attraction – is aimed directly against His Majesty.

Marshall – Burn (1900). After 1 ♕h7+ the black monarch calmly moves away to f8, but **1 ♖h8+!** (of course, not too polite, but with chess kings there is no other way...) **1 ... ♔xh8 2 ♕h7X**.

When the queen's own pieces stand in the way of her attack, she cold-bloodedly condemns them to death so as to free lines for the attack

Urban – Schoneberg (1961): **1 ... ♗g2!** White resigned (2 ♗xg2 ♘xf3+ 3 ♗xf3 ♕xh2+ 4 ♔f1 ♕xf2X or 2 ♔xg2 ♘xf3 and 3 ... ♘e3+).

Kislova – Orlova (1973): **1 ♗f8!** Black resigned. On any capture of the

bishop follows 2 ♖xf6.

Rather – Belcher (1940): The diagonal, along which the white queen dreams of making a date with the black king, is occupied by ill-fated subjects. To pave the way to 'high society', it is necessary to give each of them a combat mission. The 'order' starts with the bishop.

1 ♗a6! ♗xa6. After 1 ... ♗xe4 2 ♕xe4 the h7 square and rook c8 each find themselves under attack. Now the knight gets a job to do.

2 ♘exg5 ♖fe8. The diagonal is cleared. But after 3 ♕h7+ the meeting with the king turns out to be fleeting. However we already know in such situations that one can resort to the 'painful' method of enticement.

3 ♖h8+! Black resigned.

In the next two examples the freeing of a square for the queen (unblocking) is supported by a multi-stage mating construction. Together with this comes a bishop sacrifice, creating intermediate mating threats.

Vis – Barcza (1939): **2 ... ♗h2+ 3 ♔h1 ♗g1!** White resigned.

Gumprich – NN (1929): **1 ♗g7!** Black resigned.

In both cases, a bishop and a knight indirectly supported each other, allowing the enemy king himself to choose the form of execution. But the main role was still intended for the knight. And it was namely the knight, advancing to g5 (g4) and taking aim at the critical h7 (h2) square, which prompted the queen to provide him with immediate assistance.

A bishop might yield its place not only to its immediate supervisor but also to reprsentatives of other kinds of troops.

Landsetter – Janos (1971): **1 ♗e7! ♕d7** (1 ... ♕xe7 2 ♗xd5 ♕xh4 3 ♗xe6+) **2 ♖xe6!** Black resigned (2 ... ♕xe6 3 ♘g5).

Dvoretsky (Black), in a game against Podgaets (1974), constructed an original zugzwang position.

1 ... ♖f8! 2 ♗h1 (2 ♕xh4 ♘xf3+) **2 ... ♘g4 3 ♕g2 ♖f3! 4 c4 ♔h6!** Both sad, and funny. White's queen has to keep watch on the h2 square, the rook is riveted to defence of the f2 square, and the bishop is serving a life sentence. When the pawn moves run out, complete zugzwang ensues. White resigned.

An attack against the h7 (h2) squares can also come via the 7th (2nd), rank, if the queen is be able to get there.

Keres – Gligoric (1959). White's queen is ready for a dialogue with the foreign king, but he lacks an interpreter. The g5 square is inaccessible to the knight, but for how long?

1 ♘xf6! If 1 ♘gxe5!? Black could still fight off the attack by 1 ... ♖de8 2 ♘f7 ♔g7. Such errors are often made in time trouble.

1 ... ♖xf6 2 ♘g5. All right, an interpreter has appeared, but at a time when the black knight cannot take part in the conversation because of the pin. Two more 'desperation checks' – **2 ... Ξxf2+ 3 ⌀g1** (3 ⌀xf2? ♕c5) **3 ... Ξf1+ 4 ⌀h2**, and Black resigned.

Hill – Caldwell (1978): Here the queen is already needed to support the knight, which he does after a massive artillery attack: **1 ... ♗xg3! 2 fxg3 Ξxd4.** White resigned (3 exd4 ♕d2).

And here is a combination from the game Tal – Carleton (1974), in the course of which the ex-world champion penetrated to the 7th rank in a very tricky way.

Hoping to weaken the opponent's onslaught, Black returned the extra exchange – **1 ... Ξxd5.** But what is material for Tal, when he has an attack! **2 ♗xh6!** Pieces still don't count. But if Black tries to go over to defence, for example with the move 2 ... ♗e8, then after 3 ⌀g5+ ⌀g8 4 Ξxf8+ ♗xf8 5 ♕xe8 he will be back to square one. It seems that it is possible to play 'fortissimo', – 2 ... Ξxf3, but then 3 ♗xg7+ ⌀xg7 4 Ξxf3 leads to a

position where mate is inevitable. He has to go into the mouth of the tiger. **2 ... ♗xh6 3 ⌀g5+ ⌀g7 4 Ξf7+!** Black resigned.

Upon advancing the knight to f6 (f3) the target of the queen's attack becomes the h6 (h3) square. The path to it is via the c1-h6 (h3-c8) diagonal or the h-file.

The knight invades on f6 (f3) with his characteristic lack of ceremony, exploiting the squares d5 (d4), e4 (e5), g4 (g5) and h5 (h4) as a transfer base.

Vujanovic – Konopleva (1970): **1 ⌀f6+ ⌀h8 2 ♕h4 h6 3 Ξh5**, and Black resigned, since he cannot repulse the threat of 4 Ξxh6+ gxh6 5 ♕xh6X.

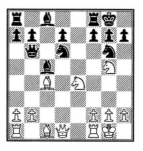

Kreschmar – Vasitsa (1938): **1 ♕h5 h6 2 ♕xg6 hxg5 3 ⌀f6+.** Black resigned.

Boey – Makles (1971): **1 ... ♖f2!
2 ♕xf2 ♕xh3+ 3 ♔g1 ♘f3+.** White
resigned.

A.Donchenko – Berzhansky (1962):
Black was ready to parry the thrust
1 ♕h6 with the move 1 ... ♗f8.
Meanwhile the f6 square is inaccessible
to the white knight, since it is protected
by the queen. But is not possible to ask
this queen to step aside?
**1 ♗xf5! exf5 2 ♕h6 ♖xe1+ 3 ♖xe1
♗f8 4 ♖e8!** "Move over, please ..."
Black resigned.

The same idea, but with a greater
content of tactical resources formed the
basis of a combination played by Reti
(White) against Freiman (1912).

1 d6! ♕f8 (1 ... ♘xc4 2 ♖e7! ♘xe7
3 ♕f6+ or 1 ... cxd6 2 ♗xg8 and 3 ♖e8)
2 ♖e8! Black resigned (2 ... ♕xe8
3 ♘f6, and not a single square on the
7th rank is available to the black queen).

Let's look at a few ways of moving
forward the pieces as a prelude to the
attack.

Petrov – Alster (1950): **1 ... ♗xf3
2 ♗xf3 ♘xd4 3 ♗xd5 ♖xd5 4 ♘xd5
♘f3+.** White resigned. The king cannot
go to g2, since the queen e1 is taken
with check (otherwise White himself
threatens to win the queen by 5 ♘xe7+)
while, after 5 ♔h1 ♕h3, mate on h2 is
unavoidable.

Sahovic – Diaz (1976): **1 ♘e4! ♘b4.**
Accepting the rook sacrifice leads to
mate – 1 ... gxf5 2 ♘f6+ ♔g7 3 ♕xf5
♖h8 4 ♕g5+ ♔f8 5 ♕h6X.
**2 ♕d2 dxe5 3 ♘f6+ ♔g7 4 ♖h5!
♕c7** (4 ... ♕xf6 5 ♕h6+; 4 ... ♔xf6
5 ♖f1+; 4 ... gxh5 5 ♕g5+ ♔h8 6 ♕h6)
5 ♖f1, Black resigned.

Sure – Knaak (1976): **1 ♕g5 ♕c5**. The threat was 2 ♘f6+ ♗xf6 3 exf6 ♖g8 4 ♕h5X. Now, however, the e5 pawn is pinned.

2 ♕h5+ ♔g8 3 ♘h6+ ♗xh6 4 ♕xh6. Black resigned. Why? Because in reply to 4 ... ♕xe5 the second knight joins in the ambush – 5 ♘g4 and he rushes towards the attack at a gallop.

The f7(f2) pawn is subjected to a combined attack by the queen and knight most often in the opening stage of the game or in positions where the enemy king has not managed to castle.

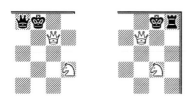

The danger arises already in the opening itself, if there is a bishop on the a2-g8 (g1-a7) diagonal, ready to sacrifice itself at the first signal.

In the game Cheron – Polike (1927) this signal is sounded at a time when the interaction of the black pieces (after ♘b8-d7) is disrupted: **1 ♗xf7+! ♔xf7 2 ♘g5+ ♔g8** (otherwise after 3 ♘e6 he loses the queen) **3 ♕d5+**, and mate in two moves.

The poor position of black king was vigorously exploited by Maroczy (White) against Vidmar (1923).

The black queen prevents the mate on f7. But she is at the same time protecting the d5 square and could not cope with these two duties after the splendid move **1 ♖e7!**. This is not only an interference but also a deflection. Black has a great choice but this does not make it any easier: **1 ... ♗xe7** (1 ... ♘xe7) 2 ♕f7X or 1 ... ♕xe7 2 ♕d5, while after 1 ... ♘e5 2 ♖xe5 he is left a piece down. Therefore, the Yugoslav grandmaster resigned.

Pytlakowski (White) found a cunning manoeuvre in a game against Makarczyk (1947).

It seems that also sufficient was the simple 1 ♕xa8+ ♔e7 2 ♕d5 (but not 2 ♕xh8? ♕xe4+ 3 ♔d1 ♕a4+ with perpetual check), but White played more elegantly: **1 ♗a3! ♕xa1 2 ♕d5!**, and it is clear that mate is inevitable.

Friedman – Tornblum (1974). 1 ... ♘h3? suggests itself, but after 2 e3 the white king obtains an air-hole. Therefore it is necessary to brick up the front: **1 ... ♖e3!** Now 2 ... ♘h3 leads inevitably to mate (incidentally there is also the threat of 2 ... ♖xf3 and 3 ... ♕h1X). White resigned.

When the king does not manage to escape to the flank, an attack by the queen, supported by a knight placed on the central squares, is usually successful. However, such a knight is good because it keeps up with the whole 'mass'.

Lovas – Csanadi (1964): **1 ♕h5+ ♔e6** (1 ... g6 2 ♖xf6+ ♗xf6 3 ♕f3) **2 ♗xf6 ♗xf6 3 ♖xf6+ gxf6 4 ♕f5+.** Black resigned. (4 ... ♔f7 5 ♕xf6+ and mate next move.

Winawer – De Vere (1870). Here it is Black's move. He exploits the exclusion of the white queen from the action of the main theatre of war, to bring his pieces into attacking positions: **1 ... ♕c4+ 2 ♔e1 ♘c6 3 ♕b7 ♘d4!** White resigned.

There is no peace for the king even in the endgame.

Batnikov – Borovoi (1957). **1 ... ♕b1+ 2 ♗c1 ♖e1+!** White resigned.

Let's look at methods of attack against the g7 (g2) squares. It excites heightened interest for attacking pieces because the knight can support the queen from four points on the chessboard.

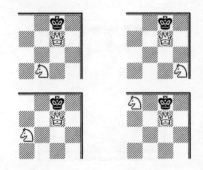

It is clear that the enemy king can also be on h8 (h1) or b7 (b2).

Most frequently the knight moves to the f5 (f4) square. In this case the g-file and the c1-h6 (h3-c8) diagonal serve as lines of military communication for the queen.

Yates – Rubinstein (1926). **1 ♗xf6 gxf6 2 ♗xe6**. Black resigned (2 ... fxe6 3 ♕g4+ or 2 ... ♗xe6 3 ♕g4+).

Osnos – Shofman (1970): **1 ... ♘f4! 2 ♕c3+ ♔h7 3 ♖xd6 ♕h3+**. White resigned.

Upon a transfer of the queen to the g-file there is a widely utilised tactical device – the freeing of squares.

Huber – Akatz (1957). The threat of mate on the 1st rank does not allow him to wait: **1 ♖xh7+! ♔g8 2 ♖h8+! ♔xh8 3 ♕h3+**. Black resigned (3 ... ♔g8 4 ♕g4+ and 5 ♕g7X).

Karpov – Csom (1977). After 1 ... ♘g5! the world champion would still have to prove whether his attack was worth the sacrificed piece. However the Hungarian grandmaster played **1 ... ♘f8?** and the struggle concluded with one point of contact: **2 ♘f5!** .

A thundering blow! The knight frees the g3 square for long-distance 'zero transportation' of the white queen – 2 ... ♘xd7 3 ♕h2+ ♔g8 4 ♕g3+ or 2 ... exf5 3 ♕h2+ mating in both cases. But a very spicy dish is served on the rank: one more unblocking manoeuvre is threatened – 3 ♖h7+! ♘xh7 4 ♕g7X, and against this there is no escape. Black resigned.

The concluding attack on the g-file is usually preceded by the elimination or deflection of the g7 (g2) pawn.

Muller – Pichler (1972): **1 ♘gh6+! gxh6**. Also declining the sacrifice leads to mate: 1 ... ♔h8 2 ♘f7+ ♔g8 3 ♘5h6+! gxh6 4 ♕g4+ ♔g7 5 ♘xh6+.

2 ♕g4+ ♔h8 3 ♖g7! Black resigned: 4 ♖g8X is threatened, and if **3 ... ♗c5**, then 4 ♖xh7+ ♔xh7 5 ♕g7X.

Upon a diagonal attack the queen heads for h6 (h3) with all speed.

Svensson – Berg (1966): **1 ... ♖xf3 2 gxf3 ♕h3**, and White resigned. Note how the queen makes her headlong dash from deep defence.

A similar idea is applied upon an attack against a king castled on the long side. Only in this case the queen dreams of landing on the a6 (a3) square.

Bilguer – Angerstein (1835). White has three pawns for the piece – a quite sufficient equivalent. However ... **1 ... ♘c3! 2 bxc3 ♕a3+ 3 ♔b1 ♘b6!** Well, who would not here give a check with the rook on b8? However after 3 ... ♖ab8+ 4 ♘b3 White retains

defensive possibilities (4 ... ♘b6 5 ♔a1). But now White resigned, since there is no defence against the threat 4 ... ♘a4; in the event of 4 ♔a1 the move 4 ... ♕xc3+ returns the king to its previous square. So, how about that, our predecessors really were able to play combinations!

The short dash of the queen (between the a3 and c3 squares in the previous example) is typical for operations on the king's flank.

Skuja – Abrosimov (1965). Mate on g7 is prevented by the rook g8, while the f6 square is defended by the enemy queen. White carries out a combination, the aim of which is to deflect one of the black pieces from carrying out its duties: **1 ♖xd5 exd5 2 ♖e8!** Black resigned.

Although the following combination is also built on this fairly straightforward tactical method, it is far from easy due to a number of additional subtleties.

Ragozin – Boleslavsky (1941): **1 ♗h6!** yet another typical device, opening the g-file. 1 ... g6 is no good because of 2 ♕e2, and Black loses the exchange.

1 ... gxh6 2 b3!. An important intermediate move. If immediately 2 ♘f5 (2 ♕xh6 ♕d7), then 2 ... ♗f4 3 ♕g4+ ♗g5 4 h4 ♘d6, and Black, by returning the piece, manages to drive away the knight from its dangerous outpost.

2 ... ♘b6. On 2 ... ♗f4 White replies simply 3 bxc4, restoring material equality while retaining all the benefits of his position.

3 ♘f5 ♔h8. After 3 ... ♗f4 4 ♕g4+ ♗g5 5 h4 ♔h8 6 hxg5 hxg5 7 ♖e3! the transfer of the rook to the h-file is decisive.

4 ♕xh6 ♖g8

Now compare this diagram with the position in the game Skuja – Abrosimov and you will without difficulty find the move **5 ♖e8!**, disorganising the interaction of the opponent's pieces. True, Black has a defence against the immediate threats: **5 ... ♗f8**. White has no other choice as **6 ♖xd8 ♗xh6 7 ♖xa8 ♖xa8 8 ♘xh6**. As a result he wins only a pawn (with the better position) which, however, is quite enough for victory. (Never mind that this did not happen in the game. After **1 ♗h6!** Boleslavsky did not enter

the main variation of the combination but played 1 ... ♕d7, which, however, hastened his defeat: 2 ♗xg7 ♔xg7 3 ♘f5+ ♔h8 4 ♖e4 ♗xh2+ 5 ♔h1, and Black resigned.)

An attack on the g7 square often accompanies the threat of a discovered double attack. Here's how it happens.

Kryysiayk – Fokina (1975): **1 ♖xe7!** ♗xe7 2 ♕g4. A typical position – mate is threatened on g7 as well as a discovered attack on the queen (3 ♘h6+). Black resigned.

The tactical pre-requisites of the operation are the vis-à-vis of the queens on the diagonal together with a knight on f5 (f4). Together with this, of course, the enemy queen must be, so to speak, 'hanging', that is without protection, and the g7 (g2) squares weakened.

Keres – Gligoric (1959): **1 ♖xg7+!** ♗xg7 2 ♕g4. Black resigned.

Here is the design layout of this construction: a knight is moved up to f5 (f4), the enemy queen enticed to the diagonal, and then the attacking queen completes the formation with a thrust to g4 (g5).

All these operations were placed on the conveyer belt in the game Savaleta – de Vicente (1958) whereupon White wanted to win (and did win) the exchange by **1 ♘d5? ♘xd5 2 ♛xd3**.

Now the black machine goes to work: **2 ... ♘f4** (one) **3 ♛e3 ♖xd2!** (two) **4 ♛xd2 ♛g5** (three). White resigned.

If one of the knights sacrifices himself to destroy the enemy castled position, the other can replace his lost comrade in the line of duty.

Bilek – Gligoric (1962): **1 ♘ef5! gxf5 2 ♘xf5**, and Black loses his queen (2 ... ♖f7 3 ♘xe7+), since she has no square from which she might defend her king against the check on g4. For example: 2 ... ♛f7 3 ♘h6+ or 2 ... ♛e8

3 ♛g4+ ♛g6 4 ♘e7+. Such a situation occurs quite often.

It is very important that the second knight manages to get to the vacant square in a timely manner.

Boleslavsky – Nezhmetdinov: **1 ... ♘xg2! 2 ♚xg2 ♘f4+ 3 ♚h1** (3 ♚g1 ♘h3+ 4 ♚g2 ♛xf2+ 5 ♚xh3 ♗d7+) **3 ... ♛xf2**. White resigned.

Landa – Klaman (1978): **1 ♛c1!** Black resigned (1 ... ♗xf5 2 ♛h6 ♚g8 3 ♘h5). A refined joke!

Engert (Black) in a game against Gulsman (1965) managed to create an amusing mating position.

1 ... ♘xg2! 2 ♔xg2? (he should reconcile himself to the loss of a pawn – 2 **♕xg2 ♗xc4**) **2 ... ♗h3+! 3 ♔xh3 ♕xf3**. White resigned: there is no defence against 4 ... ♘f4+.

A knight gets to e6 (e3) or e8 (e1) as a result of a rough and tumble brawl, so it is quite difficult to systematise typical methods of attack in these cases. We give some examples where different tactical means and direction of blows were utilised. They are united only by the ultimate goal – the queen and knight's endeavour to stay with the enemy king without witnesses. This often has to proceed at material expense, which, however, pays off ...

Moiseev – Iljevski (1974): **1 ♖xg7+! ♗xg7 2 ♖xg7+ ♔h8 3 ♖g8+!** Black resigned.

Grdzelishvili – Kasparov (1975): **1 ... ♖g2+! 2 ♗xg2 ♕b2 3 ♖c2 ♘xc2 4 ♕d7 ♘e3 5 ♗f3 ♕c1+ 6 ♔f2 ♕f1+**, White resigned.

Ljubislavlevic – Albano (1973): **1 ♘d6! ♘xd6 2 ♖h8+** (the king is lured into a discovered check) **2 ... ♕xh8 3 ♖xh8+ ♔xh8 4 ♘e6+ ♔h7 5 ♕g7X**.

As we are talking about a discovered check, we mention a typical attacking formation, based on this tactical element.

Henkin – Aronson (1954): **1 ♖xd6! exd6 2 ♘f6+ ♔g7** (2 ... ♔h8 3 ♕h6) **3 ♕d4**. White has created a menacing battery on the long diagonal. He threatens to jump away with the knight to the d5, e8 and h5 squares, in the last two cases with a double check. Such positions are usually indefensible, because the opponent, with all the will in the world, cannot break the construction of a discovered or double check with a single move.

3 ... ♕e7 4 ♘e8+ ♔h6 5 ♕g7+ ♔h5 6 ♘f6+ ♔h4 7 ♕h6+ ♔g3 8 ♕g5X.

Sabotage by the white knight in the game Botvinnik – Sharov (1928) led to the win of the exchange.

The black queen is tied to the defence of the rook c7, therefore: **1 ♘f6+! ♚h8 2 ♘e8!** Black resigned.

The study composers' idea of interference lies at the basis of the tactical operation carried out by Keller (White) against Nievergelt (1960).

A direct attack on the g7 square – 1 ♘e8 is parried by the move 1 ... ♛xb2. But what if he first blocks the a1-h8 diagonal?

1 ♗e5! ♖xe5 2 ♘e8 ♘f5 3 ♘f6+. Black resigned (3 ... ♚h8 4 ♛g8X).

Upon an advance of the knight to e7 (e2) either he himself inflicts the final blow or he offers this possibility to the queen operating on the h-file.

Here is the blitzkrieg scheme.

Kirillov – Khalilbeili (1959): **1 ♗xh7+! ♚xh7 2 ♛h5+ ♚g8 3 ♘e7X**
And its variants.

Cherubim – Orsch (1959): **1 ♗xh7+! ♚xh7 2 ♛h5+ ♚g8 3 ♘d5.** Black resigned, there is no way he can defend the e7 square (3 ... g6 4 ♛h6). In addition, he cannot prevent the mate with a move of the f-pawn, since the queen on h5 also controls the f7 square.

The same song, but with a refrain.

Katz – Shulman (1962): **1 ... ♗xh2+! 2 ♚xh2 ♛h5+ 3 ♚g1 ♖xe4 4 ♘xe4 ♘e2+** White resigned. But where is the chorus? Here it is – **3 ♚g3 ♖xe4 4 ♘xe4 ♘e2+.**

In the presented schemes, one of the squares around the king is blockaded by a pawn. If it disappears from the board, then the queen should stand close to the enemy king in close opposition, in order to deny it the maximum number of squares.

Muller – Hase (1959): **1 ♖xe6 fxe6 2 ♘e7+ ♔h7 3 ♕g6+ ♔h8 4 ♕h6X**.

As a rule, the final operation is preceded by the destruction of the castled position.

V.Romanovsky – Kharazian (1959): **1 ♘e7+ ♔g7 2 ♖xg6+ fxg6 3 ♕xg6+ ♔h8 4 ♕h6X**.

Destruction of the castled position is also the most common part of the method in combinations of the following type.

In the game Vorobil – Marek (1961) White achieved his objective with a sacrifice of two rooks.

1 ♖xg7+! ♔xg7 2 ♖xf7+! Black resigned (2 ... ♖xf7 3 ♕g6+ ♔h8 4 ♘xf7X).

Foguelman – Olivera (1960): **1 ♖xg7+! ♔xg7 2 ♕g3+!** The queen, with tempo, is engaged in an ambush, and must observe the future movements of the enemy. If the king moves away to f6, f8 or h8, then the knight takes the bit between his teeth and delivers a blow against it, respectively, on the g4 or g6 squares, and the queen comes out of hiding and slays her black rival on c7. The only square inaccessible to the knight is h7. But then the commander himself is taken prisoner: **2 ... ♔h7 3 ♕g6+ ♔h8 4 ♘f7X**.

In both examples, the queen drove the king into a corner, occupying the g6 square. But she can achieve the same result by occupying the f7 (f2) square.

Shmelev – Estrin (1971): **1 ... ♖c1!
2 ♖b1** (2 ♖xc1 ♕f2+ 3 ♔h1 ♘xg3X)
2 ... ♕e3 3 ♖bxc1 ♕xg3+ 4 ♔h1 ♘e3.
White resigned.

We have already mentioned the
particular properties of the 'double
check'. Here is a naive but instructive
miniature, in which the first check was
both a double check and the last one.

Milev – Chernei (1935): **1 e4 e5
2 ♘f3 ♘c6 3 d4 exd4 4 ♘xd4 ♘f6
5 ♗g5 ♗e7 6 ♘f5 d5 7 exd5 ♘e5
8 ♘xe7 ♕xe7 9 ♗xf6?? ♘f3X.**

The queen and knight together
sometimes create amazing mating
patterns. The following 'game', which
is not worth annotating in view of its

complete absurdity, has an amusing
final position: **1 e4 e5 2 f4 exf4 3 b3
♕h4+ 4 g3 fxg3 5 h3 g2+ 6 ♔e2
♕xe4+ 7 ♔f2 gxh1=♘X!.**

A bad joke with three knights!

Incidentally, a similar final pattern
was met in an international tournament
and the victim was a well-known
grandmaster.

Bogoljubow – Monticelli (1930):
**1 ... ♘e2+! 2 ♖xe2 ♖f1+! 3 ♔xf1
♕h1+ 4 ♔f2 ♘g4X.**

If the 'extra' pawn on h3 is removed
from the board, then we have a 'pure
mate', no less beautiful than the
previous diagram!

392. Imbish – Goring, 1899

White to move

Trojan horse.

393. Royen – Petersen, 1951

White to move

Trojan ... but not a horse!

394. Johner – Tartakower, 1928

White to move

1 ♗xe7. Exchange?

395. Dely – Mengarini, 1937

White to move

Who, where, and we are on the attack!

396. Makarov – Smit, 1964

White to move

Of course the b-file. But not at once.

397. Kupert – Muhl, 1962

Black to move

One, two, three ...

398. Richter – Tarrasch, 1892

Black to move

Resurrection of the queen.

399 Gottschall – Alef

White to move

Oblivious to luck.

400. Zolotarev – Steblyanko, 1976

Black to move

Fire torpedo ...

401. Plachetka – Sveshnikov, 1979

White to move

First came 1 h4, then ...

402. Golditz – Legel, 1959

White to move

1 ♘g5. "If you like, you can take either knight". Black captured the knight at d6.

403. Sandor – Navarovsky, 1954

Black to move

Preparing the artillery.

404. Bailey – McKeown, 1966

White to move

Three is not a crowd.

405. Bernstein – Tartakower, 1937

Black to move

Better to know how than to have.

406. Balashov – Grigorian, 1976

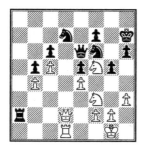

White to move

Taking the bit between your teeth ...

407. Balashov – Biyiasis, 1976

Black to move

1 ... ♗xc1. But chess is not checkers.

408. Moe – Hoen, 1972

Black to move

Gatecrashing.

409 Fomina – Epstein, 1971

White to move

Don't step back!

293

410. Nezhmetdinov – Estrin, 1951

White to move

Changing of the sentries.

411. Alexandria – Kristol, 1969

White to move

All the king's men ...

412. Portisch – Gligoric, 1975

White to move

Intrepid cavalry.

413. Strautmanis – Pashy, 1928

Black to move

Without fear and doubt.

414. Berqvist – Timman, 1972

White to move

Combination with a dual.

415. Bohm – Kochiev, 1977

Black to move

A little more pressure – and the enemy is on the run!

416. Yanofsky – Golombek, 1952

White to move

Draw, if not for ...

417. P.Williams, 1917

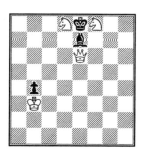

White mates in 2 moves

Mirror image.

418. W.Shinkmann, 1938

White mates in 3 moves

Scientific knowledge notwithstanding.

419 G.Zakhodyakin, 1969

White mates in 6 moves

Sleepy cowboy.

420. J.Gunst, 1926

White to move and win

Incredible but true.

14. Three Pieces

In one of the funniest books in the world, *Three Men in a Boat (To Say Nothing of the Dog)*, by Jerome K. Jerome, there's an episode in which the heroes of the story are stretching a canvas cover over the boat after hammering in the support arches.

"We got them fixed at last, and then all that was to be done was to arrange the covering over them. George unrolled it, and fastened one end over the nose of the boat. Harris stood in the middle to take it from George and roll it on to me, and I kept by the stern to receive it. It was a long time coming down to me. George did his part all right, but it was new work to Harris, and he bungled it.

How he managed it I do not know, he could not explain himself; but by some mysterious process or other he succeeded, after ten minutes of superhuman effort, in getting himself completely rolled up in it. He was so firmly wrapped round and tucked in and folded over, that he could not get out. He, of course, made frantic struggles for freedom – the birthright of every Englishman, – and, in doing so (I learned this afterwards), knocked over George; and then George, swearing at Harris, began to struggle too, and got himself entangled and rolled up."

"When there's no agreement among friends", on the chessboard the same confusion arises: the pieces get mixed up under each other's feet, creating a senseless scuffle. Meanwhile, in capable hands three pieces are a formidable brigade that can accomplish any military task quickly and precisely.

More than 200 years before, to be exact in 1787, in Paris, an amusing mini-game was played. Though it lasted only 7 moves, it went on to have a surprisingly long life.

Legall – Saint Brie: **1 e4 e5 2 ♘f3 ♘c6 3 ♗c4 d6 4 ♘c3 ♗g4 5 ♘xe5? ♗xd1?? 6 ♗xf7+ ♔e7 7 ♘d5X**.

You don't have to be a grandmaster to condemn White's light-hearted play and Black's greed – the 'modest' 6 ... ♘xe5 would have consigned to oblivion the name of the 85 year old Kermur Sire de Legall, though in his time he was the first chess teacher of the great Philidor.

However by a happy coincidence Legall's opponent was not, to put it mildly, too strong a chess player, and possibly also simply a lover of aethetics, valuing beauty over result. One way or the other, the final position pleased his contemporaries greatly, and they dubbed it 'Legall's mate'. We might suggest that he repeatedly performed such tricks even in his youth.

Since that time much water has flowed under the bridge and the military hardware of the chess army has modernised beyond recognition, yet 'Legall's mate' has not been removed from the armaments. It is just that it has been transformed into an elementary tactical operation, from time to time also appearing like a flash in great and small battles.

The game Bebchuk – Bakulin from the Moscow championship 1964 reached the position after the 4th move. White made the seemingly innocuous move **5 h3.** But when the bishop retreated to h5, **5 ... ♗h5**, the sacrifice **6 ♘xe5** became correct: **6 ... ♘xe5 7 ♕xh5 ♘xc4** (7 ... ♘f6 8 ♕e2) **8 ♕b5+**, and White won a pawn.

Of course, it is difficult to suspect master H.Bakulin of such blatant ignorance, but, as they say, 'everybody makes mistakes'.

These words of wisdom apply to an even greater extent to the game Tarrasch – Chigorin (1893).

Black's last move – ♘e6-e7?? astonished the venerable German maestro, who had obtained a rare opportunity to play, against one of the strongest players in the world, a 'combination' typical for a game in a simultaneous exhibition: **1 ♘xe5.**

Incidentally we mention that this game was played in a famous match (+9 –9 =4), which grandmaster D.Bronstein described as one of the most error-free!

Chigorin, of course, reconciled himself to the loss of a pawn and an inferior position (1 ... dxe5 2 ♘xf6+

gxf6 3 ♕xg4), since after **1 ... ♗xd1**
the black king is mated in 3 moves –
2 ♘xf6+ gxf6 3 ♗xf7+ ♔f8 4 ♗h6X.

This finish differs from the original
in its design, therefore such operations
have obtained the broader name
'Legall's legacy'. Here is another
version of it.

Tylor – NN (1924): **1 ♘xe5! ♗xd1**
(1 ... dxe5 2 ♗xf7+) **2 ♗xf7+ ♔e7
3 ♗g5X**.

In all these examples we have
looked at, the mating formation was

constructed by three minor pieces.
Their material equivalent is that of a
queen. But the 'light trio' in view of its
great mobility, as a rule is stronger than
the queen, it is important only to sort
out the interaction between the
'performers'. Such ideal interaction
manifests itself in combinations on the
'Legall theme'. In tactical terms this
theme highlights the illusory nature of
a pin. With a surprising jump, the
knight is freed from enemy restraint to
support his own comrades in a swift
attack on the king.

The following legendary performance
was a 'casual' game with the opponents
playing 'just' for their own satisfaction.
But the example set by the great
German, who sent his minor pieces on
an unprecedented heroic expedition,
has made it a model of chess beauty.

Anderssen – Kieseritzky (1851).
White has already sacrificed a rook and
bishop and in the heat of the attack will
stop at nothing: **1 e5! ♕xa1+ 2 ♔e2**.

Now Black has a tremendous
advantage in force but the threat of
mate (3 ♘xg7+ ♔d8 4 ♗c7X!) limits
his possibilities. For half a century this
position has been subjected to the most
thorough analysis, even by some of the
strongest players in the world.
However no satisfactory defence has
been found. Kieseritzky's move,

covering the c7 square, allowed a grandstand finish.

2 ... ♘a6 3 ♘xg7+ ♔d8 4 ♕f6+ ♘xf6 5 ♗e7X.

A fantastic position! White has sacrificed all his 'extra' pieces, he is now missing a queen, two rooks and a bishop, but on the board is a 'pure mate' which would have satisfied even the most exacting requirements for a composition.

Contemporaries called this game 'immortal'. With such an epithet it made history and still continues to amaze chess fans. In no way claiming it to be comparable, we'd like to show that even in our day we see beautiful combinational attacks completed with unusual finishes.

Christoffel – Platt (1948): 1 ... ♘g4! 2 ♘b3.

Actually the piece sacrifice should be accepted. After 2 exd5 Black can be satisfied with a draw – 2 ... ♘xf2 3 ♘b3 (weaker is 3 ♖f1 ♕xd5! 4 ♖xf2 ♗xf2+ 5 ♔xf2? ♕c5+) 3 ... ♘h3+ (bad is 3 ... ♘xd1+? 4 ♘xc5 bxc5 5 ♗f4, and the knight d1 perishes) 4 ♔h1 ♘f2+ etc. If you want to win then 2 ... ♕xd5 is worth considering. For example: 3 ♕e4 ♗xf2+ 4 ♔h1 ♕h5 with two pawns for a piece and a variety of threats (5 ... ♗xg3, 5 ... ♘xh2, 5 ... ♘e3).

White, apparently, placed great hopes on the move 2 ♘b3 as if now 2 ... ♘xf2 3 ♘xc5 ♘xd1, then 4 ♘xa6, and White obtains the advantage. After 2 ... ♗xf2+ 3 ♔h1 maintains the pin on the knight along the d-file. But Black has a worthy refutation.

2 ... ♘c3! 3 ♖xd8 ♘e2+ 4 ♔f1 ♖fxd8 5 ♘xc5 (threatening a discovered check, therefore White takes aim at the bishop a6, incidentally eliminating the other bishop, but trouble comes from the other side) 5 ... ♖d1+ 6 ♘e1 ♘xh2X.

A beautiful finish, brilliantly illustrating the interaction of pieces.

Among the multitude of positions, where three minor pieces force the capitulation of the enemy king, it is possible to identify a number that are typical and widely known in practical play. The main condition of a successful attack is to have a significant superiority in forces in the main direction of the breakthrough.

An elementary scheme of operating against a weakened kingside was illustrated by the end of the game Koblents – Jameson (1936).

All White's pieces are already on the battle line and waiting for the signal to attack: **1 ♕xh5!** Black resigned (1 ... gxh5 2 ♗h7X).

Gorshkov – Nikolaev (1973): **1 d5!** White opens the diagonal of the bishop b2 and at the same time parries the threat of mate on g2. Black resigned (1 ... ♕xd5 2 ♕xh7+ ♘xh7 3 ♗xh7X).

A similar mating threat can be exploited to gain time.

Ekstrom – Schoeberg (1977): **1 ♕h5!?** Using his 'extra-territory' (1 ... gxh5 2 ♗h7X), the queen frees the h3 square for the second wave of artillery fire.

1 ... ♗e8 (else 2 ♗xg6) **2 ♖f3 ♘b2? 3 ♖h3** Black resigned (3 ... ♘xd3 4 ♕xh6).

And here is how Black prepared the decisive blow in the game Korody – Benko (1951).

1 ... ♘e5! 2 ♘xd4 ♖xg2+ 3 ♔h1 ♖h2+!, and White resigned (4 ♔xh2 ♘g4+ 5 ♔g1 ♗h2X).

In the game NN – Tarrasch (1932) the white queen has already devoured two rooks and now, like a lazy python, is digesting its food in a secluded corner. Meanwhile Black carries out a successful king hunt. *(see next diagram)*

1 ... ♘e2+ 2 ♔h1 ♗xf2 (the simplest, the threat is 3 ... ♘g3X) **3 h3 ♕xh3+! 4 gxh3 ♗c6+ 5 ♔h2 ♗g3X.**

The final attack is not always so obvious in character. The contours of the mating position in the game Markus – Toma (1937) are not as simple.

A catastrophe occurs on the f7 square, the way to which will be penetrated by the bishop. The basic idea is accompanied by additional tactical ideas.

1 ♗h6+! ♔g8 (1 ... ♔xh6 2 ♘xf7+) **2 ♗e8!!** A very beautiful move. Black resigned. The threat is 3 ♗xf7X, and if 2 ... ♕xe8, then 3 ♘xd5 ♗xe5 (or 3 ... ♗g7 4 ♘f6+) 4 ♘f6+ ♗xf6 5 ♕xf6, and White wins.

The bishop, supported by the knight, can also deliver the final blow from the g7 (g2) square.

Oraevsky – Bubnov (1926): **1 ... ♘d3! 2 ♕xc7 ♗xf2+ 3 ♔h1 ♘xe1 4 cxd5 ♗g2X.**

The long diagonal also becomes the main artery of the attack in the following schemes.

The bishop's range allows it to hit its target from a distance. The knight does not directly defend the mating bishop, and along with the other bishop limits the living space of the enemy king.

A standard technical method of operation is a queen sacrifice on h6 (h3).

Abraham – Janine (1923). There is no time for the manoeuvre 1 ... ♕g3? 2 hxg4 ♕h4X in view of the threat 2 ♕xf7+. Therefore: **1 ... ♕xh3+! 2 gxh3 ♗f3X.**

In the game Exner – Englund (1902) the white queen is attacked. Since the bishop sacrifice on h6 does not work, White started to look at this square through 'telescopic sights' and found a decisive blow: **1 ♕xh6+! gxh6 2 ♗f6X**.

Let's get acquainted wiith the ending of the game NN – Blackburne (1880), in which the famous English master swiftly introduced his pieces into attacking positions.

1 ... ♘g4 2 h3 ♗xf2+ 3 ♔h1 If the black queen were not tied down to defence of the h7 pawn, then the move 3 ... ♕g3 (4 hxg4 ♕h4X) would decide. But Blackburne had already seen another finish.

3 ... ♗f5! 4 ♕xa8 ♕xh3+! 5 gxh3 ♗xe4X

When two bishops are operating on adjacent diagonals, the knight can deliver the final blow from three different points.

In the game Marshall – Soldatenkov (1928) the black bishops stalemate the enemy king on short diagonals.

The knight draws closer to the white king, overcoming all obstacles: **1 ... ♖xd2! 2 ♘xd2 ♘d4** (also sufficient is 2 ... ♕xf4) **3 ♕h5 ♕g5+!** White resigned (4 fxg5 ♗f2X or 4 ♕xg5 ♘e2X).

I.Zaitsev – Aparts (1963): **1 ... ♗h3!** Black, with tempo, brings new pieces into play. Not possible is 2 gxh3 in view of 2 ... ♖f8+ 3 ♔g2 ♖f2+ 4 ♔g1 ♘e2X (4 ... ♘f3X). Meanwhile the bishop h3 paralyses the g2 and h2 pawns, freezing the whole enemy kingside.

2 ♘c3 ♖f8+ 3 ♔g1 ♖f2 4 d3 ♖xg2+ 5 ♔f1 ♖g1+! 6 ♔xg1 ♘f3X.

Turunen – Maeder (1969): Here the bishops are placed on long diagonals while the knight endeavours to deliver a blow from the other side: **1 ♕xh6?** (1 ... gxh6 2 ♘xh6X) **1 ... ♖d8? 2 ♕h7+ ♔f8 3 ♗xg7+ ♔e8 4 ♗g6 d4 5 ♕g8+**. Black resigned.

A similar pattern is seen in the game Holmes – Tenner (1942) which is drawn with other tactical colours.

The white queen is under attack. On the e-file there are no free squares for her (1 ♕e3 ♘xc2+), for the same reason 1 ♕xf2 is no good. But the queen also does not need to move, the great advantage in development allows her to decide the battle with 3 checks in 2 moves: **1 ♘xd7+!** (discovered check) **1 ... ♘xe2 2 ♘f6X** (double check, it's also mate!).

When a cavalry attack is directed at the enemy castled position, then with the support of a bishop, it can lead to these mating finishes.

We show the scheme of dashing sabotage, step by step.

Lombardy – Sherwin (1959): **1 ♕xh7+ ♘xh7 2 ♗xh7+ ♔h8 3 ♘g6**.

If the king has the free f8 (f1) square, a similar operation brings success when the e8 (e1) square is blocked.

Shashin – Dashkevich (1955): **1 ♕xh7+ ♘xh7 2 ♗xh7+**, and wherever the black king goes it is caught by the knight on g6.

Chistiakov – Romkin (1946): **1 ♘g5 h6 2 ♕h7+**. Black resigned.

Readers will probably have noticed the characteristic arrangement of the attacking pieces: a queen and a bishop targeting the h7 pawn, a cavalry squadron on f4 and g5, ready to go.

Also possible is another distribution of troops: the queen operating along the h-file, and one of the knights moving up to e5 (e4).

Baturina – Belyaeva (1976): **1 ♕h5! h6** (1 ... ♘xh5 2 ♗xh7+ ♔h8 3 ♘g6X) **2 ♘ef7 ♕e8 3 ♗g6 hxg5? 4 ♕h8X.**

With a bishop on the a2-g8 (g1-a7) diagonal, the direction of the blow is changed.

Alvarez – Karpov (1972): **1 ... ♘f2+ 2 ♔h2 ♘6g4+ 3 ♔g1 ♘e4+.** White resigned: on each move of the king follows 4 ... ♘xg3X.

Mieses – NN (1990): **1 ♕g6!** The main task is to deflect the f7 pawn, in order to bring into action the mechanism of double check. For the present he threatens 2 ♘xf6+ and 3 ♕h7X. Nothing is changed by 1 ... hxg5 2 hxg5, and the function of the knight g5 is taken over by the rook h1.

1 ... fxg6 2 ♘xe7+ ♔h8 3 ♘xg6X.

When the bishop is on a short diagonal the knight makes even deeper raids into the enemy's rear.

Soika – Kolta (1925): **1 ♘xc6! ♕xc3 2 ♘xe7+ ♔h8 3 ♘f7X.**

The rook, in collaboraton with the two bishops, creates a mating position that is familiar to us from the chapter 'Rook and Bishop'.

Thus, in the first scheme, the bishop on e6 can be removed from the board and a black pawn placed on f7, in the second – a black pawn can be added on g7, when the bishop will be superfluous on e5. If, in the third scheme, a black rook were placed on g8, then the bishop e6 is not needed at all, in the fourth – the black pawn on h7 can successfully replace the white squared bishop. In other words, in each final episode, one of the bishops strikes a square which in other situations might be blocked by an enemy piece or a pawn.

Chigorin – NN (1880): **1 ♖xe5+ fxe5 2 ♕d8+ ♘xd8 3 ♖xd8X**. The f7 square can be blocked by any black piece (except the knight).

Alekhine – NN (1933): **1 ♕xg7+! ♔xg7 2 ♖g3+ ♔h6 3 ♗c1+ ♔h5 4 ♗e2+ ♔h4 5 ♖h3X**. Here the enemy king was drawn out from its hiding place and driven to the edge of the board.

Smolink – Asafarov (1956). In the next position White smoked out the black king from its refuge with a sacrifice followed by a discovered check: **1 ♕xg6+! ♔xg6 2 ♗h5+ ♔h7 3 ♗f7+ ♗h6 4 g6+ ♔g7 5 ♗xh6+ ♔h8 6 ♗xf8+**. Black resigned.

Waring – Fersht (1962): **1 ♗c4+ ♔h8 2 ♕xh7+! ♔xh7 3 ♖h3+ ♔g7 4 ♗h6+ ♔h7 5 ♗xf8X**.

In this and previous examples we see how the rook lies in wait, behind one of the bishops. At a crucial moment the bishop makes a dash to the side, opening the way for the rook to the king. White carried out the same operation in the following game.

Charousek – NN (1896): **1 ♕e8+! ♖xe8 2 fxe8=♕+ ♗xe8 3 ♗xd6X**. The difference lies only in the fact that the last check was delivered simultaneously by the rook and bishop.

A double check, which turned out to be mate, was also seen in the game Rudolph – NN (1912).

1 ♕h3! ♕xh3 2 ♖xg7+ ♔h8 3 ♖xf7+ ♔g8 4 ♖g7+ ♔h8 5 ♖g8X.

A typical combination where the final blow is delivered by one of the bishops.

Farago – Hazai (1976): **1 ... ♕xf2+! 2 ♔xf2 ♗d4+ 3 ♔e3 ♖xe3**. (in the game 1 ... ♖ce8? was played)

Balogh – Gromer (1931): **1 ♕a8+ ♘b8 2 ♕xb7+!** (White cannot delay, his king is already in danger) **2 ... ♔xb7 3 ♗xd7+ ♔a8** (also leading to mate is 3 ... ♔a6 4 ♗c8+ ♔a5 5 ♘c4+ ♔a4 6 ♖b4X) **4 ♖xb8+! ♔xb8 5 ♖b1+ ♔a8 6 ♗c6X**.

The fire power of the pieces was exploited to the maximum

by Vizantiadis (Black) against Sigurjonsson (1972).

1 ... ♖xf3! 2 ♕xd5 ♖h3+! 3 gxh3 ♗xd5+ 4 ♔h2 ♗e5X.

Let's look at mating finishes with the participation of the rook, bishop and knight.

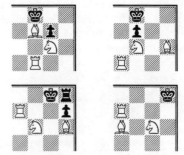

In all schemes the final check is delivered by one of the minor pieces, while the rook gives them 'specific gravity'. The method of attack depends on the overall picture of the position.

In the game Horwitz – Bledow (1837) the pre-requisites for a combination are created by the bishop b6 and rook f8, targeted on the f2 square. The tactical operation has something in common with 'Legall's legacy'.

1 ... ♞xe4! 2 ♗xe7 ♗xf2+ 3 ♔f1 ♞g3X.

The weakness of the white squares in the opponent's camp allowed Keller (Black) to penetrate the royal line against Barda (1956).

1 ... ♖xf4! 2 gxf4 ♗f5! The knight f3 is invulnerable, 3 ... ♗e4 is threatened. At the same time Black frees the g4 square for the queen.

3 ♕d5 ♕g4+ 4 ♔f1 ♕h3+! White resigned.

Bachman – Frechtel (1887). Sacrificing his queen, White smashes the pawn barrier and frees a whole complex of squares for his pieces. **1 ♕xf6+! gxf6 2 ♗h6+ ♔g8 3 ♞xf6X.**

Velikov – Perline (1972). The black queen is attacked, but the bishop and knight are eager for a fight. Who will be the third? The rook: **1 ... ♖xe4!** White resigned (2 ♖xb8 ♖e2+ 3 ♔h1 ♞g3X).

A delightful combination was played by N.Rossolimo in a simultaneous exhibition (1944). It does not fit into any scheme and can adorn any collection of chess masterpieces.

1 ♖xf5! (for the present, things are still not quite clear and therefore doubly interesting) **1 ... exf5 2 ♕xh6+!! ♔xh6** (not possible is 2 ... gxh6 3 ♞f6+ ♔h8 and 4 ♖g8X) **3 ♖h1+ ♔g6** (White has already given up enough pieces, but the result is still not apparent...) **4 ♔f4!!.**

An absolutely incredible move. On a full board of pieces the king rushes into the attack, in order to take away the g5 square from its black rival. Now White threatens 5 ♗h5+ ♔h7 (h6) 6 ♗xf7X.

4 ... ♖e6 (so that in the above mentioned variation he can cover with the rook on h6) **5 ♖h8!** Black resigned: there is no defence against the threat of 6 ♗h5X.

When the king is situated on the queenside, an important role in the attack, as we have already repeatedly mentioned, is played by the bishop, posted on the h2-b8 (b1-h7) diagonal. It nails the opponent's king to the c8 (c1) square, giving the knight the honourable right to deliver the decisive blow. Meanwhile the rook cuts off the king from the d-file.

The tactical operation and the movement of pieces to attacking positions, is similar to the methods looked at in the chapter 'Bishop and Knight'.

In the game Spanier – Lorenz (1965) a deadly check by the knight on b3 is prevented by the white queen. Black's task is to deflect it from its defence of critical squares.

1 ... ♕a5! White resigned. On 2 ♕xa5 follows 2 ... ♘b3X. Nor is there any escape on other replies, for example: 2 ♕d1 ♘b3+ 3 ♕xb3 ♕d2X.

Muse – Reinhardt (1935): **1 ... ♖xd2! 2 ♔xd2 ♕e5**. With a sacrifice of the exchange Black entices the king out of its refuge into the outside world. The threat is 3 ... ♕xb2+.

3 ♕b5 ♖d8+ 4 ♔c1. A familiar picture appears (see the previous diagrams).

4 ... ♘d4!, and White resigned (5 ♕xe5 ♘b3X or 5 ♕a4 ♕a5; however if 5 ♕b4, then even possible is 5 ... ♕xe2 with an unstoppable mate).

Rytov – Skuja (1971). Here things are already more serious. If he plays directly 1 ♘d5, then after 1 ... ♗c5 Black trembles but holds on. However it is possible to send the other knight on another route, only first it is necessary to carry out a little regrouping.

1 ♘b3! ♕b4 (1 ... ♕f5 2 ♕xa6) **2 ♘d5! ♗e6** (2 ... b5 3 ♕c3! ♕xc3 4 ♘xe7+ ♔b7 5 bxc3 ♖he8) **3 ♕xc6+!** Black resigned (3 ... bxc6 4 ♗xa6+ ♔b7 5 ♘xe7X).

A rook, supported by one of the minor pieces, can enter into direct contact with the enemy king. The third piece fulfils the function of 'stopper'.

The tactical operation in the next game is based on a double check.

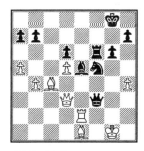

Langeweg – Casa (1968): **1 ... ♕f1+!** (attraction) **2 ♔xf1 ♘e3+ 3 ♔g1 ♖f1X**.

Kaeste – Nilsson (1957): **1 ♕h6+!** (deflection) **1 ... ♗xh6 2 ♘g5+ ♔h8 3 ♖h7X**.

Shiyanovsky (White), playing against Rumyantsev (1968), exploited other tactical elements.

1 ♗h6+ ♔g8 2 ♘xd5 ♕xd5 3 ♘f5! A discovered attack: the queen is under fire, also there is a threat of mate with the knight on e7.

3 ... ♕c5+ 4 ♗e3! Freeing a square: the bishop makes way for the knight which in this situation is a more useful piece. Black resigned (4 ... ♕c7 5 ♘h6+ ♔f8 6 ♖xf7X).

Sanz – Franco (1962): **1 ... ♕xh2+ 2 ♔xh2 ♘g4+ 3 ♔g1 ♘h3+ 4 ♔g2 ♖xf2+ 5 ♔xh3 ♖h2 mate**

Karlsson – Josefsson (1977): **1 ... hxg3 2 fxg3 ♗d5+**. White resigned. The queen is forcibly deflected from the 2nd rank, and the rook mates on h2.

The following final positions have a study-like character. They are delicate, light, beautiful, and not stolen from the museum but taken from tournament practice.

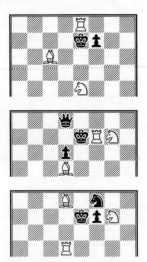

The operation in the game King – Benjamin (1962) is essentially a scheme.

1 ♕xe5! ♕xe5 2 ♖d8+ ♔e7 3 ♖e8X.

The same finish was intended by Euwe (White), when making his splendid move against Benitez (1948). **1 ♕a3! g6** (1 ... ♕xa3 2 ♖d8+ ♔e7 3 ♖e8X; there is no escape by 1 ... f6 2 ♖d8+ ♔f7 3 ♗e8+ ♔f8 4 ♗g6X) **2 ♖d8+**. Black resigned (2 ... ♔g7 3 ♖xg8+).

There was a good finish in an old game between Arnous de Riviere and Journoud (1848).

1 ♘e5! ♘xb3 2 ♘exf7+ ♕xf7 3 ♘xf7+ ♔d7 4 ♗b5+! (an important move, forcing Black to block his own king) **4 ... c6 5 ♖e7X**.

White also exploited a blockaded king in the next game.

Hebert – Shickley (1975): **1 ♖xf7+! ♗xf7 2 ♘f5+ ♔e6 3 ♘g7+ ♔e7 4 ♗d8X**

With a significant advantage in development, three pieces can carry out acts of sabotage even in the opening.

As a rule, such situations arise when there is a heavy concentration of forces in a central line of advance.

In the game Kumin – Grob (1961) Black could restore material equality by taking the knight on a7. However, to exploit his advantage in development, he starts an attack on the king stuck in the centre.

1 ... ♗g4 2 d4 exd3 3 ♕xd3 ♖d8. Only three moves are needed by Black to bring his main troops into battle.

4 ♕e3+ It seems that White has saved himself, since on 4 ... ♗e7? possible is 5 0-0. But the queen is no longer needed.

4 ... ♕xe3+! 5 fxe3 (otherwise 5 ♗xe3 ♖d1X) **5 ... ♖d1+ 6 ♔f2 ♘e4X.**

In the game Dorazil – NN (1958) White pretended that he wanted to exchange queens. But in fact he was creating one of the funniest, but typical, mating positions.

1 ♘xe5 ♕xd1 2 ♗xf7+ ♔e7 (2 ... ♔d8 3 ♖axd1+ ♗d6 4 ♘xc6+ bxc6 5 ♗xg7) **3 ♘g6+! ♔xf7 4 ♘xh8X.**

Potter – Matthews (1897): **1 ♘xe5!** (according to Legall's legacy) **1 ... ♗xd1 2 ♗b5+ ♔e7 3 ♗g5+ f6 4 ♘g6+ ♔f7 5 ♘xh8X.**

And here are two schemes and two examples of the interaction between rook and knights.

In the game Bronstein – Kottnauer (1946) the white cavalry attacked.

1 ♘e8! Black resigned. Bad is 1 ... ♕xe5+ 2 ♕xe5 ♖xe5 3 ♘g6+, while after 1 ... ♕b6 (with the threat of 2 ... ♕g1+) White forces mate: 2 ♕h7+! ♔xh7 3 ♖xg7+ ♔h8 4 ♘g6X.

Kamyshov – Estrin (1951): **1 ... ♘fg3+ 2 ♔g1 ♕xh2+! 3 ♔xh2 ♖h8+ 4 ♗xh8 ♖xh8+ 5 ♔g1 ♖h1X**.

Upon a combined attack of two rooks and a minor piece, the final picture often leads to the usual linear mate, with the only difference that one of the rooks enters into combat with the enemy king, being supported by the bishop and knight. It may be the minor piece robs the king of free squares.

When heavy pieces are taking aim at the royal fortress, a demolition sacrifice should be sought.

Suetin – Didishko (1975): **1 ♕xh7+!** Black resigned (1 ... ♔xh7 2 ♖dg2 or 2 ♖h2+ ♗h6 3 ♖xh6X).

Rellstab – Petrov (1937): **1 ... ♗xf4+! 2 ♕xf4 ♖g3!** (the h3 square is defenceless) **3 ♕xf5 ♖g2+**. White resigned.

The same mating construction was the tactical objective of the operation in the game between Smyslov (White) and Magrin (1968).

1 ♘f7+! (with tempo, freeing the g5 square for the rook) **1 ... ♖xf7 2 ♖g5 ♘g6** (the only defence against the threat of 3 ♖xh5X) **3 ♖xg6+ ♔h7 4 ♖6g5 d5** (Black opens the rank for his rook b6, in order to have the possibility of covering it after 5 ♖xh5+ ♖h6) **5 ♘xd5 ♘xd5 6 ♗xd5 ♖f8 7 ♖xh5+ ♖h6 8 ♗g8+!** Black resigned.

In the next position from the game Mista – Kloza (1955) Black had just played 1 ... ♗f8-c5, relying on the pin on the bishop d4. However, even in such a poor state he was able to give support to his rooks.

1 ♕h7+! Luring the king to the h7 square, so as to have the possibility of taking the rook g7 with check.

1 ... ♔xh7 2 ♖xg7+ ♔h8. Not possible is 2 ... ♔h6 because of 3 ♖1g6X, but now a volley of checks can be heard, allowing White to forcibly regroup his rooks for a decisive attack.

3 ♖g8+ ♔h7 4 ♖1g7+ ♔h6 5 ♖g6+ ♔h7 6 ♖8g7+ ♔h8 7 ♖h6X.

In the following three examples the bishop supplements the construction of the linear mate, making its own contribution.

Besser – Hackert (1968): **1 ♗g5 ♕e5 2 ♕xh7+! ♔xh7 3 ♖h4+ ♘h5 4 ♖xh5+ ♔g7 5 ♗e7+.** Black resigned.

Ward – Brown (1901): **1 ♕xf6+! gxf6 2 ♗h6+ ♕g7 3 ♖xf6X.**

Fulds – Lang (1956): **1 ♕xd5+! exd5 2 ♗b6+! axb6 3 ♖e8X.**

With a surprising sacrifice, T.Petrosian (White) brought his pieces into an attacking position in a game against Kupreychik (1976).

1 ♘xe4! ♕xe4 2 ♗d3 ♕b4+ 3 ♕xb4 ♘xb4 4 ♗xh7+ ♔h8 5 ♗b1+ ♔g8 6 ♗c4! a5 7 ♗h7+ ♔h8 8 ♗f5+! Black resigned (8 ... ♔g8 9 ♖ch4 f6 10 ♗g6 or 9 ... g6 10 ♖h8+ ♔g7 11 ♖1h7+ ♔f6 12 ♖xf8 with an easy win).

Also the knight can support the rook in its linear aspirations.

Sigurdsson – Kristiansson (1952): **1 ♕e8! ♖xe8 2 ♖xe8 ♗f7** (Otherwise 3 ♖fxf8+) **3 ♖xf7 h6 4 ♖exf8+**. Black resigned (4 ... ♔h7 5 ♖xg7X).

* * * *

421. Zheliandinov – Gusev, 1967

Black to move

A notch in the wood. 1 ... h6.

422. Anderssen – Schallopp, 1864

White to move

A genius smiles.

423. Pollock – Halle, 1884

White to move

From this story ...

424. NN – Kruger, 1920

Black to move

... many ...

425. Nyberg – Leepin, 1941

Black to move

... learn nothing.

426. Lykovnikov – Alekseev, 1973

Black to move

Someone is rushing somewhere ...

427. Duncan – Engheim, 1920

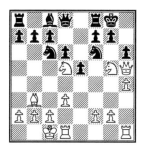

White to move

For the sake of a check ... but what a check!

428. Muller – Visel, 1955

Black to move

Fragment of the monarchy.

429 Jamieson – Gungaabazar, 1974

White to move

Crowded house.

430. Rudolf – NN, 1912

White to move

'Piano' and 'forte'.

431. Janowski – Samisch, 1925

White to move

The sapper queen.

432. Malmgren – Cuabrado, 1953

White to move

The Commander is out in front.

433. Kutur – Kozma, 1959

White to move

The mailed fist.

436. Tal – Petrosian, 1975

White to move

Blitz game – blitz solution.

434. Emmerich – Moritz, 1922

Black to move

Leapfrog.

437. Lemaire – Tibo, 1960

Black to move

Who comes first?

435. Lokasto – Zakrevsky, 1974

Black to move

1 ... ♘f5? And ...

438. Torber – Menke, 1966

White to move

Forced into the daylight.

439 Fischer – Miagmasuren, 1967

White to move

In three ... precisely.

440. Durao – Olivera, 1958

White to move

Critical mass.

441. Kellner – Zagorovsky, 1963

Black to move

What follows on 1 ... ♚d8?

442. Popova – Kasinova, 1974

White to move

In the land of the Amazons.

443. Bartushat – Hirsch, 1935

Black to move

Double somersault.

444. Dely – Donner, 1961

White to move

Getting the green light.

445. Timofeev – Shishkin, 1957

White to move

A steep hill.

448. Sikora – Chefranov, 1963

White to move

Nowhere to run.

446. Druganov – Panteleev, 1956

Black to move

1 ... ♘xb1? 2 ♖xe8X. However ...

449 NN – Charle, 1903

Black to move

The fall of Pompeii.

447. Perlaska – Grassi, 1907

White to move

Commotion in the land of Nod.

450. Kunin – Oksenhoit, 1958

White to move

Not much yet, still ...

451. Yudovich – Ragozin, 1937

White to move

And he did not play 1 ♘f5. But if he did ...

452. V.Masman, 1935

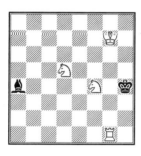

White mates in 3 moves

Head spinning.

453. O.Wurzburg, 1941

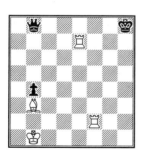

White mates in 3 moves

Sleeping beauty.

454. B.Lindgren, 1967

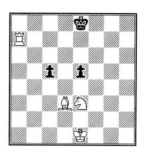

White mates in 4 moves

Link arms.

455. A.Mandler, 1959

White mates in 4 moves

Go out, in order to return.

456. V.Masman, 1950

White mates in 4 moves

Trading places ...

15. Solutions

When checking your answers to the exercises with the solutions, in a number of cases you might come across alternative versions. Not all the positions have only one solution. In some the win is obtained not only with the help of tactics, but also positional means. In practical play it will also frequently be like this: the side having the advantage has several ways leading to victory. In the answers are given continuations occurring in the games, or mentions of missed opportunities.

If you find another way to win, that's good. But even better, if you find a combination or tactical blow on the theme of the corresponding chapter. You know, in the end, to win a game quickly and effectively is always more pleasant than carrying out a technical realisation of the advantage.

Differing from the usual manuals in chess literature, the listing of the names of the opponents is not given in the solutions to the exercises, but right after the diagrams with the puzzles. We think that to a large extent this format is more conducive to mastering the material, since fixed in the memory at the same time are both the contours of the positions and their co-authors.

1. Rook

1. **1 ... ♖b3!** White resigned.

2. **1 ♕a7!** Black resigned.

3. **1 ♕f6+!** Black resigned.

4. **1 ♕e5!** Black resigned.

5. **1 ♗b8!** Black resigned (1 ... ♖xb8 2 ♕d7+ ♔f8 3 ♕d8+).

6. **1 ♖e1? ♖xe1+ 2 ♘xe1 ♕f4! 3 ♘f3 ♗xf3** White resigned.

7. **1 ♖xf6? ♕c6!** White resigned.

8. **1 ... ♖xc6 2 ♖f7!** Black resigned.

9. **1 ... ♖a8?** (Correct is 1 ... ♗d7) **2 ♘d8!** Black resigned.

10. **1 ♕e8! ♖xe8 2 ♖xe8 ♗d7 3 ♖d8** Black resigned.

11. **1 ♘e4!** Black resigned (On 1 h3? Black would have defended by 1...♕e6).

12. **1 ♗e6!** Black resigned (1 ... ♗xe6 2 ♕a8+ ♗d8 3 ♕xd8+).

13. **1 ♕xb4!** Black resigned (1 ... ♖xb4 2 ♖c8+ ♘g8 3 ♖xg8+ or 1 ... ♖e8 2 ♕xe7).

14. **1 ♖xd8+ ♖xd8 2 ♕f7!** Black resigned.

15. **1 ♗h6! ♕xh6 2 ♕h4!** Black resigned.

16. **1 ... ♕f4!** White resigned.

17. **1 ♕xd6!** Black resigned (1 ... cxd6 2 ♘f7+).

18. **1 ♖d8+ ♘e8 2 ♕b2! ♕e7 3 ♕xb7! ♕xd8 4 ♕xf7+** Black resigned.

19. **1 g6!** Black resigned. 1 ... hxg6 2 ♖e8 threatening 3 ♖xf8+ and 4 ♖h8X.

20. **1 ♕b4! ♖d8 2 ♖cd5** Black resigned.

21. **1 ... ♕f4 2 ♔g1?** (2 ♕b5) **2 ... ♕d4+ 3 ♔h1 ♕f2!** White resigned (4 ♖g1 ♖e1).

22. **1 ♕xe7 ♕d4+ 2 ♗e3 ♕xa1 3 ♕xf8+!** Black resigned (3 ... ♔xf8 4 ♗c5+ ♔g8 5 ♖e8X).

23. **1 ... ♖xa2? 2 ♗d5!** Black resigned.

24. **1 ♖xd5? ♕f2!** and Black wins. (In the game 1 ... ♕a6?? 2 ♘g3! was played and White maintained equality).

25. **1 ♗xc7? ♖xc7 2 ♖xb4 ♖ac8!** White resigned.

26. **1 ... ♘e4 2 ♖xe4 ♖xf6 3 ♘g6+!** Black resigned (3 ... fxg6 or 3 ... ♖xg6 – 4 ♕xh7+! ♔xh7 5 ♖h4X).

27. **1 ♕f6+! ♘xf6 2 ♗c5+!** Black resigned (2 ... ♗xc5 3 gxf6+ ♔f8 4 ♖h8X).

28. **1 ♘d5! ♗xd5** (1 ... ♖xc3 2 ♕h6) **2 ♕h6 ♖g8 3 ♕xh7+ ♔xh7 4 ♖h3X.**

29. **1 ... ♗xf4? 2 ♘f5+! exf5 3 exf5+** Black resigned (3 ... ♔f8 4 ♖xc6!).

30. **1 ♗xc7+! ♖xc7 2 ♕e8+! ♔xe8 3 ♖b8+** Black resigned.

31. **1 ... ♕xg3! 2 ♖xd5+ ♖xd5 3 fxg3 ♖xh2+!** White resigned.

32. **1 ♖d5+ ♔f4 2 ♔f2!** Black resigned as 2 ... ♕d7 3 ♖hh5! with an unstoppable mate on f5).

33. **1 ♕e1! ♕d8 2 ♕e5** (simpler than 2 ♖e6) **2 ... ♔g8 3 ♕e6+ ♔h8 4 ♕xd7** Black resigned.

34. **1 ... ♘g3+! 2 hxg3 ♖f6!** White resigned.

35. **1 ... f4!** White resigned (2 ... ♗c5+ 3 bxc5 bxc5X is threatened, and if 2 ♘b3 then 2 ... ♖c4X).

36. **1 ♗b1? h4+ 2 ♔g4 f5+! 3 ♖xf5** (now the rook is pinned) **3 ... ♖g2X.** White obtained a draw after 1 ♗xf7+! ♔xf7 2 ♖xg5.

37. **1 ♖f3! ♕xf3 2 ♕g7+ ♔h5 3 ♕xg6+! hxg6 4 ♖h8X.**

38. **1 ♖d8+! ♕xd8 2 ♕xe5** (threatening mate on g7) **2 ... ♕d7 3 ♕h8+! ♔xh8 4 ♖f8X.** 'Clearing the table' as they say in snooker.

39. **1 ... ♕g1+! 2 ♖xg1 f2+ 3 ♔h1 fxe1=♕** Black resigned.

40. **1 ♕d2! ♕a8** (1 ... ♕f8 2 ♕e3) **2 ♕a5 ♕b8 3 ♕xc7** Black resigned.

41. **1 ♖d8!** and White wins (the threat is 2 ♖b7X, if however 1 ... ♖xd8 2 c7+ ♔b7 3 cxd8=♕+). In the game 1 c7+? was played and White lost.

42. **1 ... ♖xf3! 2 ♕xg5 ♖xf2!** White resigned.

43. **1 ... ♖g8+ 2 ♔h6 ♕xh2+ 3 ♖h5 ♕d2+! 4 ♕xd2 ♖g6X.**

2. Bishop

44. **1 ... h6? 2 ♕f6+!** Black resigned (2...♔xf6 3 ♗e5X).

45. **1 ... ♖xd6! 2 ♖xd6 ♖f3+!** Black resigned (3 gxf3 ♗f1X).

46. **1 ♖xf7! ♕xf7 2 ♕xh7+! ♕xh7 3 f7X.**

47. **1 ... ♕g1+ 2 ♔f5? ♕g6+! 3 ♕xg6 ♗e6X.**

48. **1 ... ♔xg6 2 ♗g5 ♖f4+!** White resigned (3 gxf4 ♗f2X; 3 ♗xf4 ♗e7+ 4 ♗g5 ♗xg5X).

49. **1 ... ♗xh2! 2 ♖xe8 ♔h6** White resigned.

50. 1 d7 f2 2 d8=♕ f1=♕ leads to a draw [in fact 3 ♗c2+! ♔b4 4 ♕d2+ ♔c4 5 ♗e4! ♕b3 6 ♗d5+ ♔a4 7 ♕d4+ wins - ed]. The cramped position of the black king allows White to start a mating attack with little material. **1 ♔c5!** (threatening 2 ♗c2X) **1 ... ♔b3.** If 1 ... a2 2 ♗xa2 f2, then 3 ♗c4, and White wins. It seems the black king breaks out of the danger zone, but soon it must return to its previous position: **2 d7 f2 3 d8=♕ f1=♕ 4 ♕d5+ ♔c3** (4 ... ♔b2 5 ♕a2+ ♔c3 6 ♕c2X) **5 ♕d4+ ♔b3 6 ♕a4+! ♔xa4** (6 ... ♔b2 7 ♕c2+) **7 ♗c2X.**

51. **1 ♔f3 g1=♕** (1 ... g1=♘+ 2 ♔f2+) **2 ♘f2+ ♕xf2+ 3 ♔xf2X.**

52. **1 ♘d4+ ♔b1 2 ♘b5! a2 3 ♘a3+ ♔b2 4 ♗f6+! ♔xa3 5 ♗a1! b5+ 6 ♔c3 b4+ 7 ♔c4 b3 8 ♔c3 b2 9 ♗xb2X.**

53. **1 ♘c6!** This move gains an important tempo; in view of the threats of 2 ♘b4+ or 2 ♘xd4 it is necessary to eliminate the knight. **1...♔xc6 2 ♗f6 ♔d5** (Of course on 2 ... ♔c5 follows 3 ♗e7+) **3 d3!! a2 4 c4+! ♔c5** (Naturally not 4 ... dxc3 5 ♗xc3 with an easy win for White) **5 ♔b7!!** (Crowning of the idea. On 5...a1=♕ White delivers mate in the centre of the board – 6 ♗e7X, while after 5 ... ♔b4 or 5 ... ♔d6 6 ♗xd4 Black can quietly resign. And so, six moves in all, but what moves!).

3. Queen

54. **1 ... ♖xh2+!** White resigned.

55. **1 ♕h6!** Black resigned.

56. **1 ... d2? 2 ♖xb8+** Black resigned.

57. **1 ... ♖e3+** White resigned.

58. **1 ♖xh6+!** Black resigned.

59. **1 ♖b4!** Black resigned.

60. **1 ... ♕xe5? 2 ♕h6!** Black resigned (2 ... ♕xf6 3 ♖d8+! ♗xd8 4 ♕f8X).

61. **1 d5! ♕xd5 2 ♕h6 ♖xf6 3 ♖xf6** Black resigned.

62. **1 ... ♖f7!** White resigned.

63. **1 ... ♕a1+!** White resigned (2 ♔h2 ♕e5+ 3 ♕g3 ♕h5+ 4 ♔g1 ♖d1+ 5 ♗f1 ♖xf1+ 6 ♔xf1 ♕d1X).

64. **1 ♖d5!** Black resigned (1...♕xd5 2 ♖e8+).

65. **1 ♕f8+ ♔g5** (1 ... ♔h7 2 ♗g8+ ♔h8 3 ♗f7+ ♔h7 4 ♕g8+) **2 ♖xf5+!** White resigned (2 ... gxf5 3 ♕g7X or 2 ... ♔g4 3 ♖g5+! ♔h3 4 ♕c8+).

66. **1 ♕g3+ ♔h8 2 ♕e5+ ♔g8 3 ♕g5+ ♔h8 4 ♖xf7 ♕xf7 5 ♕d8+ ♕g8 6 ♕f6+ ♕g7 7 ♕xg7X** (In the game 1 ♕e6? was played).

67. **1 ♖xg7+! ♔xg7 2 ♕e7+ ♔g8 3 ♕f8+ ♔h7 4 ♕f7X.**

68. **1 ... ♖h5+! 2 ♔xh5 ♕h3+ 3 ♔g5 h6+ 4 ♔f4 g5+ 5 ♔e5 ♕e6X.**

69. **1 ... f5+ 2 gxf5 ♕f5+ 3 ♔h4 ♕h5X.**

70. **1 ... ♖f1+! 2 ♗xf1 ♕e4+! 3 ♕xe4 exf1=♕X.**

71. **1 ... ♗e3+! 2 ♗xe3 ♘f2! 3 ♗xf2 ♕d2+ 4 ♔b1 ♕d1+ 5 ♔a2 ♕xc2X.**

72. **1 ♗f5+ ♔h8 2 ♖g6!** Black resigned (2 ... fxg6 3 ♖xh6+).

73. **1 ... ♖c1+! 2 ♕xc1 ♖xa3+! 3 ♔b1 ♖a1+! 4 ♔xa1 ♕a8+ 5 ♔b1 ♕a2X.**

74. **1 ... f6+ 2 ♔g4** (2 ♕xf6 ♕g3X) **2 ... ♕g2+ 3 ♔g3 f5+ 4 ♔f4 e5+! 5 dxe5 ♕d2X.**

75. **1 ♕e8+ ♔h7 2 ♘g5+! hxg5 3 ♖h3+ ♔g6 4 ♖h6+!** Black resigned (4 ... gxh6 5 ♕g8X or 4 ... ♔xh6 5 ♕h8+ ♔g6 6 ♕h5X).

76. **1 ... ♘d1+** was played (1 ... ♘c2! 2 ♖b1 ♕e3+ 3 ♕xe3+ fxe3+ 4 ♔e2 exd2 wins), and after **2 ♔g1 ♘c3!** (threatening 3 ... ♕e3X) **3 h3** (White could have fought on with 3 ♘b1! ♗a4 4 bxc3 ♗xb3 5 axb3 ♗d6 6 c5 ♗xc5 7 ♖a2) **3 ... ♗a4!** White resigned.

77. **1 ♔g3! ♔h7 2 ♕f8 ♔g6 3 ♕g8X.**

78. **1 ♔d7!** (1 ♘g5 is not decisive because of 1 ... ♕h5 2 ♔xh5 ♘f6) **1 ... ♘d6 2 ♔xd6 ♕xh7 3 ♕e8X.**

79. **1 ♕d6! ♔e4 2 g4 ♔e3 3 c3 ♔e4 4 ♕d4X.**

80. **1 ♕c3!** (threatening 2 ♕e3X; if 1 ... ♔g5 2 f4+ ♔h6 3 ♕h8X) **1...♕xf3 2 ♕c1+! ♔e4 3 ♕c4X.**

4. Knight

81. **1 ♖e8+ ♗d8 2 ♖xd8+! ♖xd8 3 ♘c7+ ♔b8 4 ♘a6+ ♔a8 5 ♕b8+! ♖xb8 6 ♘c7X.**

82. **1 ♖e8+!** Black resigned. **1 ... ♖xe8** (1 ... ♔xe8 2 ♘xd6+ or ♘xg7+) **2 ♕xd6+ ♔g8 3 ♘e7+ ♔f8** (3 ... ♖xe7 4 ♕d8+) **4 ♘g6+ ♔g8 5 ♕f8+ ♖xf8 6 ♘e7X.**

83. **1 ♖h6!** Black resigned. (1 ... ♕xh6? 2 ♘f7X or 1 ... c5 2 ♖xf6 cxd4 3 ♘f7+ ♖xf7 4 ♖xf7 ♖g7 5 ♖xg7 ♔xg7 6 cxd4).

84. **1 ♘d8! ♖xg2+** (Desperation; if 1 ... ♕xd5 2 ♖e8+ ♔g8 3 ♘f7X) **2 ♔h1** (2 ♔xg2? was actually played but should have lost to 2 ... ♕xd5+, however the game went 2 ... ♕g6+ 3 ♖g3 Black resigned.)

85. **1 ♖xe6! ♕xe6 2 ♘g5 ♕g6 3 ♖xh7+ ♔xh7 4 ♘f7X.**

86. **1 ... b6 2 cxb6 axb6 3 ♕xb6?** ♕xb4! White resigned; he cannot hold the f2 square without serious loss (4 ♕e3 f4!; 4 ♖gb1 ♕xb6 5 ♖xb6 ♖ag8).

87. **1 ... ♘e4!** White resigned.

88. **1 f4 exf4 e.p. 2 ♖xd5! ♖xe1+ 3 ♕xe1 cxd5 4 ♕e6+** Black resigned (4 ... ♔h8 5 ♘f7+).

89. **1 ... ♕h3 2 ♕f1 ♘g4!** White resigned. For the cadre there remains the additional stroke 3 ♕g1 ♕g2+ 4 ♕xg2 fxg2+ 5 ♔xg2 ♖xf2+ or 3 ♗g1 ♕xf1 4 ♖xf1 f2.

90. **1 ... ♖c2!** Now on 2 ♕e3 could follow 2 ... ♘e2+ 3 ♔f2 ♘g4+. He has to take the rook – **2 ♗xc2** but then **2...♘e2X.**

91. **1 ... ♕h5! 2 ♕xd5+ ♔h7 3 ♕xa2 ♖xh3+ 4 gxh3 ♕xh3+ 5 ♕h2 ♘f2X.**

92. **1 ♗d4+! cxd4 2 cxd4+ ♔f4 3 ♘e6X.**

93. **1 ♘h8!** and there is no defence against **2 ♘g6X.**

94. **1 ♕xd4! ♕xd4 2 ♘f5 h5 3 ♘xd4 ♖e8 4 ♘f5 d4 5 e6** Black resigned.

95. **1 ♘e7+ ♔h5? 2 g4+! ♔xh4 3 ♔g2** and Black resigned; the knight returns to f5, punishing the right hand excursion.

96. **1 ... g5** (2 ... ♖h4+ 3 gxh4 g4+ 4 ♔g3 ♘e2X is threatened) **2 ♖fe1 ♖f4!** (forcing White to block this square) **3 gxf4 g4+ 4 ♔g3 ♘f5X.**

97. **1 ... Ⓧxc4! 2 Ⓧxc4 ♘b6** (the threat of mate forces a transfer to a winning pawn endgame) **3 Ⓧc5 ♘d5+ 4 Ⓧxd5 exd5 5 e4 fxe4 6 fxe4 dxe4 7 ♔xe4 ♔e6** White resigned.

98. **1 ♗f6!** (zugzwang) **1 ... gxf6 2 ♔f8 f5 3 ♘f7X.**

99. **1 ♘g5+ ♔h6 2 Ⓧh8+! ♔xh8 3 ♔g8 ♘d6 4 ♔xh8** (zugzwang) and **5 ♘f7X.**

100. **1 Ⓧd2! ♘xd2** (1 ... ♘a3+ 2 ♔b3) **2 ♘c1!** (zugzwang) and **3 ♘xb3X.**

101. **1 ♔f3! ♔h1 2 ♔f2 ♔h2 3 ♘c3 ♔h1 4 ♘e4 ♔h2 5 ♘d2 ♔h1 6 ♘f1 h2 7 ♘g3X.**

102. **1 ♔f2 h4 2 ♘d3 ♗f5** (2 ... ♗c6 3 ♔f1 ♗b5 4 ♗h7 ♗xd3+ 5 ♗xd3 f2 6 ♗e4X) **3 ♗d5 ♗e4!** (counting on continually pursuing the white bishop) **4 ♗a8! ♗xa8 5 ♔f1** and **6 ♘xf2X.**

103. **1 ♘c5!** (but not 1 ♘d4? e2+ 2 ♘xe2 ♘f1 3 ♘d4 ♘e3+ 4 ♔d2 ♘f1+ etc). **1 ... e2+ 2 ♔d2 ♘f1+ 3 ♔c1! ♔xe1 4 ♘d3X.**

104. **1 ♘d6+ ♔g3! 2 ♘f5+ ♔g2! 3 ♕g4+** (3 ♘xh6? f2+ – draw) **3 ... ♔h1!** (if 3 ... ♔h2, then 4 ♕g3+ ♔h1 5 ♘xh6) **4 ♕xh6 f2+ 5 ♔f1 ♗xg4 6 ♘xg4** (zugzwang) **6...♗h2 7 ♘xf2X.**

105. **1 ♔xe1 ♕a1 2 h3!!** (a very difficult move, the point of which becomes clear later) **2 ... ♕a2 3 h4 ♕a1 4 h5 ♕a2 5 h6 ♕a1 6 h7 ♕a2 7 h8=♘!** (the pawn has noticeably increased in weight) **7 ... ♕a1 8 ♘f7 ♕a2 9 ♘d8 ♕a1 10 ♘e6 ♕a2 11 ♘xc5 ♕a1 12 ♘e4 ♕a2 13 ♘d6 ♕a1 14 ♘xc4 ♕a2 15 ♘a5 ♕a1** (now it is clear why he had to lose a tempo and play 2 h3! and not 2 h4; in this case the queen would now go to a2) **16 ♘xb3X.**

106. **1 f3+ gxf3 2 exd3+ cxd3 3 ♗f5+ exf5 4 Ⓧe6+ dxe6 5 Ⓧd4+ cxd4 6 a8=♗+ ♕d5 7 ♗xd5+ exd5 8 ♘f6+ gxf6 9 ♕e5+ fxe5 10 ♘g5X.**

5. Pawn

107. **1 ♕xd4+!** Black resigned (1...Ⓧxd4 2 b6X).

108. **1 ♕e1+!** Black resigned (1 ... Ⓧxe1 2 g3X).

109. **1 Ⓧf4+ ♔h5 2 Ⓧh4+! gxh4 3 g4X.**

110. **1 Ⓧg7+ ♔h5 2 ♔g2!** Black resigned (3 ♔h3 and 4 g4X is unstoppable).

111. **1 ♘f5+! ♔h5** (1 ... gxf5 2 ♕xf6+ ♔h5 3 ♕g5X) **2 ♕xh7+! ♘xh7 3 g4X.**

112. **1 c5! ♘e6** (1 ... bxc5 2 ♘c4+ ♔b5 3 a4X; or 1 ... b5 2 a3! – zugzwang) **2 ♘b7+ ♔b5 3 a4X.**

113. **1 ♗g8+ ♔g6 2 Ⓧc6+ Ⓧf6 3 h5+!** Black resigned (3 ... ♔xh5 4 ♗f7+! and 5 g4X). There is also no salvation in 2 ... ♗f6 3 g4 Ⓧxf4 4 h5+ ♔g5 5 Ⓧc5+.

114. **1 Ⓧb6! cxb6 2 c3 b5 3 ♔c5 b4 4 cxb4X.**

115. **1 Ⓧb7! ♕xb7 2 ♗xg6+ ♔xg6 3 ♕g8+ ♔xf5 4 ♕g4+ ♔e5 5 ♕h5+ Ⓧf5 6 f4+ ♗xf4 7 ♕xe2+ ♗xe2 8 Ⓧe4+ dxe4 9 d4X!** This really is doing it single-handedly in the field of battle!

116. **1 ♔f3!** (1 ♔e4? c5 2 ♔d3 ♔e8 3 ♔c4 ♔f7 with a draw) **1 ... c6** (1 ... c5 2 ♔e4 ♔e8 3 ♔d5!) **2 ♔f4 c5 3 ♔e4** (zugzwang) **3...♔e8 4 ♔d5! ♔d7 5 ♔c4** (zugzwang again) **5...♔e8 6 ♔xc5 d3 7 ♔d6 d2 8 ♔e6 d1=♕ 9 f7X.**

117. **1 ♔g2 a5** (or 1 ... ♔xf5 2 ♔f3 ♔g5 3 g4 a5 4 ♔e4 ♔xg4 5 h6) **2 ♔f3 a4 3 h6! ♔xh6 4 ♔g4 a3 5 ♔h4 a2 6 g4 a1=♕ 7 g5X.**

6. Two Rooks

118. **1 ♖c1!** (White wins the queen, since 1 ♕xa4 is not possible because of 1...♘xc8X) **1 ... ♖f6 2 ♖xc6 ♖fxc6 3 ♖xa7** Black resigned.

119. **1 ... ♕xe4+!** White resigned (2 ♕xe4 ♖6f2X).

120. **1 ♖xh6+! ♔xh6 2 ♕h3+ ♔g7 3 ♕g3+ ♔h7 4 ♕h4+ ♔g7 5 ♕g5+ ♔h7?** (5 ...♔h8 6 ♖d3 f6) **6 ♖d3** (only now, when the king is restricted to the edge, and the queen does not obstruct the transfer of the rook along the third rank) Black resigned. If 6...♖xc3 the queen is allowed to go back down a short flight of stairs to the third rank, and Black loses a rook).

121. **1 ♘c6+! bxc6 2 ♖b1+ ♔a7 3 ♕f2+** Black resigned.

122. **1 ♕xf7+!** Black resigned.

123. **1 ♕xc7+!** Black resigned.

124. **1 ♗c5!** Black resigned.

125. **1 ♗g5! hxg5 2 hxg5** Black resigned.

126. **1 ♗e7!** and White wins; 1...♘d7 (1 ... ♖xe7 2 ♖d8+) 2 ♗xe6 ♖xe7 3 ♗xd7 ♖d8 4 ♖gd3.

127. **1 ♕c6!** Black resigned.

128. **1 ♕xh7!** Black resigned.

129. **1 ♖b1 ♕a5 2 ♕xf7+!** Black resigned.

130. **1 ♗xb7!** Black resigned (1 ... ♕xb7 2 ♖d8+ or 1 ... ♗xb7 2 ♖d7).

131. **1 ... ♘h4? 2 ♕xh6+!** Black resigned. Correct was 1 ... ♕xg2+ 2 ♔xg2 ♘xf4+.

132. **1 ♘e6!** Black resigned (1 ... ♗xe6 2 ♕xh7+!).

133. **1 ... ♕c3!** Black resigned.

134. **1 g6+!** Forcing Black to close the only airway, since on 1 ... ♔xg6 follows 2 ♖g8+ ♔f7 (2 ... ♔h5 3 ♖h1+) 3 ♖bg1 with the unstoppable ♖g1-g7X.

But after **1 ... hxg6** a blow was delivered from the other side – **2 ♖b7X**.

135. **1 ... ♘xe5** The rook is deflected from the first rank. **2 ♖xe5 ♖c1+** White resigned (3 ♔h2 ♘g4+!).

136. **1 ... ♖xe3 2 ♕f8+!** Black resigned.

137. **1 ♖xd7! ♖xd7 2 ♘f6+ ♔h8** (2 ... gxf6 3 ♕xg4+ ♔h7 4 ♕h5+ and 5 ♖g1X). **3 ♕xg4 g6 4 h5** Black resigned.

138. **1 ... ♕g1+!!** – what a beautiful move! **2 ♖xg1 ♘f2X** or **2 ♔xg1 ♖gxg2+ 3 ♔h1 ♖xh2+ 4 ♔g1 ♖bg2X**.

139. **1 ... ♘xf2+! 2 ♖xf2 ♗g2+! 3 ♖xg2 ♖e1+** White resigned.

140. **1 ♖xh5? ♖g8!** (freeing himself from the pin and threatening mate on the first rank. **2 ♕d3 ♕g1+** White resigned in view of 3 ♖d1 ♖c1+ 4 ♖xc1 ♕xc1X.

141. **1 ♖xe4! ♕xe4 2 ♕g3+ ♔h8 3 ♘xf7+** Black resigned (3...♖xf7 4 ♖a8+).

142. **1 ♘f6+! gxf6 2 ♕g4+ ♔h7 3 ♖ee3!** Black resigned (there is no defence against the threat of 4 ♖xh6+).

143. **1 ♖xg7+! ♔xg7 2 ♘e6+! dxe6 3 ♖d7+** Black resigned.

144. Not 1 h6? because of 1...♖xh6, but first **1 ♘d5!** (threatening 2 ♖f7+). Black resigned. (1 ... ♖xd5 2 h6).

145. **1 ♖e5+ ♔f4 2 ♖dd5! a4** (in the hope of a pawn endgame – 3 ♖f5+ etc) **3 ♖e4+ ♔f3 4 ♖dd4!** Black resigned as mate with the rook from e3 is unavoidable.

146. **1 ♗xe6! fxe6 2 ♖d8!** Black resigned.

147. **1 ... ♖c7 2 g3 ♖c1+ 3 ♔e2 ♘f4+! 4 gxf4 ♖g2+ 5 ♔e3 ♖e1X**. A very beautiful finish!

148. **1 ... ♘e4+! 2 fxe4 fxe4+ 3 ♔e1 ♕xg3+!** White resigned (4 ♖xg3 ♖h1+

5 ♗f1 ♖hxf1+ 6 ♔e2 ♖7f2X).

149. 1 ... ♖fc8 2 fxe5 ♘f4! 3 ♗d3 ♘xd3+ 4 ♕xd3 ♕e3+! White resigned.

150. 1 ... 0-0 2 ♘f6+! gxf6 3 ♖g2+ ♔h8 4 ♖xh7+! ♔xh7 5 ♕e4+ Black resigned.

151. 1 ♗xh7+! ♔xh7 2 ♖h3+ ♔g8 3 ♗xg7! Black resigned.

152. 1 ... g4? 2 ♖xf7! ♖xc3 3 ♕h4! ♖xh4 4 ♖xf8X.

153. 1 ♖a8 ♕e7 (1 ... ♔d7 2 ♕xb7+! ♖xb7 3 ♖xb7X) 2 ♕xc6+! ♕c7 3 ♖xb7! Black resigned.

154. 1 ... d3! 2 exd3 ♖a1+ 3 ♔g2 ♖ee1 4 f4 ♖e2X. Nor is there is any salvation in other moves: 2 ♖e7 ♖xe7 3 ♖xe7 ♖a1+ 4 ♔g2 d2; 2 ♖xf7 dxe2+ 3 ♔g2 ♖f3 4 ♖g7+ ♔f8 5 ♖xh7 ♖xf2+; 2 e3 ♖a1+ 3 ♔g2 d2 4 ♖xf7 ♖g1+ 5 ♔xg1 d1=♕+.

155. 1 ... ♗c5+! (1 ... f3? 2 ♖f4+) 2 ♖xc5, and only now 2 ... f3! White resigned.

156. 1 ♖xg6+! fxg6 2 ♕xe6+ ♔g7 3 ♕xg6+ ♔f8 4 ♕f6+ ♔g8 5 ♗h7+! Black resigned.

157. 1 ♕f5! (1 ... ♖xf5 2 ♖h8X or 1 ... ♗xf5 2 ♖h4X).

158. 1 ♕h1! ♕xh1 2 ♖xh1 and 3 ♔g2X; 1 ... ♕e1+ 2 ♔g2; 1 ... ♕g4(g6) 2 ♖xg4(g6); 1 ... ♕e2+ 2 ♖xe2; 1 ... ♕d3+ 2 ♔g2+.

159. 1 ♖b3 ♘d5 2 ♖b2 ♘e3 3 ♖hh2 ♔d1 4 ♖b1X; 1 ... ♘f5 2 ♖h2 ♘e3 3 ♖bb2.

160. 1 ♖c2! (closing the diagonal of the bishop g6 in the event of 1 ... e3.) 1 ... ♔b1 2 ♖d2 ♔c1 3 ♖e2 ♗g3 4 ♔g2+ ♗e1 5 ♖hxe1X.

161. 1 ♖h7+ (if at once 1 ♖f7?, then 1 ... ♕d6 and Black keeps in his sights the critical squares b8 and f8) 1 ... ♔g8 2 ♖he7 ♔h8 3 ♖bc7! (the point of this move is shown in the variation

3 ... ♕g8 4 ♔f1, and the c4 square is inaccessible to the black queen) 3 ... ♔g8 4 ♖a7 ♔h8 5 ♖f7 (now the queen can hold the eighth rank only by standing directly on it) 5 ... ♕e8+ 6 ♔f2 ♔g8 (6 ... ♔g8 7 ♖ae7) 7 ♖g7+ ♔f8 8 ♖h7 ♔g8 9 ♖ag7+ ♔f8 10 ♖h8+ and White wins.

162. 1 f7 ♔g7 2 f8=♕+ ♔xf8 3 ♖f1+ ♔g7 4 ♖g2+ ♔h6 5 ♖h1+ ♖h3 6 ♖gh2 ♖bc3+ 7 ♔b4 ♖b3+ 8 ♔a4, and White wins the rook.

163. 1 ♖a3! h2 (the rook d8 cannot abandon the eighth rank because of ♖a3-a8+) 2 ♖e3+ ♔f8 3 ♖g2 (with the threat of 4 ♖f3+ and 5 ♖e2X) 3 ... ♔f7 4 ♖f2+ ♔g6 5 ♖g3+ ♔h6 6 ♖f6X! An epaulette mate with two rooks – a rare finish.

7. Rook and bishop

164. 1 ... ♕d1+! White resigned (2 ♔xd1 ♗g4+).

165. 1 ♕f7+ Black resigned.

166. 1 ♗d1? ♕h6! White resigned.

167. 1 ♕xh7+! Black resigned (1 ... ♔xh7 2 ♖h5X or 1 ... ♖xh7 2 ♖g8+).

168. 1 ♗h6 ♗g7(?) 2 ♕xf7+! ♖xf7 3 ♖e8+ ♗f8 4 ♖xf8X.

169. 1 ♕xe7+! ♕xe7 2 ♗d6 ♕xd6 3 ♖e8X.

170. 1 ♘c7+! ♖xc7 2 ♕xc6+! Black resigned.

171. 1 ♗b5+ ♔f8 2 ♕d8+! ♗xd8 3 ♖e8X.

172. 1 ♖xe3! ♖xe3 2 h4 ♖e1+ and Black resigned.

173. 1 ♖xe5! Black resigned (1 ... ♖xe5 2 ♕f8+).

174. 1 ... ♘xd2 2 ♕xd2 ♕h4! 3 ♗h5 ♕xh2+ 4 ♔xh2 ♖xh5+ 5 ♔g1 ♖h1X.

175. 1 ♕xh7+! Black resigned (1 ... ♔xh7 2 ♖h5+ ♔g7 3 ♗h6+ ♔h7 4 ♗f8X).

176. **1 ♕h8+! ♔xh8 2 ♗f6+** Black resigned.

177. **1 ... ♘b3+!** White resigned (2 axb3 ♖a1+ 3 ♘b1 ♖xb1X).

178. **1 ... ♕d1+!** White resigned (2 ♘xd1 ♖e1+).

179. **1 ♖f7!** Black resigned.

180. **1 ♕xa7+! ♔xa7 2 ♗c8+** Black resigned.

181. **1 ♕xg7+!** Black resigned (1...♔xg7 2 ♖g3+).

182. **1 ♘e7+! ♖8xe7** (1 ... ♖2xe7 2 ♕xe7) **2 ♖d8+ ♖e8 3 ♕f8+! ♖xf8 4 ♖xf8X.**

183. **1 ... ♗xd4?** (1 ... ♘f5 was necessary) **2 ♕h8+! ♗xh8 3 ♖xh8X.**

184. **1 ♕xh7+! ♔xh7 2 ♘g5+ fxg5 3 ♖h3X.**

185. **1 ♗xe4 dxe4 2 ♘xd7 ♕xd7 3 ♕h5** Black resigned.

186. **1 ♕b7!** (1 ♗e3? ♗c4!) and White won.

187. **1 gxh7+ ♔xh7 2 ♕g6+! ♘xg6 3 hxg6+ ♔g8 4 ♖h8X.**

188. **1 ♕xd7+! ♖xd7 2 ♘c7+!** Black resigned (2 ... ♖xc7 3 ♖d8X).

189. **1 ♖e8+! ♘xe8 2 ♖d7X.**

190. **1 ♖b5+ ♔xa4 2 ♖b7** Black resigned.

191. **1 ♗h5+! ♘xh5 2 ♕xh5+!** Black resigned (2 ... ♖xh5 3 ♖g8X).

192. **1 ... ♕xf3! 2 gxf3 ♖e1+ 3 ♔g2 ♖g1X.**

193. It seems there is no defence against the threat of ♕xf8+ and ♖e8X but **1 ... ♕c4+! 2 ♗xc4 ♖xh2** White resigned.

194. **1 ♖xb2! ♖xb2 2 ♕d4 ♕e5 3 ♖e1!** Black resigned.

195. **1 ... ♕xd1+! 2 ♘xd1 ♘f3+ 3 ♕xf3 ♖e1+** White resigned.

196. **1 ... ♕e1+! 2 ♕xe1 ♗e3+ 3 ♕xe3 ♖f1X.**

197. **1 ♕f8+! ♔xf8 2 ♗h6+ ♔g8 3 ♖e8X.**

198. **1 ... ♗d3!** White resigned.

199. **1 ♕a3+ ♕e7** (1 ... ♔g8 2 ♗xh7+) **2 ♗c6!** Black resigned.

200. **1 ... ♘e4 2 ♗e6!** Black resigned.

201. **1 ... ♖xf2! 2 ♕xd7 ♖xg2+** White resigned (3 ♔h1 ♖g3+).

202. **1 ... ♕c6?** (1 ... ♖xd1+) **2 ♖xd7! ♕xa4 3 ♖d8+ ♗f8 4 ♗h6** Black resigned.

203. **1 ♘xf6+ ♗xf6 2 ♕xf6!** Black resigned (2 ... gxf6 3 ♖g3+ ♔h8 4 ♗xf6X).

204. **1 ... ♗b5 2 ♕a3 c4! 3 b4 ♘g3+ 4 hxg3 hxg3+ 5 ♘h2 ♖xh2X.**

205. **1 ... ♖xh3+! 2 gxh3 ♕h2 3 ♔xh2 ♖f2+ 4 ♔h1 ♖h2X.**

206. **1 ♕xg7+ ♘xg7 2 ♖xg7+ ♔h8 3 ♖g8+! ♔xg8 4 ♖g1+** Black resigned.

207. **1 ... ♕xf3! 2 gxf3 ♖dg8+ 3 ♗g3 ♖xg3+ 4 hxg3 ♗xf3** White resigned.

208. **1 ♖e5 ♕c2 2 ♖g5+ ♔h6 3 ♕f8+! ♖xf8 4 ♗g7X.**

209. **1 ... ♕xe4! 2 ♕xe4 ♖d6+ 3 ♕d4 ♖xd4+ 4 exd4 ♖d2X.**

210. **1 ♕xc7+! ♔xc7 2 ♘b5+ ♔b8 3 ♖d8+! ♖xd8 4 ♗f4+ ♔a8 5 ♘c7+ ♔b8 6 ♘xa6+ ♔a8 7 ♘c7+ ♔b8 8 ♘d5+ ♔a8 9 ♘b6+ axb6 10 ♖a1X.**

211. **1 ... ♗f2!** White resigned (the threat is 2...♗c1+, and if 2 ♗c3, then 2...♖e3).

212. **1 ... ♖xd4 2 cxd4?** (2 ♖xd4 ♕h5 3 ♔g1 ♗c5) **2 ... ♕e1+!** White resigned. (3 ♔xe1 ♗b4+).

213. **1 ♘g6+! ♘xg6 2 ♕xh7+! ♔xh7 3 ♖h5X.**

214. **1 ♘g6+!** Black resigned (1 ... hxg6 2 h5).

215. **1 ♕b8! ♖xb8 2 ♖c8X. 1 ... ♖f8 2 ♖h4X.**

216. **1 ♗b7! ♗f7 2 ♖a3 ♗b3 3 ♗e4 ♗d5 4 ♖g3X; 1 ... ♗h7 2 ♖f8 ♗f5 3 ♖g8+!; 1 ... ♗e8 2 ♖a3** and then **3 ♖g3+.**

217. 1 ♖g1 ♔d8 2 ♖c1 ♗c7 3 ♖c5! ♔e8 4 ♖g5 ♔d8 5 ♖g8X.

218. Any bishop check could be fatal for the black king, therefore the rook must keep in its sights two points from where the bishop could deliver a blow. 1 ♗h4 ♖d1 2 ♗g3 ♖c1 3 ♗f4 ♖c2 4 ♗g5! Now the rook is powerless, and the white bishop goes either to d8 or d2.

219. White is playing for mate, whilst at the same time avoiding stalemate. 1 ♔g6 ♖a6+ 2 ♗e6 ♖a5 3 ♖e4 ♖a4 4 ♗c4; 1 ... ♖g1+ 2 ♔f7 ♖f1+ 3 ♗f5 g6 4 ♔xg6 ♖g1+ 5 ♔f6 ♖g8 6 ♗g6 ♖g7 7 ♖e1.

8. Rook and knight

220. 1 ♘e5! Black resigned (1 ... ♕xa2 2 ♖d8X).

221. 1 ♕xf5? ♘xe1! White resigned. Because of the threat 2...♘f3 mate, he loses a piece.

222. 1 ♖g6! Black resigned.

223. 1 ♕xg7+! ♘xg7 2 ♖f8+ ♔h7 3 ♘f6X.

224. 1 ... ♖f2+ 2 ♔h1 ♖h2+! 3 ♔xh2 ♘f3+ 4 ♔h1 ♖xg1X.

225. 1 ... ♘xd3! White resigned (2 ♗xd3 ♗xe4+ or 2 ♕xh3 ♘f2X).

226. 1 ♖xg7+! ♔xg7 2 ♖g1+ ♔h8 3 ♕xf7! Black resigned.

227. 1 ... cxd4? 2 ♕xf7+! Black resigned.

228. 1 ... ♕g2+! White resigned (2 ♖xg2 ♘f3+ 3 ♔h1 ♖d1+).

229. 1 ... ♖xd5! 2 ♖xd5 ♘f3 3 ♖5d2 ♖xd2 4 ♖xd2 ♘xd2 5 b5 ♘c4 White resigned.

230. 1 ... ♕h4! White resigned.

231. 1 ... ♕d1+! White resigned (2 ♔xd1 ♘e3+ 3 ♔e1 ♖d1X).

232. 1 ... ♘e2+ 2 ♔h1 ♕xh2+! White resigned.

233. 1 ♕xe7+! ♖xe7 2 ♖xe7+ ♔f7 3 ♘e6+ ♔g8 4 ♖e8+ ♖f8 5 ♖xf8X.

234. 1 ♗d2! Black resigned. In view of the threat of mate on e7, he loses one of the pieces.

235. 1 ♘f5+ ♔g8 2 ♕f8+! ♔xf8 3 ♖c8+ Black resigned.

236. 1 ♘c8+! Black resigned (1 ... ♕c5 or 1 ... ♘c5 – 2 ♕xc5+ and 3 ♖d8X).

237. 1 ... ♕xe4! White resigned (2 dxe4 ♖xd1+! 3 ♕xd1 ♘g3+ 4 hxg3 hxg3+).

238. 1 ♘g6+ ♔e8 2 ♕xf7+! ♘xf7 ♖xf7 ♔xf7 4 ♖f1+ ♔e8 5 ♖f8X.

239. 1 ♖a5+! ♔xa5 (1 ... ♔b6 2 ♕xc5X) 2 ♕xc5+! dxc5 3 ♘c4+ ♔b5 4 ♖b6X.

240. 1 ♘g4? ♘e2+ 2 ♔h1 ♕xg4! 3 hxg4 ♖h5+ 4 gxh5 ♖h4X.

241. 1 ♕xc5! ♖xc5 2 ♘e7+ ♔h8 3 ♖xh7+ ♔xh7 4 ♖h1+ Black resigned.

242. 1 ... ♕xh2+! 2 ♔xh2 ♘g4+ 3 ♔h1 ♖h3+! 4 gxh3 ♖h2X.

243. 1 ♕xb6+! axb6 2 ♘c7+ ♔a7 3 ♖a8X.

244. 1 ♖g5! Black resigned. (1 ... ♕xc2 2 ♖h5X).

245. 1 ♖d5 ♗f6 and now instead of the played 2 ♘f4(?) better is 2 ♖d1! with the threat of 3 ♘d4 or 3 ♘f4, and if 2 ... ♗e5 3 ♘g5 d5 4 ♖xd5.

246. 1 ... ♖xh2! 2 ♔xh2 (2 ♕xh2 ♘f3+) 2 ... ♖h8+ 3 ♔g1 ♘e2X.

247. 1 ♕b7+! ♘xb7 2 ♘c6+ ♔a8 3 axb7+ ♔xb7 4 ♖xa7X.

248. If 1 ... ♘g4+!? 2 ♖xb6 axb6, then 3 ♔f1 and White holds. 1 ... ♖g2+ 2 ♔h1 ♘f5! leads to mate as there is no defence against the two threats – 3...♖g1X or 3...♘xg3X.

249. 1 ... ♔h5! White resigned. 2...♘e4+ is threatened. If 2 ♕xf6, then 2...h1=♘X!

250. **1 ♘a5!** Black resigned.

251. The game went **1 ... ♘g4 2 ♗xg7 ♖xg7?.** Instead **2 ... ♕xh3+!** leads to mate.

252. **1 ... ♖xc3! 2 ♕xc3 ♕xc3** White resigned (3 ♖xc3 ♖d1+ 4 ♘e1 ♖xe1+ 5 ♔g2 ♘f4+ 6 ♔g3 ♖g1+ 7 ♖g2 ♖xg2X).

253. **1 ... h4 2 ♘c4 hxg3 3 ♔b4!** and the threat of mate on d6 decides.

254. **1 ... ♕xh2+! 2 ♔xh2 ♖h4+ 3 ♔g1 ♘g3!** White resigned.

255. **1 ♕g6!** Black resigned (1...hxg6 2 ♖h3X).

256. **1 ♘f6!** Black resigned (one of two mating finishes is unavoidable – 1...gxf6 2 ♕xf7X or 1 ... ♕xc4 ♖e8+ ♖xe8 3 ♖xe8X).

257. **1 ♘xe4! ♗xd2 2 ♘xf6+ ♔f8 3 ♗d6+! ♕xd6 4 ♖e8X.**

258. **1 ♗xh7+! ♔xh7 2 ♘h3+ ♔g8 3 ♕h5 ♕h6 4 ♘f5! ♕xh5 5 ♘e7+ ♔h8 6 ♖xh5X.**

259. **1 ... ♖xe7! 2 ♕xe7 ♕xf3! 3 gxf3 ♖g8+ 4 ♔f1 ♗a6+ 5 ♖e2 ♘d2+ 6 ♔e1 ♘xf3+ 7 ♔d1 ♖g1+ 8 ♖e1 ♖xe1X.**

260. **1 ... ♘xd1! 2 bxa5 ♘c3!** White resigned (3 ♖b2 ♖f1+ or 3 ♘xc3 ♖f1+ 4 ♘b1 ♖fxb1X).

261. A similar motif to the game Levitsky-Marshall (1912): **1 ♕g6! ♕xg6 2 ♘e7+ ♔h8 3 ♘xg6+ ♔g8 4 ♘e7+ ♔h8 5 ♖xh7+ ♔xh7 6 ♖h3+ ♖h4 7 ♖xh4X.**

262. **1 e8=♘+!** Black resigned. (1 ... ♖xe8 2 ♖d7X or 1 ... ♔d5 2 ♖d7+ ♔e4 3 ♘d6+). 1 e8=♕? is no good because of 1 ... ♘d5+.

263. **1 ♖e8 ♕c7 2 ♕xg5+! fxg5 3 ♘h5X.**

264. **1 ♖g5!** (threatening 2 ♖g8X) **1 ... ♕xh4 2 ♖g4!** Black resigned.

265. **1 ♖h8+ ♔f7 2 ♗e8+!!** (a study-like move) **2...♘xe8 3 ♖g5!** Black resigned.

266. **1 ♕h7+! ♔xh7 2 ♘f6+ ♔h8** (2 ... ♔xh6 3 ♖h3+ ♔g5 4 ♖g3+ ♔xf6 5 ♖g6X). **3 ♗xg7+! ♔xg7 4 ♖g3+** Black resigned (4 ... ♔xf6 5 ♖g6X; 4 ... ♔h6 5 ♖g6X; 4 ... ♔h8 or 4 ... ♔f8 – 5 ♖g8X).

267. **1 ♖f7+ ♔e8** (1 ... ♔g8 2 ♖g7+ ♔f8 3 ♘g6+ ♔e8 4 ♖g8+) **2 ♖e7+** and now **2...♔f8 3 ♘g6+ ♔g8 4 ♖g7X** or **2 ... ♔d8 3 ♘f7+ ♔c8 4 ♘d6+ ♔b8** (4 ... ♔d8 5 ♔e6) **5 ♖b7X.**

268. **1 ♖d7! ♗b8** (1 ... ♗xd7 2 ♕xf7+ ♖xf7 3 ♖xf7X) **2 ♘xf7 ♗xd7 3 ♘d8+!** Black resigned.

269. **1 ... ♘f3+!** White resigned. (2 gxf3 ♖g6+ 3 ♔h1 ♘f2X).

270. **1 ♘f8+ ♔c8** (1 ... ♔c7 2 ♘e6+) **2 ♖c1+ ♔b8** (2 ... ♔d8 3 ♘e6+) **3 ♘d7+ ♔a7 4 ♖a1X; 1 ... ♔e8 2 ♘e6! ♖g8** (2 ... ♖f7 3 ♖d8X; or 2 ... ♖h7 3 ♖d8+ ♔f7 4 ♘g5+) **3 ♘c7+ ♔f7 4 ♖f1+ ♔g7 5 ♘e6+ ♔h6** (h8,h7) **6 ♖h1X.**

271. **1 ♔e3+ ♔b3 2 ♖xh5! ♕xf7 3 ♖b5+ ♔c2** (3 ... ♔a2 4 ♘xc3+ ♔a1 5 ♖b1X) **4 ♘xa3+ ♔c1 5 ♖b1X.**

272. White places his opponent in a zugzwang position. For this he has to manoeuvre with his king in order not to allow a rook check along the rank. **1 ♔g7! fxg6 2 ♔h6! g5 3 ♔h5 g4 4 ♔h4 g3 5 ♔xg3** and **6 ♖xb2X; 1 ... f5 2 ♔h6 f4 3 ♖d2 f3 4 ♖f2** and **5 ♖xb2X.**

273. **1 ♔e7 ♖h7+** (1 ... ♔h7 2 ♖xc5) **2 ♔e6 ♖a7 3 ♘f6+ ♔g7 4 ♖g8+ ♔h6 5 ♔f5** and there is no defence against mate; **1 ... c4 2 ♔e6 ♔f8 3 ♘d6+ ♔g7 4 ♘f5+ ♔h7 5 ♖c7+ ♔g6 6 ♖g7+ ♔h5 7 ♔e5 ♖a8 8 ♔f4.** In both variations the white king is shielded from checks from the black rook.

274. **1 h5+ ♔h6** (1 ... ♔f6 2 ♖f7X) **2 ♘f7+ ♔xh5** (2 ... ♔g7 3 ♘g5+ ♔g8 4 ♖e8+ ♔g7 5 h6+ ♔g6 6 ♔g4! f1=♕**

7 ♖e6+ ♛f6 8 ♖xf6+ ♚xf6 9 ♚h5! and White wins) **3 ♖e5+ ♚h4 4 ♞g5 f1=♕+ 5 ♞f3+ ♚h3 6 ♖h5+ ♚g2 7 ♖h2X**.

9. Two Bishops

275. **1 ... ♕f3+! 2 gxf3 ♗h3X**.

276. **1 ... c6? 2 ♖h5! ♕xh5 3 ♕xc6+ bxc6 4 ♗xa6X**.

277. **1 ... ♗xg4! 2 ♕xf6 ♗h3X**.

278. **1 ... ♗e7?** 2 ♕a5+ Black resigned (2 … b6 3 ♕xb6+ or 3 ♗xb6+).

279. **1 ... ♗g8? 2 ♕xh6+!** Black resigned. 2 … gxh6 (2 ... ♗h7 3 e6) 3 e6+ ♚h7 4 ♗e4+.

280. **1 ... ♞d8? 2 ♖xf5!** Black resigned. (2 … gxf5 or 2 … exf5 3 ♗d4X).

281. **1 ... ♕d8 2 ♖e8+!** Black resigned.

282. **1 ... b5? 2 ♖e8!** Black resigned.

283. **1 ♞b6+! axb6 2 ♕xc6+ bxc6 3 ♗a6X**.

284. **1 ... ♗d4+ 2 ♚h1 ♖e1+!** White resigned.

285. **1 ♞b5 cxb5 2 ♕xb8+! ♖xb8 3 ♗xb5X**.

286. **1 ♖f8+! ♗xf8 2 d6+** Black resigned.

287. **1 ... ♗xf2+ 2 ♚h1?** (correct was 2 ♚f1 ♖xd1+ 3 ♕xd1 ♖xb2 4 ♕d8 h6 5 ♞f7+ ♚h7 6 ♕d7 and White ought not lose) **2 ... ♖xd1+ 3 ♕xd1 ♖c1! 4 ♕xc1 ♗d5+ 5 ♞f3 ♗xf3X**.

288. **1 ... ♞f3+! 2 ♞xf3 e2+ 3 ♞d4 exd1=♕+ 4 ♕xd1 ♖e1+!** White resigned.

289. **1 ♗h7!** Surprising! Black resigned (1 … ♕xe2 2 ♗xh6X).

290. **1 ♗xg6!** Black resigned (1 fxg6 2 ♕xe6X; 1 ... hxg6 2 ♕h8X).

291. **1 ♕e6!** Black resigned (1 … dxe6 2 ♗a3+). There is also no salvation in 1 ... g6 2 ♗a3+ ♚g7 3 ♕e5+ ♚f7 4 ♕e7X.

292. **1 d8=♕+! ♗xd8 2 ♖xd8+!** Black resigned (2…♕xd8 3 ♕c3+).

293. **1 ♕xe5+!!** Black resigned.

294. **1 ♞c7+! ♕xc7 2 ♗xf7+ ♚d7** (2 ... ♚f8 3 ♗e6+) **3 ♕f5+!** (deflecting the knight from its defence of the e6 square) **3…♞xf5 4 e6X**.

295. **1 ♗a8! a5 2 b6 a4 3 b7 ♚h1 4 b8=♗(♕)X**.

296. **1 ♚f6+ ♚g8 2 ♚g6 ♚g7 3 ♗d5+ ♚h8 4 ♗xg7X**.

297. **1 ♗g6+ ♚a1 2 ♚f7 ♞c4 3 ♗d4+ ♞b2 4 ♗g7 a3** (Stalemate? No!) **5 ♚f6! ♞c4 6 ♚e6+ ♞b2 7 ♚e5 ♞c4+ 8 ♚d5+ ♞b2 9 ♚d4 ♞a4 10 ♚c4+ ♞b2+ 11 ♚c3 ♞a4+ 12 ♚b3+ ♞b2 13 ♗f8! ♞d3 14 ♚xa3 ♞c5+ 15 ♚c2 ♞a4 16 ♚c1** and **17 ♗b2X**.

298. **1 ♗e5+ ♞c7+ 2 ♚b6 ♗d8 3 ♗d7!** (any other waiting move fails to provide a win. For example: 3 ♗h3? ♚a8 4 ♗g2+ ♞d5+ 5 ♚a6 ♗c7! 6 ♗xc7 – stalemate. White must go around the d5 square.) **3 ... ♚a8 4 ♗c6+ ♚b8 5 ♗b7! any 6 ♗xc7X**.

299. **1 ♗f2 ♗a5 2 e4! ♗xe4 3 a8=♕+! ♗xa8 4 ♗e2+ ♚b7 5 ♗f3+ ♚a6 6 b7! ♗xb7 7 ♗e2X**.

10. Two Knights

300. **1 ... ♞hg3+ 2 ♚h2 ♞f1+ 3 ♚h1 ♕h2+! 4 ♞xh2 ♞fg3X**.

301. **1 ♕h7+! ♞xh7 2 ♞hg6+ ♚g8 3 ♞xe7+ ♚h8 4 ♞5g6X**.

302. **1 ♕xh7+! ♚xh7** (1 ... ♚f7 2 ♕h5+) **2 ♞xf6+ ♚h8 3 ♞g6X**.

303. **1 ♖xe5! ♕xe5 2 ♞g6! ♕xd5** (2 ... ♕xh2 3 ♞de7X) **3 ♞e7+ ♚h8 4 ♕xh7+! ♚xh7 5 ♖h1+** Black resigned. More tenacious would have been 2 … hxg6).

304. **1 ♞f6! ♞g8** (1 ... ♕xf7 2 ♞xf7X; or 1 ... gxf6 2 ♕h7X) **2 ♕h5+ ♞h6 3 ♕g6!** Black resigned.

305. **1 ... ♗d6? 2 ♕xh7+ ♖xh7 3 ♘g6X.**

306. **1 ♗a3! ♕xa3 2 ♕e6 ♘d8** (2 ... ♔g7 3 ♘h5+) **3 ♕f7+! ♘xf7 4 ♘e6X.**

307. **1 ... ♖d5+! 2 ♘xd5 g6+ 3 ♔h6 ♘g4X.**

308. **1 ♘d8.** Now the bishop must let the knight have the f7 square and the mating formation is ready. The next move of the bishop depends on the move of the black rook. **1 ... ♖a1** (b1, c1, d1, e1, g1, h1) **2 ♗a2** (b3, c4, d5, e6 g6, h5).

309. **1 ♖a8+ ♔b6 2 ♖a6+ ♔xa6 3 c8=♘! ♘ any 4 ♘c5X or ♘xc5X.**

310. **1 ♘e3 ♗g3 2 ♘c4 ♗f4** (otherwise 3 ♘d2 4 ♘e3 ♗e5 5 ♘c5 ♗f4 6 ♘e6 ♗h6 7 ♔g3) **3 ♘a5 ♗e3** (3 ... ♗d6 4 ♘c6, 5 ♘d4 or d8, 6 ♘c6) **4 ♘b7!** (4 ♘c6? ♗b6) **4 ... ♗f4 5 ♘bd8 any 6 ♘e6 ♗h6 7 ♔g3** and mate on the next move.

311. **1 ♘e4! ♘d3** (after 1 ... g1=♕+ 2 ♘f2+ Black loses the queen, whereas now he again threatens to promote the pawn) **2 ♕f2!! ♘xf2 3 ♘g3+ ♔g1 4 ♘g5!** An interesting zugzwang position; on any move by any knight Black is mated.

312. **1 g6 ♘h4 2 ♘g7+ ♔g5** (2 ... ♔h6 3 ♔xh4 ♔xg7 4 ♔h5 ♔xf8 5 ♔h6 ♔g8 6 g7 ♔f7) **3 ♘ge6+ ♔h6** (now he has to take into account that 4 ♔xh4 is stalemate) **4 g7! ♘f5+ 5 ♔g4 ♘xg7 6 ♘d4!.**

11. Bishop and Knight

313. **1 ♘xc6!** Black resigned.
314. **1 ... ♕h3!** White resigned.
315. **1 ♕h6!** Black resigned.
316. **1 ... ♕xf3! 2 ♗xd8 ♘f4!** White resigned.
317. **1 ♗h6 ♗h8? 2 ♘d5!** Black

resigned.
318. **1 ♗e6+ ♔f8 2 ♕h5!** Black resigned.
319. **1 d6!** Black resigned (2 ♘h6X is threatened, if 1 ... ♕xd6, then 2 c5+).
320. **1 ♕xb7? ♘b4!** White resigned.
321. **1 ♖e8+ ♖xe8 2 ♘xe8 ♕e6 3 ♕g4+!** Black resigned.
322. **1 ♕h6+! ♘xh6 2 ♗xh6+ ♔g8 3 f7X.**
323. **1 ♘d5! ♕a5 2 ♕a3!** Black resigned.
324. **1 ♖xf5! gxf5 2 ♕xh5+ ♖xh5 3 ♗f7X.**
325. **1 ♘f6+!** Black resigned (1 ... ♘xf6 2 ♖d8X or 1 ... gxf6 2 ♕xe6+ fxe6 3 ♗h5X).
326. **1 ... ♖xb4! 2 ♘xb4 ♗h2+ 3 ♔f1 ♕b6!** White resigned: on any move, defending the f2 square, follows none the less 4 ... ♕xf2+ 5 ♖xf2 ♘g3X.
327. **1 ♘g4 ♗xg2 2 ♕xe5+!** Black resigned (2 ... dxe5 3 ♗f6+ ♔g8 4 ♘h6X).
328. **1 ... ♘e2+ 2 ♔h1 ♖xf1+ 3 ♖xf1 ♘g3X.**
329. **1 ... ♖xd2! 2 ♗xd2 ♘g5!** White resigned (3 ♕xg5 ♕f3; 3 h4 ♘f3+; 3 ♕xe2 ♘h3X).
330. **1 ♖xe4! ♘xe4 2 ♖xe4 fxe4 3 ♗f4+ ♔c8** (3 ... ♔a8 4 ♘b6+ axb6 5 ♕a4X) **4 ♕b6!** Black resigned.
331. **1 ... ♕xb2+! 2 ♔xb2 ♘c4+** White resigned.
332. **1 ♕xh5+! gxh5 2 g6+ fxg6 3 fxg6X.**
333. **1 ♗d4! ♕xe1** (1 ... ♕c6 2 ♘e7) **2 ♕g7+! ♗xg7 3 fxg7+ ♔g8 4 ♘h6X.**
334. **1 ♕xh7+! ♔xh7 2 ♘g6+ ♔g8 3 ♖h8+ ♔f7 4 ♖f8+! ♕xf8 5 d6X.**
335. **1 ♕xe4! fxe4?** (1 ... ♗xf1) **2 ♗xe4+ ♔h8 3 ♘g6+ ♔h7 4 ♘xf8+ ♔h8 5 ♘g6+ ♔h7 6 ♘e5+ ♔h8 7 ♘f7X.**

336. **1 ... ♖d3!** White resigned (2 ♘xd3
♗e6X; 2 ♘e2 ♘xa3X; 2 ♖a1 ♖c3X).

337. **1 g8=♗ ♔g1 2 ♘e2+ ♔h1
3 ♗d5X.**

338. **1 ♗c7 d3 2 ♘c1 d2 3 ♘a2** and
4 ♘b4X.

339. **1 ♔c7 ♔a5 2 ♗f6 ♔a6 3 ♗d8
♔a5 4 ♔b7X.**

340. **1 ♗a4 e5+** (otherwise the
knight cannot be saved) **2 ♘xe5 ♘f2** (if
2 ... ♘b2 3 ♗c2 ♔g8 4 ♔c3) **3 ♔e3
♘h3** (3 ... ♘h1 4 ♔f3) **4 ♗d7 ♘g5
5 ♔f4 ♘h7** (finally the knight takes
shelter from the pursuit, but now he
takes away the free square for his king)
6 ♘g6+ ♔g8 7 ♗e6X.

341. **1 ♖h1 ♖h3 2 ♗d7 ♖h5 3 ♘g4!
♖f8+** (3 ... ♖xh1 4 ♗f5X) **4 ♔xf8
♖xh1 5 ♗f5+ ♔h8 6 ♘e5** (Threatening
7 ♘f7X – there is only one defence)
6...♖h7 7 ♘g6X.

342. **1 ♗c3 e1=♕!** (intending
the following exchanging operation)
**2 ♗xe1 ♖d5+ 3 ♔b6 ♖xa5 4 ♗c3!
♖a8 5 ♔b7 ♖f8** (the only square where
the rook can take cover from the
threats) **6 ♘f5+ ♔g8 7 ♘h6X.**

12. Queen and bishop

343. **1 ♗d6!** Black resigned
(1 ... ♖xd6 2 ♖c8+ ♖d8 3 ♖xd8+
♕xd8 4 ♕xf7X).

344. **1 ♖xg7+!!** Black resigned
(1 ... ♔xg7 2 ♕g5+).

345. **1 ♗xh7+ ♔xh7 2 g8=♕+!
♖xg8 3 ♕h5X.**

346. **1 ♗h8!** Black resigned. Mate is
threatened and after 1 ... ♕d6+ 2 ♔f2
any check leads to loss of the queen.

347. **1 ... ♖d1!** White resigned
(2 ♕xd1 ♕g2X; 2 ♖xd1 ♕xf3; 2 ♕xc6
♖xe1X; 2 ♕xh3 ♖xe1+).

348. **1 ♘e6!** Black resigned
(1 ... fxe6 2 ♗xe6+ ♔f8 3 ♕h8X).

349. **1 ... ♕d2!** White resigned.

350. **1 ♘f6+ ♔h8 2 ♕h4 gxf6**
(2 ... h6 3 ♗xc4) **3 ♗d3 f5 4 ♕xe7
♘xd2 5 ♕f8X.**

351. **1 ... ♖d4!** White resigned
(2 ♕xd4 ♕b1X).

352. **1 ♖xh7+! ♘xh7 2 ♗b2+ e5 3
♕xd5 ♔g7 4 ♕d7+** Black resigned.

353. **1 c3!** Black resigned (2 ♗c2
cannot be averted). Also possible are
1 ♗d5 or 1 c4.

354. **1 ... ♖xb2! 2 ♔xb2 ♕xc3+
3 ♔c1 ♖b8!** White resigned: there is no
satisfactory defence against 4...♖b1+.

355. **1 ♖h8+! ♗xh8 2 ♖xh8+ ♔g7
3 ♖h7+!** Black resigned (3...♔f8 or
♔xh7 – 4 ♗f6, and the threat of
5 ♕h2+ decides).

356. **1 ... ♘xe5! 2 dxe5 ♕c6** and
Black wins a pawn.

357. **1 ... ♖xa3+!** and however White
takes the daring rook he is immediately
mated.

358. **1 ... ♘g3+ 2 hxg3 ♗g2+ 3 ♔xg2
♕xg3+** White resigned.

359. **1 ♖xh6! gxh6 2 ♖g5+!** Black
resigned (2 ... hxg5 3 ♕g6+).

360. **1 ♗g7+! ♔xg7 2 ♖xh7+ ♔xh7
3 ♕xg6+** Black resigned.

361. **1 ... ♖f2+! 2 ♔xf2 ♕xh2+
3 ♔f1 ♕h3+** White resigned.

362. **1 ... ♘xd4? 2 ♗xd4 ♗b5
3 ♘f6+!** Black resigned.

363. **1 ♖f8+! ♖xf8 2 ♖xf8+ ♕xf8
3 ♕xe5+ ♕g7 4 ♕e8+** Black resigned.

364. **1 ♘f6+! gxf6 2 ♗xe7 ♕xe7
3 ♕g4+ ♔h8 4 ♕h4 ♗xh2+ 5 ♔h1**
(5 ♔xh2? ♕d6+ 6 f4 f5) Black
resigned.

365. **1 ♖c8+! ♗xc8 2 ♕e8+ ♖f8
3 ♖xg7+! ♔xg7 4 ♕g6+ ♔h8 5 ♕h7X.**

366. **1 ... ♗g1+! 2 ♕xg1 ♘g4+!
3 hxg4 ♕h6+ 4 ♗h4 ♕xh4X.**

367. **1 ♖xf6! ♖a1+ 2 ♔g2 gxf6
3 ♕e8+ ♔g7 4 ♕e7+ ♔g8 5 ♗h7+**

♔h8 6 ♗g6 Black resigned.

368. **1 ♖h7+! ♔xh7 2 ♕f7+ ♔h8 3 ♖xe8+ ♖xe8+ 4 ♕xe8+ ♔g7 5 ♕f7+ ♔h8 6 ♕g8X.**

369. **1 g4 ♘d4?** (1 ... ♘g7) **2 ♖xc5! ♕xc5 3 ♗xd4** Black resigned.

370. **1 ... ♘xd4 2 ♕h5+ ♔g8 3 ♕e5!** Black resigned.

371. **1 ♗xe6 ♖xd1** (Black assumes that there will be a usual exchanging operation – 2 ♕xd1? ♕xe6 with a draw, but White intends something quite different...) **2 ♕a8+!** Black resigned: after 2 ... ♔h7 3 ♗xf7 and there is no defence against mate.

372. **1 ♖xg7! ♔xg7 2 ♕f6+ ♔f8** (2 ... ♔g8 3 ♖xh6 and there is no defence against the standard method 4 ♗h7+ ♔h8 5 ♗g6+ ♔g8 6 ♕h7+ ♔f8 7 ♕xf7X) **3 ♗g6** Black resigned.

373. Black wins with the move **1 ... ♕e1! 2 ♕xa8+ ♔f7** and there is no defence against 3 ... ♘g4+ 3 hxg4 ♕h4X or 3 ... ♗g1+ 4 ♔h1 ♗f2+ 5 ♔h2 ♕g1X. If 3 ♕e3, then 3... ♘g4+ 4 hxg4 ♕h4+ 5 ♔g1 ♗xe3+ and 6 ... ♕f2X.

374. **1 ♕b4 ♔h8? 2 ♖xc5! bxc5 3 ♕h4** Black resigned.

375. **1 ♘f6+! gxf6** (1 ... ♔h8 2 ♕h5) **2 ♗xf6** (threatening 3 ♖g5X) **2...♖d5 3 ♕d2!** Black resigned.

376. **1 ♖xg7! ♔xg7 2 ♗h6+ ♔g8 3 ♗g6!** Black has no way of defending the critical f7 square and he resigned, since 3...hxg6 leads to mate – 4 ♕xg6X.

377. **1 ... ♘e1** (The knight frees with tempo the f3 square for the queen.) [But better was 1 ... ♗g4 2 ♕d8+ ♔g7 3 ♕d6 ♘xd2...] **2 ♖xe1?** [...since White now has 2 ♕xf7+! ♔xf7 3 ♖xd7+ ♔e8 4 ♖d8+ ♔e7 5 ♖8d7+ – ed] **2 ... ♕f3+ 3 ♔g1 ♗h3** White resigned.

378. **1 ... ♘xd5 2 exd5 c4! 3 ♗xc4** (3 ♗f5 ♕f6 or 3 ♗e4 f5) **3 ... ♕h4** White resigned.

379. **1 ... ♖d4! 2 exd4 ♕a4** White resigned.

380. **1 d5! ♕xc4? 2 ♗f8!** Black resigned.

381. **1 ♕d6 2 ♘b5 ♕c6!** White resigned.

382. **1 ♖c7? ♖e1+ 2 ♔h2 ♖h1+!** White resigned (3 ♔xh1 ♕h3+).

383. **1 ... ♖fe8! 2 ♗xc7** It turns out that, after taking the bishop, Delannoy ironically noted: "It is not worth travelling from America to Europe in order to make this blunder!". Morphy announced mate in six moves: **2 ... ♖xf2 3 ♔xf2 ♖e2+! 4 ♔xe2 ♕xg2+ 5 ♔e1 ♕g1+ 6 ♔d2 ♕f2+ 7 ♔d1 ♗h5X.**

384. **1 ♖xf7+! ♔xf7 2 ♗xg6+ ♔g8 3 ♗h5+ ♔h7 4 ♕g6+ ♔h8 5 ♕f6+!** Black resigned. (5 ... ♔h7 6 ♗g6+ ♔h6 7 ♗f7+ ♔h7 8 ♕g6+ ♔h8 9 ♕h6X).

385. **1 ♖af1 ♘xf1 2 ♕h5! g6 3 ♖xg6+ ♔h8 4 ♖g8+** Black resigned (4 ... ♔xg8 5 ♕xh7X).

386. **1 ... ♖g3! 2 ♕xg3 ♗h4!** White resigned (3 ♕xh4 ♕e3+).

387. **1 ♗e7+ ♔h6 2 ♖xh7+! ♔xh7 3 ♗f8+** Black resigned.

388. **1 ♗xe6 ♖xc5** (if 1 ... ♕xe6, then 2 ♖xg7+! ♔xg7, and now the black queen can be taken with check 3 ♘xe6+; also bad is 1 ... fxe6 2 ♕xg6; with the irresistible threats of 3 ♕xg7X or 3 ♖h8X; on 1 ... ♗d3! there is the strong 2 ♕c3!) **2 ♖h8+!** Black resigned (2...♗xh8 3 ♕xg6+).

389. **1 ♖xf6! ♔xf6 2 ♖e6+ ♔g7 3 ♖xg6+! fxg6 4 ♕xg6+ ♔f8 5 ♕h6+ ♔f7 6 ♗g6+ ♔f6 7 ♗h7+ ♔e5 8 ♕g7+ ♔f4 9 ♕g3X.**

390. The queen endeavours to penetrate to the seventh rank: **1 ♘xc5**

♗xc5 2 ♖xc5! dxc5 (now the line is open) 3 ♕g3+ ♔h8 (3 ... ♔f7 4 ♕c7+ ♔e8 5 ♕d7X) 4 ♕c7 Black resigned. The march-route of the queen is reminiscent of the 'mark of Zorro' – 'Z'.

391. By creating mating threats over the following moves, White surprisingly traps the black queen: 1 ♕a1+ ♔h7 2 ♕b1+ ♔h8 3 ♕b2+ ♔h7 4 ♕c2+ ♔h8 5 ♕c3+ ♔h7 6 ♕d3+ ♔h8 7 ♕h3+! (forcing the black bishop to abandon the eighth rank, since 7 ... ♕h7 is not possible because of 8 ♕c3+) 7...♗h7 8 ♕c3+ ♔g8 9 ♕c8! (now a discovered check is threatened with the bishop going to c5, and in the event of 9 ... ♕f7 matters are concluded with a mate – 10 ♗h6+) 9...♔f7 10 ♗c5! and the black queen is trapped.

13. Queen and knight

392. 1 ♘g5! Black resigned (the threats are 2 ♕f7X or 2 ♕d5X).

393. 1 ♖e8! Black resigned.

394. 1 ♗xe7? ♘d4! White resigned.

395. 1 ♘d5! exd5 2 ♗xf6 Black resigned.

396. 1 g4 ♕xc2 2 ♖h8+! Black resigned.

397. 1 ... ♗g1! 2 ♖xg1 ♘f3+ White resigned.

398. 1 ... ♘e2+ 2 ♔h1 ♖xh2+! 3 ♔xh2 ♖h8+ 4 ♗h6 ♕h4X.

399. 1 ♗xh7+! ♔xh7 2 ♕h5+ ♔g8 3 ♘c6! Black resigned: the threat of 4 ♘e7X leads to the win of the queen.

400. 1 ... ♖xc2! White resigned (2 ♔xc2 ♘f2+ or 2 ♕xc2 ♕e1+).

401. 1 h4? ♖c4 White resigned (2 ♕e3 ♕h3+ 3 ♔g1 ♖xh4!).

402. 1 ... ♗xd6 (better is 1 ... ♗xg5) 2 ♗h7+ ♔h8 3 ♗g8! Black resigned.

403. If at once 1 ... ♘g4 then 2 ♕xe4 or 2 ♗xe4. Therefore 1 ... ♖xd5! 2 ♖xd5 ♖xc6! 3 ♗c5 (3 ♕xc6 ♘g4) 3 ... ♖xc5 4 ♖xc5 ♗xc5 White resigned.

404. 1 ♘f5! ♕c7 2 ♖xh7+ ♔xh7 3 ♕h4+ Black resigned.

405. 1 ... ♘xd4! 2 ♕xa8+ ♔f7 3 ♕xh8 ♕b5 White resigned.

406. 1 ♘xg5+! hxg5 2 ♕xg5 ♘e8 3 ♖d6 Black resigned.

407. 1 ... ♗xc1? 2 ♖xd7! ♕xd7 3 ♕g4! ♕xf5 (otherwise 4 ♘xh6+) 4 ♕xf5 and White won.

408. 1 ... b3! 2 cxb3 ♘cb4 White resigned.

409. 1 ♖xf7! ♕xf7 (1 ... ♔xf7 2 ♘h6+) 2 ♕xg5+ ♔h7 3 ♕h6+ Black resigned.

410. 1 ♘xg7! ♔xg7 2 ♘d4! ♕c8 3 ♘f5+ ♔g8 4 ♕g3+ ♘g4 5 ♕xg4+ Black resigned.

411. 1 ♘f7+ ♔g8 2 ♕d5! ♘b6 (otherwise the discovered check mechanism comes into operation, but now other threats are generated) 3 ♘h6+ ♔h8 4 ♖xf8+ ♖xf8 5 ♖xf8+ and Black resigned, since on 5...♕xf8 follows 6 ♕e5+ ♕g7 7 ♕e8+ and mate on the next move.

412. 1 ♘xh7! ♘f5 (1 ... ♗xh7 2 ♘d8!) 2 ♖xf5 ♗xf5 3 ♘e7 Black resigned (3 ... ♗xh7 4 ♕f6X).

413. 1 ... ♘f6! 2 ♕xh8 ♘g4! 3 ♕xg7+ ♗e7 4 ♘f3 e4 5 ♘e5+ ♘cxe5 6 ♗f4 ♘f3+ 7 ♔h1 ♘fxh2 White resigned.

414. 1 ♘h5! gxh5 2 ♘e6 fxe6 3 ♖g5+ ♔f7 4 ♕g6X. Also possible is the alternative 1 ♖e6! fxe6 2 ♕xg6+ ♔h8 3 ♘h5 with unstoppable mate.

415. 1 ... ♖xh3! 2 cxb6+ ♔b8 3 bxa7+ ♔xa7 4 ♔xh3 ♖h8+ 5 ♔xg3 ♖h3+! White resigned (6 ♔xh3 ♕h5+).

416. 1 ♕g3+ ♔h1 (1 ... ♔f1 2 ♘d2+)

2 ♕h3+! (but not 2 ♘f2+? ♕xf2 3 ♕xf2 – stalemate) **2 ... ♕h2+ 3 ♘g3+ ♔g1 4 ♕f1X.**

417. **1 ♕e5!** (1 … ♔xf8 2 ♕h8X or 1 ... ♔xd8 2 ♕b8X).

418. **1 ♘a8! ♔d6 2 ♔d4 ♔c6 3 ♕d5X.**

419. **1 ♕e6 ♔g5 2 ♕f7 ♔h6 3 ♕g8 ♔h5 4 ♕g7 ♔h4 5 ♕g6 ♔h3 6 ♕g3X** or **1 ... ♔f3 2 ♕e5 ♔g4 3 ♕f6 ♔h5 4 ♕g7** etc.

420. **1 ♕a5+ ♔b8 2 ♕b6+ ♔a8 3 ♘b5!** (threatening 4 ♘c7+) **3 ... ♕b7 4 ♕d8+ ♔b8 5 ♕d5+ ♕b7 6 ♕a2+ ♗a4** With this bishop sacrifice Black postpones inevitable defeat: 6 ... ♔b8 7 ♕g8+ ♕c8 8 ♕g3+! ♔a8 (8 ... ♔b7 9 ♘d6+) 9 ♕a3+ ♔b8 (9 ... ♔b7 10 ♘d6+) 10 ♕a7X. **7 ♕xa4+ ♔b8 8 ♕f4+ ♔a8 9 ♕f8+ ♔b8 10 ♕f3+ ♕b7 11 ♕a3+ ♔b8 12 ♕f8+ ♕c8 13 ♕f4+ ♔a8 14 ♕a4+ ♔b8 15 ♕a7X.** An elegant finish!

14. Three pieces

421. **1 ... h6? 2 ♕h7+** Black resigned.

422. **1 ♕xe4+! ♘xe4 2 ♗xf7X.**

423. **1 ♘xe5! ♗xd1?** (1 ... ♘fxd5) **2 ♘xf6+ gxf6 3 ♗xf7+ ♔f8 4 ♗h6X.**

424. **1 ... ♘xe4! 2 ♗xd8 ♗xf2+ 3 ♔e2 ♘d4X.**

425. **1 ... ♘xe4!** White resigned.

426. **1 ... ♘b4! 2 ♕h3+ ♔b8** White resigned. Not possible are 3 ♗xa4 ♘a2X or 3 ♗xb4 ♖xd1+ 4 ♖xd1 ♕c2X.

427. **1 ♕g6!** Black resigned (1 … fxg6 2 ♘e7+ ♔h8 3 ♘xg6X).

428. **1 ... ♕xg2+ 2 ♔xg2 ♖g6+ 3 ♔h1** (3 ♔f3 ♘d2X) **3 ... ♘xf2X.**

429. **1 ♖a8+!** Black resigned (1...♘cb8 2 ♖xb8+ ♘xb8 3 ♖c7X or 1 ... ♗xa8 2 ♗a6+ ♔b7 3 ♗xb7X).

430. **1 ♕h5 h6 2 ♗xf7+ ♔h8 3 ♕xh6+! gxh6 4 ♗e5X.**

431. **1 ♕h6!** Black resigned.

432. **1 ♕xh6!** Black resigned.

433. **1 axb7+ ♖xb7 2 ♖xa7+! ♖xa7 3 ♖xa7+ ♔xa7 4 ♖a1+ ♔b7 5 ♗a6+ ♔a7 6 ♗c8X.**

434. **1 ... ♕xh2+! 2 ♔xh2 ♘g4+ 3 ♔g1 ♘h3+ 4 ♔f1 ♘h2X.**

435. **1 ... ♘f5? 2 ♘b5+! cxb5 3 ♘b7X.**

436. **1 ♕a4+!** Black resigned (1...♕xa4 2 ♖c8+ ♔d8 3 ♖xd8X).

437. **1 ... ♕xf1+! 2 ♔xf1 ♗c4+** White resigned (3 ♔e1 ♖b1X).

438. **1 ♕xg7+!** Black resigned (1...♔xg7 2 ♖g3+ ♔h6 3 ♗c1+ ♔h5 4 ♗e2+ ♔xh4 5 ♖h3X).

439. **1 ♕xh7+! ♔xh7 2 hxg6+ ♔xg6 3 ♗e4X.**

440. **1 ♕xa6+! bxa6 2 ♖xa6+ ♔b8 3 ♗d6+** Black resigned (3...♔c8 4 ♖c6+ ♔d8 5 ♖d7X).

441. **1 ... ♔d8? 2 ♘b7+!** Black resigned (2...♔xe7 3 ♖f7X). This happened in a correspondence game.

442. **1 hxg6 fxg6 2 ♕xh7+! ♔xh7 3 ♖h1+** Black resigned (3...♔g8 4 ♖h8+ ♔f7 5 ♘g5X).

443. **1 ... ♘xe4! 2 ♕xd8 ♘g3+ 3 ♔g1 ♘f3X.**

444. **1 ♕xd6+! ♔xd6 2 ♖xb7+ ♔a8 3 ♖b4+** Black resigned (3...♔a7 4 ♖a3+ ♕a6 5 ♖b7+ ♔a8 6 ♖xa6X).

445. **1 ♖xh7! ♘xc4 2 ♖dh1 g5 3 ♗e4 ♘xe5 4 fxe5 f5 5 ♗d5+** Black resigned. (5...♔f8 6 ♖h8+ ♔g7 7 ♖1h7+ ♔g6 8 ♗f7X).

446. **1 ... ♕d1+!** (1 ... ♘xb1? 2 ♖xe8X) **2 ♖xd1 ♘e2+! 3 ♔xe2 ♘b3X.** Beautiful!

447. **1 ♕xe8+! ♔xe8 2 ♘d4+ ♔f8** (2 ... ♕e5 3 ♖g8+ ♔e7 4 ♘f5X) **3 ♖e8+! ♔xe8 4 ♖g8+ ♔e7 5 ♘f5X.** Only one of Black's pieces got into play!

448. **1 ♕xf7+! ♔xf7 2 ♖f1+ ♔e8 3 ♖g8+ ♔e7 4 ♖g7+ ♔e8 5 ♗g6X.**

449. **1 ... ♕g3! 2 fxg3 ♗xg3+ 3 ♔e2 ♗d1X**.

450. **1 ♗b5!** (White threatens mate with the knight on e5 and at the same time includes the bishop in the attack.) **1 ... ♘c6** (it seems that Black has defended against the immediate threats and covered all critical squares...) **2 ♘e5+! ♘xe5 3 ♗e8+ ♔f8 4 ♗g6X**.

451. **1 ♘f5! ♕g5** (1 ... ♘xd2 2 ♘xg3 ♗xg2 3 ♔xg2 ♘b3 4 ♖c7; or 1 ... ♕xg2+ 2 ♕xg2 ♗xg2 3 ♗xg7+ ♔g8 4 ♖c7! h5 5 ♔xg2) **2 ♕xd8+! ♕xd8 3 ♖c8 ♕xc8 4 ♗xg7+ ♔g8 5 ♗d5+ ♕e6 6 ♗xe6X**.

452. **1 ♖g2** (threatening 2 ♘g6+ and 3 ♘df4X) **1 ... ♗e8(c2) 2 ♘e7(♘e3)** and mate on the next move.

453. **1 ♖a2!** Now the queen cannot simultaneously keep under control both critical squares a8 and h2 – and on one of them the rook will deliver a fatal check.

454. **1 ♘d5!** c4 2 ♗g6+ ♔d8 (2 ... ♔f8 3 ♘f6 and 4 ♖f7X) 3 ♘b6 and 4 ♖d7X; **1 ... e4 2 ♘f6+ ♔d8** (2 ... ♔f8 3 ♗c4 and 4 ♖f7X) 3 ♗a6 and 4 ♖d7X; **1 ... ♔d8 2 ♗b5 ♔c8 3 ♗c6** and 4 ♖a8X. 1 ♘f5? ♔f8! would be a false trail.

455. **1 ♖b8 d5 2 ♘ab3 d4 3 ♘c5+ ♔a5 4 ♘1b3X**; **1 ... a6 2 ♘c2 d5 3 ♖b4+ ♔a5 4 ♘b3X**; **1 ... d6 2 ♘c2 ♔a5 3 ♘b3+ ♔a6** (3 ... ♔a4 4 ♖b4X) **4 ♘b4X**.

456. It seems sufficient to make a waiting move, so that after 1...d4 he can bring into operation the mating mechanism – 2 ♘e4, 3 ♘f6 and 4 ♘g6X. However 1 ♔d2? leads to stalemate: 1 ... d4 2 ♘e4 d3 3 ♘f6. The solution is **1 ♗h6! d4 2 ♘d5** (White constructs the same position by changing the places of the knights.) **2...d3 3 ♘f6 d2 4 ♘f7X**.